Toshiba Air Fryer Oven Cookbook

600 Delicious and Affordable Air Fryer Recipes tailored for Your Toshiba Air Fryer Toaster Oven

Mildred J. Thomas

Copyright© 2021 By Mildred J. Thomas All Rights Reserved

The content contained within this book may not be reproduced, duplicated or transmitted without direct written permission from the author or the publisher.

Under no circumstances will any blame or legal responsibility be held against the publisher, or author, for any damages, reparation, or monetary loss due to the information contained within this book, either directly or indirectly.

Legal Notice:

This book is copyright protected. It is only for personal use. You cannot amend, distribute, sell, use, quote or paraphrase any part, or the content within this book, without the consent of the author or publisher.

Disclaimer Notice:

Please note the information contained within this document is for educational and entertainment purposes only. All effort has been executed to present accurate, up to date, reliable, complete information. No warranties of any kind are declared or implied. Readers acknowledge that the author is not engaged in the rendering of legal, financial, medical or professional advice. The content within this book has been derived from various sources. Please consult a licensed professional before attempting any techniques outlined in this book.

By reading this document, the reader agrees that under no circumstances is the author responsible for any losses, direct or indirect, that are incurred as a result of the use of the information contained within this document, including, but not limited to, errors, omissions, or inaccuracies.

Table of Contents

Chapter 1 Breakfast

Maple Granola	1
Bacon Knots with Maple Sugar	1
Cheddar Ham Toast	1
Cinnamon Monkey Bread	2
Vanilla French Toast withBourbon	2
Hash Brown Cups with Cheddar Cheese	2
Buttermilk Biscuits	2
Grits with Cheddar Cheese	3
Tater Tot and Chicken Sausage Casserole	3
Egg and Bacon Bread Cups	3
Baked Cornmeal Pancake	3
Bell Pepper Rings with Eggs	4
English Muffins with Spinach and Pear	4
Corn Frittata with Avocado Dressing	4
Cheese and Bacon Muffin Sandwiches	4
Breakfast Sausage Quiche	5
Blueberry Cake with Lemon	5
Cinnamon Apple Turnovers	5
Beef Hash with Eggs	5
Maple French Toast Casserole	6
Honey Cashew Granola with Cranberries	6

Chapter 2 Poultry

Chicken and Ham Rochambeau	7
Breaded Chicken Fingers	7
Breaded Chicken Livers	7
Breaded Chicken Tenders with Thyme	8
Barbecue Chicken with Coleslaw	8
Mustard Chicken Thighs in Waffles	8
Gochujang Chicken Wings	9
Chili Chicken Skin with Dill	9
Chicken Drumsticks with Cajun Seasoning	9
Ginger Chicken Bites in Sherry	9
Honey-Ginger Chicken Breasts	10
Parmesan Chicken Cutlets	10
Rosemary Chicken Breasts with Tomatoes	10
Chicken Tacos with Lettuce	11
Buttermilk Chicken Drumsticks	11
Chicken Thighs with Cherry Tomatoes	11
Mozzarella Chicken Breasts with Basil	12
Chicken Thighs with Cabbage Slaw	12
Buttery Chicken with Corn	13
Vinegary Chicken with Pineapple	13
Chicken Gnocchi with Spinach	13
Peach Chicken with Dark Cherry	13
Turkey Meatloaves with Onion	14
Paprika Hens with Creole Seasoning	14
Paprika Hens in Wine	14
Chili Chicken Fries	15

Chapter 3 Fish and Seafood

Tuna Casserole with Basil	16
Salmon Spring Rolls with Parsley	16
Cajun Tilapia Tacos	16
Hoisin Tuna with Lemongrass	16
Tilapia Meunière with Parsley	17
Tuna and Fruit Kebabs with Honey Glaze	17
Breaded Fish Fillets with Mustard	17
Cayenne Cod Fillets with Garlic	17
Tuna and Veggie Salad	18
Salmon with Roasted Asparagus	18
Salmon with Cherry Tomatoes	18
Teriyaki Salmon and Bok Choy	19
Honey-Lemon Snapper with Grapes	19
Ginger Swordfish Steaks with Jalapeño	19
Baked Salmon in Wine	19
Fried Cod Fillets in Beer	20
Parmesan Fish Fillets with Tarragon	20
Cajun Catfish Cakes with Parmesan	20
Coconut Curried Fish with Chilies	20
Shrimp and Veggie Spring Rolls	21
Orange Shrimp with Cayenne	21
Flounder Fillets with Lemon Pepper	21
Paprika Tiger Shrimp	22

Chapter 4 Casseroles, Quiches, and Frittatas

Mushroom and Beef Casserole	23
Cauliflower Casserole with Pecan Butter	23
Cheddar Chicken Sausage Casserole	23
Corn Casserole with Bell Pepper	23

Asparagus Casserole with Grits	24
Cheddar Broccoli Casserole	24
Tilapia and Rockfish Casserole	24
Parmesan Green Bean Casserole	24
Cheddar Pastrami Casserole	25
Swiss Chicken and Ham Casserole	25
Spinach and Mushroom Frittata	25
Cauliflower and Okra Casserole	25
Turkey Casserole with Almond Mayo	25
Peppery Sausage Casserole with Cheddar	26
Chickpea and Spinach Casserole	26
Beef and Bean Casserole	26
Cheddar Chicken and Broccoli Divan	27
Smoked Trout Frittata with Dill	27
Cheddar and Egg Frittata with Parsley	27
Cheddar Broccoli and Carrot Quiche	27

Chapter 5 Wraps and Sandwiches

Nugget and Veggie Taco Wraps	29
Veggie Salsa Wraps	29
Tuna and Lettuce Wraps	29
Lettuce Fajita Meatball Wraps	29
Chicken-Lettuce Wraps	29
Cheesy Chicken Sandwich	30
Smoky Chicken Sandwich	30
Cheesy Potato Taquitos	30
Chicken and Yogurt Taquitos	30
Pork Momos	31
Air Fried Cream Cheese Wontons	31
Crispy Crab and Cream Cheese Wontons	31
Cabbage and Pork Gyoza	31
Pea and Potato Samosas with Chutney	32
Bulgogi Burgers	32
Eggplant Hoagies	33
Lamb and Feta Hamburgers	33

Chapter 6 Vegan and Vegetarian

Roasted Veggie and Tofu	34
Black Bean and Salsa Tacos	34
Thai Curried Veggies	34
Eggplant and Bell Peppers with Basil	34
Vinegary Asparagus	35
Baked Eggs with Spinach and Basil	35
Cheesy Broccoli with Rosemary	35
Kale with Tahini-Lemon Dressing	35
Vegetable Mélange with Garlic	35
Garlic Carrots with Sesame Seeds	36
Thai-Flavored Brussels Sprouts	36
Honey Eggplant with Yogurt Sauce	36
Parmesan Cabbage Wedges	36
Sesame Mushrooms with Thyme	36
Ratatouille with Bread Crumb Topping	37
Butternut Squash and Parsnip with Thyme	37
Butternut Squash with Goat Cheese	37
Ginger-Pepper Broccoli	38
Parmesan Brussels Sprouts	38

Chapter 7 Appetizers and Snacks

Cheddar Baked Potatoes with Chives	39
Sausage and Onion Rolls with Mustard	39
Honey Roasted Grapes with Basil	39
Parmesan Cauliflower with Turmeric	39
Cheddar Mushrooms with Pimientos	40
Roasted Mushrooms with Garlic	40
Jalapeño Poppers with Cheddar	40
Green Chiles and Cheese Nachos	40
Pepperoni Pizza Bites with Marinara	41
Cheddar Sausage Balls	41
Tuna Melts with Mayo	41
Sugar Roasted Walnuts	41
Balsamic Prosciutto-Wrapped Pears	42
Breaded Zucchini Tots	42
Ginger Shrimp with Sesame Seeds	42
Paprika Polenta Fries with Chili-Lime Mayo	42
Lemon Ricotta with Capers	43
Deviled Eggs with Mayo	43
Honey Snack Mix	43
Parmesan Snack Mix	43
Paprika Potato Chips	44
Hush Puppies with Jalapeño	44
Fried Pickle Spears with Chili	44
Cinnamon Apple Chips	44
Avocado Chips with Lime	45
Brie Pear Sandwiches	45
Parmesan Crab Toasts	45
Buttermilk-Marinated Chicken Wings	45
Pork and Turkey Sandwiches	46
Horseradish Green Tomatoes	46
Turkey-Wrapped Dates and Almonds	46
Italian Rice Balls with Olives	46

Muffuletta Sliders with Olive Mix ... 47

Chapter 8 Desserts

Lemon Caramelized Pear Tart ... 48
Honey Walnut and Pistachios Baklava ... 48
Monk Fruit and Hazelnut Cake ... 48
Blueberry and Peach Tart ... 49
Butter Shortbread with Lemon ... 49
Chocolate Coconut Cake ... 49
Coffee Chocolate Cake with Cinnamon ... 49
Vanilla Cookies with Chocolate Chips ... 50
Chocolate Vanilla Cheesecake ... 50
Strawberry Crumble with Rhubarb ... 50
Raspberry Muffins ... 51
Peach and Apple Crisp with Oatmeal ... 51
Vanilla Walnuts Tart with Cloves ... 51
Mixed Berry Bake with Almond Topping ... 51
Vanilla Coconut Cookies with Pecans ... 52
Cinnamon Apple Fritters ... 52
Chocolate Blueberry Cupcakes ... 52
Vanilla Chocolate Chip Cookies ... 53
Vanilla Chocolate Cake ... 53
Coconut Orange Cake ... 53
Peach and Blueberry Galette ... 53
Honey Apple-Peach Crumble ... 54
Cinnamon Apple with Apricots ... 54
Honey-Glazed Peach and Plum Kebabs ... 54
Vanilla Pound Cake ... 54
Pumpkin Pudding with Vanilla Wafers ... 55
Vanilla Ricotta Cake with Lemon ... 55

Chapter 9 Rotisserie Recipes

Whiskey-Basted Prime Rib Roast ... 56
Paprika Pulled Pork Butt ... 56
Porchetta with Lemony Sage Rub ... 56
Orange Honey Glazed Ham ... 57
Ham with Dijon Bourbon Baste ... 57
Spareribs with Paprika Rub ... 58
Smoked Paprika Lamb Leg ... 58
BBQ Chicken with Mustard Rub ... 58
Sirloin Roast with Porcini-Wine Baste ... 59
Balsamic Chuck Roast ... 59
Baby Back Ribs with Paprika Rub ... 60
Teriyaki Chicken ... 60
Chicken Roast with Mustard Paste ... 61

Turkey with Thyme-Sage Brine ... 61
Pork Loin Roast with Brown Sugar Brine ... 61
Dried Fruit Stuffed Pork Loin ... 62
Feta Stuffed Lamb Leg ... 62
Mustard Lamb Shoulder ... 62

Chapter 10 Sauces, Dips, and Dressings

Cauliflower Alfredo Sauce ... 64
Red Buffalo Sauce ... 64
Avocado Dressing ... 64
Dijon and Balsamic Vinaigrette ... 64
Hemp Dressing ... 64
Lemony Tahini ... 64
Cashew Mayo ... 64
Mushroom Apple Gravy ... 65
Creamy Ranch Dressing ... 65
Creamy Coconut Lime Dressing ... 65
Garlic Lime Tahini Dressing ... 65
Fresh Mixed Berry Vinaigrette ... 65
Lemon Dijon Vinaigrette ... 65
Chimichurri ... 65
Kale and Almond Pesto ... 66
Marinara Sauce ... 66
Shawarma Spice Blend ... 66
Spicy Southwest Seasoning ... 66
Baked White Rice ... 66
Red Enchilada Sauce ... 67

Chapter 11 Dehydrate

Dehydrated Pineapple Slices ... 68
Pork Jerky ... 68
Strawberry Roll Ups ... 68
Dehydrated Strawberries ... 68
Peach Fruit Leather ... 68
Smoky Venison Jerky ... 68
Dried Mushrooms ... 69
Dehydrated Zucchini Chips ... 69
Cinnamon Pear Chips ... 69
Dried Hot Peppers ... 69
Lemon-Pepper Salmon Jerky ... 69
Kiwi Chips ... 69
Dehydrated Onions ... 70
Candied Bacon ... 70
Cinnamon Orange Slices ... 70

Chapter 12 Pizza

Simple Pizza Dough	71
Pro Dough	71
No-Knead Pan Pizza Dough	71
Garlic Tomato Pizza Sauce	71
Pepperoni Pizza with Mozzarella	72
Italian Sausage and Bell Pepper Pizza	72
Mushroom and Spinach Pizza	72
Ham and Pineapple Pizza	73
Mozzarella Meatball Pizza	73
Cheese Tomato Pizza with Basil	73
Prosciutto and Bacon Pizza	74
Arugula and Prosciutto Pizza	74
Spinach, Egg and Pancetta Pizza	74
Chicken and Butternut Squash Pizza	75
Prosciutto and Fig Pizza	75
Ricotta Margherita with Basil	75
Zucchini and Summer Squash Pizza	76
Pear Pizza with Basil	76
Black Bean Pizza with Chipotle	76
Spring Pea Pizza with Ramps	77
Zucchini Pizza with Pistachios	77
Escarole and Radicchio Pizza with Walnuts	77
Mozzarella Brussels Sprout Pizza	78
Butternut Squash and Arugula Pizza	78
Double-Cheese Clam Pizza	78
Egg and Arugula Pizza	79
Zucchini and Onion Pizza	79
Pizza Margherita	80

Appendix 1 Measurement Conversion Chart

Appendix 2 Air Fryer Cooking Chart

Appendix 3 Index

Chapter 1 Breakfast

Maple Granola

Prep time: 5 minutes | Cook time: 40 minutes | Serves 4

- 1 cup rolled oats
- 3 tablespoons maple syrup
- 1 tablespoon sunflower oil
- 1 tablespoon coconut sugar
- ¼ teaspoon vanilla
- ¼ teaspoon cinnamon
- ¼ teaspoon sea salt

1. Mix together the oats, maple syrup, sunflower oil, coconut sugar, vanilla, cinnamon, and sea salt in a medium bowl and stir to combine. Transfer the mixture to a baking pan.
2. Select Bake. Set temperature to 248°F (120°C) and set time to 40 minutes. Press Start to begin preheating.
3. Once preheated, place the pan into the oven. Stir the granola four times during cooking.
4. When cooking is complete, the granola will be mostly dry and lightly browned.
5. Let the granola stand for 5 to 10 minutes before serving.

Bacon Knots with Maple Sugar

Prep time: 5 minutes | Cook time: 7 to 8 minutes | Serves 6

- 1 pound (454 g) maple smoked center-cut bacon
- ¼ cup maple syrup
- ¼ cup brown sugar
- Coarsely cracked black peppercorns, to taste

1. On a clean work surface, tie each bacon strip in a loose knot.
2. Stir together the maple syrup and brown sugar in a bowl. Generously brush this mixture over the bacon knots.
3. Place the bacon knots in the perforated pan and sprinkle with the coarsely cracked black peppercorns.
4. Select Air Fry. Set temperature to 390°F (199°C) and set time to 8 minutes. Press Start to begin preheating.
5. Once preheated, place the pan into the oven.
6. After 5 minutes, remove the pan from the oven and flip the bacon knots. Return the pan to the oven and continue cooking for 2 to 3 minutes more.
7. When cooking is complete, the bacon should be crisp. Remove from the oven to a paper towel-lined plate. Let the bacon knots cool for a few minutes and serve warm.

Cheddar Ham Toast

Prep time: 5 minutes | Cook time: 6 minutes | Serves: 1

- 1 slice bread
- 1 teaspoon butter, at room temperature
- 1 egg
- Salt and freshly ground
- black pepper, to taste
- 2 teaspoons diced ham
- 1 tablespoon grated Cheddar cheese

1. On a clean work surface, use a 2½-inch biscuit cutter to make a hole in the center of the bread slice with about ½-inch of bread remaining.

2. Spread the butter on both sides of the bread slice. Crack the egg into the hole and season with salt and pepper to taste. Transfer the bread to the perforated pan.
3. Select Air Fry. Set temperature to 325°F (163°C) and set time to 6 minutes. Press Start to begin preheating.
4. Once preheated, place the pan into the oven.
5. After 5 minutes, remove the pan from the oven. Scatter the cheese and diced ham on top and continue cooking for an additional 1 minute.
6. When cooking is complete, the egg should be set and the cheese should be melted. Remove the toast from the oven to a plate and let cool for 5 minutes before serving.

Cinnamon Monkey Bread

Prep time: 5 minutes | Cook time: 8 minutes | Serves 4

- 1 (8-ounce / 227-g) can refrigerated biscuits
- 3 tablespoons melted unsalted butter
- ¼ cup white sugar
- 3 tablespoons brown sugar
- ½ teaspoon cinnamon
- ⅛ teaspoon nutmeg

1. On a clean work surface, cut each biscuit into 4 pieces.
2. In a shallow bowl, place the melted butter. In another shallow bowl, stir together the white sugar, brown sugar, cinnamon, and nutmeg until combined.
3. Dredge the biscuits, one at a time, in the melted butter, then roll them in the sugar mixture to coat well. Spread the biscuits evenly in a baking pan.
4. Select Bake. Set temperature to 350°F (180°C) and set time to 8 minutes. Press Start to begin preheating.
5. Once the oven has preheated, place the pan into the oven.
6. When cooked, the biscuits should be golden brown.
7. Cool for 5 minutes before serving.

Vanilla French Toast withBourbon

Prep time: 15 minutes | Cook time: 6 minutes | Serves 4

- 2 large eggs
- 2 tablespoons water
- ⅔ cup whole or 2% milk
- 1 tablespoon butter, melted
- 2 tablespoons bourbon
- 1 teaspoon vanilla extract
- 8 (1-inch-thick) French bread slices
- Cooking spray

1. Line the perforated pan with parchment paper and spray it with cooking spray.
2. Beat the eggs with the water in a shallow bowl until combined. Add the milk, melted butter, bourbon, and vanilla and stir to mix well.
3. Dredge 4 slices of bread in the batter, turning to coat both sides evenly. Transfer the bread slices onto the parchment paper.
4. Select Bake. Set temperature to 320°F (160°C) and set time to 6 minutes. Press Start to begin preheating.
5. Once the oven has preheated, place the pan into the oven. Flip the slices halfway through the cooking time.
6. When cooking is complete, the bread slices should be nicely browned.
7. Remove from the oven to a plate and serve warm.

Hash Brown Cups with Cheddar Cheese

Prep time: 10 minutes | Cook time: 9 minutes | Serves 6

- 4 eggs, beaten
- 2¼ cups frozen hash browns, thawed
- 1 cup diced ham
- ½ cup shredded Cheddar cheese
- ½ teaspoon Cajun seasoning
- Cooking spray

1. Lightly spritz a 12-cup muffin tin with cooking spray.
2. Combine the beaten eggs, hash browns, diced ham, cheese, and Cajun seasoning in a medium bowl and stir until well blended.
3. Spoon a heaping 1½ tablespoons of egg mixture into each muffin cup.
4. Select Bake. Set temperature to 350°F (180°C) and set time to 9 minutes. Press Start to begin preheating.
5. Once preheated, place the muffin tin into the oven.
6. When cooked, the muffins will be golden brown.
7. Allow to cool for 5 to 10 minutes on a wire rack and serve warm.

Buttermilk Biscuits

Prep time: 5 minutes | Cook time: 18 minutes | Makes 16 biscuits

- 2½ cups all-purpose flour
- 1 tablespoon baking powder
- 1 teaspoon kosher salt
- 1 teaspoon sugar
- ½ teaspoon baking soda
- 8 tablespoons (1 stick) unsalted butter, at room temperature
- 1 cup buttermilk, chilled

1. Stir together the flour, baking powder, salt, sugar, and baking powder in a large bowl.
2. Add the butter and stir to mix well. Pour in the buttermilk and stir with a rubber spatula just until incorporated.
3. Place the dough onto a lightly floured surface and roll the dough out to a disk, ½ inch thick. Cut out the biscuits with a 2-inch round cutter and re-roll any scraps until you have 16 biscuits.
4. Arrange the biscuits in the perforated pan in a single layer.
5. Select Bake. Set temperature to 325°F (163°C) and set time to 18 minutes. Press Start to begin preheating.
6. Once preheated, place the pan into the oven.

7. When cooked, the biscuits will be golden brown.
8. Remove from the oven to a plate and serve hot.

Grits with Cheddar Cheese

Prep time: 10 minutes | Cook time: 11 minutes | Serves 4

- ⅔ cup instant grits
- 1 teaspoon salt
- 1 teaspoon freshly ground black pepper
- ¾ cup whole or 2% milk
- 3 ounces (85 g) cream cheese, at room temperature
- 1 large egg, beaten
- 1 tablespoon butter, melted
- 1 cup shredded mild Cheddar cheese
- Cooking spray

1. Mix the grits, salt, and black pepper in a large bowl. Add the milk, cream cheese, beaten egg, and melted butter and whisk to combine. Fold in the Cheddar cheese and stir well.
2. Spray a baking pan with cooking spray. Spread the grits mixture into the baking pan.
3. Select Air Fry. Set temperature to 400°F (205°C) and set time to 11 minutes. Press Start to begin preheating.
4. Once preheated, place the pan into the oven. Stir the mixture halfway through the cooking time.
5. When done, a knife inserted in the center should come out clean.
6. Rest for 5 minutes and serve warm.

Tater Tot and Chicken Sausage Casserole

Prep time: 5 minutes | Cook time: 17 to 18 minutes | Serves 4

- 4 eggs
- 1 cup milk
- Salt and pepper, to taste
- 12 ounces (340 g) ground chicken sausage
- 1 pound (454 g) frozen tater tots, thawed
- ¾ cup grated Cheddar cheese
- Cooking spray

1. Whisk together the eggs and milk in a medium bowl. Season with salt and pepper to taste and stir until mixed. Set aside.
2. Place a skillet over medium-high heat and spritz with cooking spray. Place the ground sausage in the skillet and break it into smaller pieces with a spatula or spoon. Cook for 3 to 4 minutes until the sausage Starts to brown, stirring occasionally. Remove from heat and set aside.
3. Coat a baking pan with cooking spray. Arrange the tater tots in the baking pan.
4. Select Bake. Set temperature to 400°F (205°C) and set time to 14 minutes. Press Start to begin preheating.
5. Once preheated, place the pan into the oven.
6. After 6 minutes, remove the pan from the oven. Stir the tater tots and add the egg mixture and cooked sausage. Return the pan to the oven and continue cooking.
7. After another 6 minutes, remove the pan from the oven. Scatter the cheese on top of the tater tots. Return the pan to the oven and continue to cook for 2 minutes more.
8. When done, the cheese should be bubbly and melted.
9. Let the mixture cool for 5 minutes and serve warm.

Egg and Bacon Bread Cups

Prep time: 10 minutes | Cook time: 10 minutes | Serves 4

- 4 (3-by-4-inch) crusty rolls
- 4 thin slices Gouda or Swiss cheese mini wedges
- 5 eggs
- 2 tablespoons heavy cream
- 3 strips precooked bacon, chopped
- ½ teaspoon dried thyme
- Pinch salt
- Freshly ground black pepper, to taste

1. On a clean work surface, cut the tops off the rolls. Using your fingers, remove the insides of the rolls to make bread cups, leaving a ½-inch shell. Place a slice of cheese onto each roll bottom.
2. Whisk together the eggs and heavy cream in a medium bowl until well combined. Fold in the bacon, thyme, salt, and pepper and stir well.
3. Scrape the egg mixture into the prepared bread cups. Arrange the bread cups in the perforated pan.
4. Select Bake. Set temperature to 330°F (166°C) and set time to 10 minutes. Press Start to begin preheating.
5. Once preheated, place the pan into the oven.
6. When cooked, the eggs should be cooked to your preference.
7. Serve warm.

Baked Cornmeal Pancake

Prep time: 10 minutes | Cook time: 6 minutes | Serves 4

- 1½ cups yellow cornmeal
- ½ cup all-purpose flour
- 2 tablespoons sugar
- 1 teaspoon salt
- 1 teaspoon baking powder
- 1 cup whole or 2% milk
- 1 large egg, lightly beaten
- 1 tablespoon butter, melted
- Cooking spray

1. Line the perforated pan with parchment paper.
2. Stir together the cornmeal, flour, sugar, salt, and baking powder in a large bowl. Mix in the milk, egg, and melted butter and whisk to combine.
3. Drop tablespoonfuls of the batter onto the parchment paper for each pancake. Spray the pancakes with cooking spray.
4. Select Bake. Set temperature to 350°F (180°C) and set time to 6 minutes. Press Start to begin preheating.
5. Once the oven has preheated, place the pan into the oven. Flip the pancakes and spray with cooking spray again halfway through the cooking time.

6. When cooking is complete, remove the pancakes from the oven to a plate.
7. Cool for 5 minutes and serve immediately.

Bell Pepper Rings with Eggs

Prep time: 5 minutes | Cook time: 7 minutes | Serves 4

- 1 large red, yellow, or orange bell pepper, cut into four ¾-inch rings
- 4 eggs
- Salt and freshly ground black pepper, to taste
- 2 teaspoons salsa
- Cooking spray

1. Coat a baking pan lightly with cooking spray.
2. Put 4 bell pepper rings in the prepared baking pan. Crack one egg into each bell pepper ring and sprinkle with salt and pepper. Top each egg with ½ teaspoon of salsa.
3. Select Air Fry. Set temperature to 350°F (180°C) and set time to 7 minutes. Press Start to begin preheating.
4. Once preheated, place the pan into the oven.
5. When done, the eggs should be cooked to your desired doneness.
6. Remove the rings from the pan to a plate and serve warm.

English Muffins with Spinach and Pear

Prep time: 5 minutes | Cook time: 10 minutes | Serves 4

- 2 strips turkey bacon, cut in half crosswise
- 2 whole-grain English muffins, split
- 1 cup fresh baby spinach, long stems removed
- ¼ ripe pear, peeled and thinly sliced
- 4 slices Provolone cheese

1. Put the turkey bacon strips in the perforated pan.
2. Select Air Fry. Set temperature to 390°F (199°C) and set time to 6 minutes. Press Start to begin preheating.
3. Once preheated, place the pan into the oven. Flip the strips halfway through the cooking time.
4. When cooking is complete, the bacon should be crisp.
5. Remove from the oven and drain on paper towels. Set aside.
6. Put the muffin halves in the perforated pan.
7. Select Air Fry and set time to 2 minutes. Return the pan to the oven. When done, the muffin halves will be lightly browned.
8. Remove the pan from the oven. Top each muffin half with ¼ of the baby spinach, several pear slices, a strip of turkey bacon, followed by a slice of cheese.
9. Select Bake. Set temperature to 360°F (182°C) and set time to 2 minutes. Place the pan back to the oven. When done, the cheese will be melted.

10. Serve warm.

Corn Frittata with Avocado Dressing

Prep time: 10 minutes | Cook time: 20 minutes | Serves 2 or 3

- ½ cup cherry tomatoes, halved
- Kosher salt and freshly ground black pepper, to taste
- 6 large eggs, lightly beaten
- ½ cup fresh corn kernels
- ¼ cup milk
- 1 tablespoon finely chopped fresh dill
- ½ cup shredded Monterey Jack cheese

Avocado Dressing:

- 1 ripe avocado, pitted and peeled
- 2 tablespoons fresh lime juice
- ¼ cup olive oil
- 1 scallion, finely chopped
- 8 fresh basil leaves, finely chopped

1. Put the tomato halves in a colander and lightly season with salt. Set aside for 10 minutes to drain well. Pour the tomatoes into a large bowl and fold in the eggs, corn, milk, and dill. Sprinkle with salt and pepper and stir until mixed.
2. Pour the egg mixture into a baking pan.
3. Select Bake. Set temperature to 300°F (150°C) and set time to 15 minutes. Press Start to begin preheating.
4. Once the oven has preheated, place the pan into the oven.
5. When done, remove the pan from the oven. Scatter the cheese on top.
6. Select Bake. Set temperature to 315°F (157°C) and set time to 5 minutes. Return the pan to the oven.
7. Meanwhile, make the avocado dressing: Mash the avocado with the lime juice in a medium bowl until smooth. Mix in the olive oil, scallion, and basil and stir until well incorporated.
8. When cooking is complete, the frittata will be puffy and set. Let the frittata cool for 5 minutes and serve alongside the avocado dressing.

Cheese and Bacon Muffin Sandwiches

Prep time: 5 minutes | Cook time: 8 minutes | Serves 4

- 4 English muffins, split
- 8 slices Canadian bacon
- 4 slices cheese
- Cooking spray

1. Make the sandwiches: Top each of 4 muffin halves with 2 slices of Canadian bacon, 1 slice of cheese, and finish with the remaining muffin half.
2. Put the sandwiches in the perforated pan and spritz the tops with cooking spray.
3. Select Bake. Set temperature to 370°F (188°C) and set time to 8 minutes. Press Start to begin preheating.
4. Once preheated, place the pan into the oven. Flip the sandwiches halfway through the cooking time.

5. When cooking is complete, remove the pan from the oven. Divide the sandwiches among four plates and serve warm.

Breakfast Sausage Quiche

Prep time: 5 minutes | Cook time: 25 minutes | Serves 4

- 12 large eggs
- 1 cup heavy cream
- Salt and black pepper, to taste
- 12 ounces (340 g) sugar-free breakfast sausage
- 2 cups shredded Cheddar cheese
- Cooking spray

1. Coat a casserole dish with cooking spray.
2. Beat together the eggs, heavy cream, salt and pepper in a large bowl until creamy. Stir in the breakfast sausage and Cheddar cheese.
3. Pour the sausage mixture into the prepared casserole dish.
4. Select Bake. Set temperature to 375°F (190°C) and set time to 25 minutes. Press Start to begin preheating.
5. Once the oven has preheated, place the dish into the oven.
6. When done, the top of the quiche should be golden brown and the eggs will be set.
7. Remove from the oven and let sit for 5 to 10 minutes before serving.

Blueberry Cake with Lemon

Prep time: 5 minutes | Cook time: 10 minutes | Serves 8

- 1½ cups Bisquick
- ¼ cup granulated sugar
- 2 large eggs, beaten
- ¾ cup whole milk
- 1 teaspoon vanilla extract
- ½ teaspoon lemon zest
- Cooking spray
- 2 cups blueberries

1. Stir together the Bisquick and sugar in a medium bowl. Stir together the eggs, milk, vanilla and lemon zest. Add the wet ingredients to the dry ingredients and stir until well combined.
2. Spritz the sheet pan with cooking spray and line with the parchment paper, pressing it into place. Spray the parchment paper with cooking spray. Pour the batter on the pan and spread it out evenly. Sprinkle the blueberries evenly over the top.
3. Select Bake. Set temperature to 375°F (190°C) and set time to 10 minutes. Press Start to begin preheating.
4. Once the unit has preheated, place the pan into the oven.
5. When cooking is complete, the cake should be pulling away from the edges of the pan and the top should be just starting to turn golden brown.
6. Let the cake rest for a minute before cutting into 16 squares. Serve immediately.

Cinnamon Apple Turnovers

Prep time: 10 minutes | Cook time: 20 minutes | Serves 4

- 1 cup diced apple
- 1 tablespoon brown sugar
- 1 teaspoon freshly squeezed lemon juice
- 1 teaspoon all-purpose flour, plus more for dusting
- ¼ teaspoon cinnamon
- ⅛ teaspoon allspice
- ½ package frozen puff pastry, thawed
- 1 large egg, beaten
- 2 teaspoons granulated sugar

1. Whisk together the apple, brown sugar, lemon juice, flour, cinnamon and allspice in a medium bowl.
2. On a clean work surface, lightly dust with the flour and lay the puff pastry sheet. Using a rolling pin, gently roll the dough to smooth out the folds, seal any tears and form it into a square. Cut the dough into four squares.
3. Spoon a quarter of the apple mixture into the center of each puff pastry square and spread it evenly in a triangle shape over half the pastry, leaving a border of about ½ inch around the edges of the pastry. Fold the pastry diagonally over the filling to form triangles. With a fork, crimp the edges to seal them. Place the turnovers on the sheet pan, spacing them evenly.
4. Cut two or three small slits in the top of each turnover. Brush with the egg. Sprinkle evenly with the granulated sugar.
5. Select Bake. Set temperature to 350°F (180°C) and set time to 20 minutes. Press Start to begin preheating.
6. Once the unit has preheated, place the pan into the oven.
7. After 10 to 12 minutes, remove the pan from the oven. Check the pastries. If they are browned unevenly, rotate the pan. Return the pan to the oven and continue cooking.
8. When cooking is complete, remove the pan from the oven. The turnovers should be golden brown and the filling bubbling. Let cool for about 10 minutes before serving.

Beef Hash with Eggs

Prep time: 10 minutes | Cook time: 25 minutes | Serves 4

- 2 medium Yukon Gold potatoes, peeled and cut into ¼-inch cubes
- 1 medium onion, chopped
- ⅓ cup diced red bell pepper
- 3 tablespoons vegetable oil
- ½ teaspoon dried thyme
- ½ teaspoon kosher salt, divided
- ½ teaspoon freshly ground black pepper, divided
- ¾ pound (340 g) corned beef, cut into ¼-inch pieces
- 4 large eggs

1. In a large bowl, stir together the potatoes, onion, red pepper, vegetable oil, thyme, ¼ teaspoon of the salt and ¼ teaspoon of the pepper. Spread the vegetable mixture on the sheet pan in an even layer.

2. Select Roast. Set temperature to 375°F (190°C) and set time to 25 minutes. Press Start to begin preheating.
3. Once the unit has preheated, place the pan into the oven.
4. After 15 minutes, remove the pan from the oven and add the corned beef. Stir the mixture to incorporate the corned beef. Return the pan to the oven and continue cooking.
5. After 5 minutes, remove the pan from the oven. Using a large spoon, create 4 circles in the hash to hold the eggs. Gently crack an egg into each circle. Season the eggs with the remaining ¼ teaspoon of the salt and ¼ teaspoon of the pepper. Return the pan to the oven. Continue cooking for 3 to 5 minutes, depending on how you like your eggs.
6. When cooking is complete, remove the pan from the oven. Serve immediately.

Maple French Toast Casserole

Prep time: 5 minutes | Cook time: 12 minutes | Serves 6

- 3 large eggs, beaten
- 1 cup whole milk
- 1 tablespoon pure maple syrup
- 1 teaspoon vanilla extract
- ¼ teaspoon cinnamon
- ¼ teaspoon kosher salt
- 3 cups stale bread cubes
- 1 tablespoon unsalted butter, at room temperature

1. In a medium bowl, whisk together the eggs, milk, maple syrup, vanilla extract, cinnamon and salt. Stir in the bread cubes to coat well.
2. Grease the bottom of the sheet pan with the butter. Spread the bread mixture into the pan in an even layer.
3. Select Roast. Set temperature to 350°F (180°C) and set time to 12 minutes. Press Start to begin preheating.
4. Once the unit has preheated, place the pan into the oven.
5. After about 10 minutes, remove the pan and check the casserole. The top should be browned and the middle of the casserole just set. If more time is needed, return the pan to the oven and continue cooking.
6. When cooking is complete, serve warm.

Honey Cashew Granola with Cranberries

Prep time: 5 minutes | Cook time: 12 minutes | Serves 6

- 3 cups old-fashioned rolled oats
- 2 cups raw cashews
- 1 cup unsweetened coconut chips
- ½ cup honey
- ¼ cup vegetable oil
- ⅓ cup packed light brown sugar
- ¼ teaspoon kosher salt
- 1 cup dried cranberries

1. In a large bowl, stir together all the ingredients, except for the cranberries. Spread the mixture on the sheet pan in an even layer.
2. Select Bake. Set temperature to 325°F (163°C) and set time to 12 minutes. Press Start to begin preheating.
3. Once the unit has preheated, place the pan into the oven.
4. After 5 to 6 minutes, remove the pan and stir the granola. Return the pan to the oven and continue cooking.
5. When cooking is complete, remove the pan. Let the granola cool to room temperature. Stir in the cranberries before serving.

Chapter 2 Poultry

Chicken and Ham Rochambeau

Prep time: 25 minutes | Cook time: 30 minutes | Serves 4

- 1 tablespoon melted butter
- ¼ cup all-purpose flour
- 4 chicken tenders, cut in half crosswise
- 4 slices ham, ¼-inch thick, large enough to cover an English muffin
- 2 English muffins, split in halves
- Salt and ground black pepper, to taste
- Cooking spray

Mushroom Sauce:
- 2 tablespoons butter
- ½ cup chopped mushrooms
- ½ cup chopped green onions
- 2 tablespoons flour
- 1 cup chicken broth
- 1½ teaspoons Worcestershire sauce
- ¼ teaspoon garlic powder

1. Put the butter in a baking pan. Combine the flour, salt, and ground black pepper in a shallow dish. Roll the chicken tenders over to coat well.
2. Arrange the chicken in the baking pan and flip to coat with the melted butter.
3. Select Broil. Set temperature to 390°F (199°C) and set time to 10 minutes. Press Start to begin preheating.
4. Once preheated, place the pan into the oven. Flip the tenders halfway through.
5. When cooking is complete, the juices of chicken tenders should run clear.
6. Meanwhile, make the mushroom sauce: melt 2 tablespoons of butter in a saucepan over medium-high heat.
7. Add the mushrooms and onions to the saucepan and sauté for 3 minutes or until the onions are translucent.
8. Gently mix in the flour, broth, Worcestershire sauce, and garlic powder until smooth.
9. Reduce the heat to low and simmer for 5 minutes or until it has a thick consistency. Set the sauce aside until ready to serve.
10. When broiling is complete, remove the baking pan from the oven and set the ham slices into the perforated pan.
11. Select Air Fry. Set time to 5 minutes. Flip the ham slices halfway through.
12. When cooking is complete, the ham slices should be heated through.
13. Remove the ham slices from the oven and set in the English muffin halves and warm for 1 minute.
14. Arrange each ham slice on top of each muffin half, then place each chicken tender over the ham slice.
15. Transfer to the oven and set time to 2 minutes on Air Fry.
16. Serve with the sauce on top.

Breaded Chicken Fingers

Prep time: 20 minutes | Cook time: 10 minutes | Makes 12 chicken fingers

- ½ cup all-purpose flour
- 2 cups panko bread crumbs
- 2 tablespoons canola oil
- 1 large egg
- 3 boneless and skinless chicken breasts, each cut into 4 strips
- Kosher salt and freshly ground black pepper, to taste
- Cooking spray

1. Spritz the perforated pan with cooking spray.
2. Pour the flour in a large bowl. Combine the panko and canola oil on a shallow dish. Whisk the egg in a separate bowl.
3. Rub the chicken strips with salt and ground black pepper on a clean work surface, then dip the chicken in the bowl of flour. Shake the excess off and dunk the chicken strips in the bowl of whisked egg, then roll the strips over the panko to coat well.
4. Arrange the strips in the perforated pan.
5. Select Air Fry. Set temperature to 360°F (182°C) and set time to 10 minutes. Press Start to begin preheating.
6. Once preheated, place the pan into the oven. Flip the strips halfway through.
7. When cooking is complete, the strips should be crunchy and lightly browned.
8. Serve immediately.

Breaded Chicken Livers

Prep time: 10 minutes | Cook time: 10 minutes | Serves 4

- 2 eggs
- 2 tablespoons water
- ¾ cup flour
- 2 cups panko bread crumbs
- 1 teaspoon salt
- ½ teaspoon ground black pepper
- 20 ounces (567 g) chicken livers
- Cooking spray

1. Spritz the perforated pan with cooking spray.
2. Combine the flour, marjoram, thyme, parsley, and salt in a shallow dish. Stir to mix well.
3. Whisk the egg with lemon juice and water in a large bowl. Pour the bread crumbs in a separate shallow dish.
4. Roll the chicken halves in the flour mixture first, then in the egg mixture, and then roll over the bread crumbs to coat well. Shake the excess off.
5. Arrange the chicken halves in the perforated pan and spritz with cooking spray on both sides.

6. Select Air Fry. Set temperature to 390°F (199°C) and set time to 5 minutes. Press Start to begin preheating.
7. Once preheated, place the pan into the oven. Flip the halves halfway through.
8. When cooking is complete, the chicken halves should be golden brown and crispy.
9. Serve immediately.

Breaded Chicken Tenders with Thyme

Prep time: 15 minutes | Cook time: 5 minutes | Serves 4

- ½ cup all-purpose flour
- 1 teaspoon marjoram
- ½ teaspoon thyme
- 1 teaspoon dried parsley flakes
- ½ teaspoon salt
- 1 egg
- 1 teaspoon lemon juice
- 1 teaspoon water
- 1 cup bread crumbs
- 4 chicken tenders, pounded thin, cut in half lengthwise
- Cooking spray

1. Spritz the perforated pan with cooking spray.
2. Combine the flour, marjoram, thyme, parsley, and salt in a shallow dish. Stir to mix well.
3. Whisk the egg with lemon juice and water in a large bowl. Pour the bread crumbs in a separate shallow dish.
4. Roll the chicken halves in the flour mixture first, then in the egg mixture, and then roll over the bread crumbs to coat well. Shake the excess off.
5. Arrange the chicken halves in the perforated pan and spritz with cooking spray on both sides.
6. Select Air Fry. Set temperature to 390°F (199°C) and set time to 5 minutes. Press Start to begin preheating.
7. Once preheated, place the pan into the oven. Flip the halves halfway through.
8. When cooking is complete, the chicken halves should be golden brown and crispy.
9. Serve immediately.

Barbecue Chicken with Coleslaw

Prep time: 15 minutes | Cook time: 10 minutes | Makes 4 tostadas

Coleslaw:
- ¼ cup sour cream
- ¼ small green cabbage, finely chopped
- ½ tablespoon white vinegar
- ½ teaspoon garlic powder
- ½ teaspoon salt
- ¼ teaspoon ground black pepper

Tostadas:
- 2 cups pulled rotisserie chicken
- ½ cup barbecue sauce
- 4 corn tortillas
- ½ cup shredded Mozzarella cheese
- Cooking spray

Make the Coleslaw:
1. Combine the ingredients for the coleslaw in a large bowl. Toss to mix well.
2. Refrigerate until ready to serve.

Make the Tostadas:
1. Spritz the perforated pan with cooking spray.
2. Toss the chicken with barbecue sauce in a separate large bowl to combine well. Set aside.
3. Place one tortilla in the perforated pan and spritz with cooking spray.
4. Select Air Fry. Set temperature to 370°F (188°C) and set time to 10 minutes. Press Start to begin preheating.
5. Once preheated, place the pan into the oven. Flip the tortilla and spread the barbecue chicken and cheese over halfway through.
6. When cooking is complete, the tortilla should be browned and the cheese should be melted.
7. Serve the tostadas with coleslaw on top.

Mustard Chicken Thighs in Waffles

Prep time: 1 hour 20 minutes | Cook time: 20 minutes | Serves 4

For the Chicken:
- 4 chicken thighs, skin on
- 1 cup low-fat buttermilk
- ½ cup all-purpose flour
- ½ teaspoon garlic powder
- ½ teaspoon mustard powder
- 1 teaspoon kosher salt
- ½ teaspoon freshly ground black pepper
- ¼ cup honey, for serving
- Cooking spray

For the Waffles:
- ½ cup all-purpose flour
- ½ cup whole wheat pastry flour
- 1 large egg, beaten
- 1 cup low-fat buttermilk
- 1 teaspoon baking powder
- 2 tablespoons canola oil
- ½ teaspoon kosher salt
- 1 tablespoon granulated sugar

1. 1.Combine the chicken thighs with buttermilk in a large bowl. Wrap the bowl in plastic and refrigerate to marinate for at least an hour.
2. 2.Spritz the perforated pan with cooking spray.
3. 3.Combine the flour, mustard powder, garlic powder, salt, and black pepper in a shallow dish. Stir to mix well.
4. 4.Remove the thighs from the buttermilk and pat dry with paper towels. Sit the bowl of buttermilk aside.
5. 5.Dip the thighs in the flour mixture first, then into the buttermilk, and then into the flour mixture. Shake the excess off.
6. 6.Arrange the thighs in the perforated pan and spritz with cooking spray.

7. Select Air Fry. Set temperature to 360°F (182°C) and set time to 20 minutes. Press Start to begin preheating.
8. Once preheated, place the pan into the oven. Flip the thighs halfway through.
9. When cooking is complete, an instant-read thermometer inserted in the thickest part of the chicken thighs should register at least 165°F (74°C).
10. Meanwhile, make the waffles: combine the ingredients for the waffles in a large bowl. Stir to mix well, then arrange the mixture in a waffle iron and cook until a golden and fragrant waffle forms.
11. Remove the waffles from the waffle iron and slice into 4 pieces. Remove the chicken thighs from the oven and allow to cool for 5 minutes.
12. Arrange each chicken thigh on each waffle piece and drizzle with 1 tablespoon of honey. Serve warm.

Gochujang Chicken Wings

Prep time: 10 minutes | Cook time: 25 minutes | Serves 4

Wings:
- 2 pounds (907 g) chicken wings
- 1 teaspoon salt
- 1 teaspoon ground black pepper

Sauce:
- 2 tablespoons gochujang
- 1 tablespoon mayonnaise
- 1 tablespoon minced ginger
- 1 tablespoon minced garlic
- 1 teaspoon agave nectar
- 2 packets Splenda
- 1 tablespoon sesame oil

For Garnish:
- 2 teaspoons sesame seeds
- ¼ cup chopped green onions

1. Line a baking pan with aluminum foil, then arrange the rack on the pan.
2. On a clean work surface, rub the chicken wings with salt and ground black pepper, then arrange the seasoned wings on the rack.
3. Select Air Fry. Set temperature to 400°F (205°C) and set time to 20 minutes. Press Start to begin preheating.
4. Once preheated, place the pan into the oven. Flip the wings halfway through.
5. When cooking is complete, the wings should be well browned.
6. Meanwhile, combine the ingredients for the sauce in a small bowl. Stir to mix well. Reserve half of the sauce in a separate bowl until ready to serve.
7. Remove the air fried chicken wings from the oven and toss with remaining half of the sauce to coat well.
8. Place the wings back to the oven. Select Air Fry. Set time to 5 minutes.
9. When cooking is complete, the internal temperature of the wings should reach at least 165°F (74°C).
10. Remove the wings from the oven and place on a large plate. Sprinkle with sesame seeds and green onions. Serve with reserved sauce.

Chili Chicken Skin with Dill

Prep time: 5 minutes | Cook time: 6 minutes | Serves 4

- 1 pound (454 g) chicken skin, cut into slices
- 1 teaspoon melted butter
- ½ teaspoon crushed chili flakes
- 1 teaspoon dried dill
- Salt and ground black pepper, to taste

1. Combine all the ingredients in a large bowl. Toss to coat the chicken skin well.
2. Transfer the skin in the perforated pan.
3. Select Air Fry. Set temperature to 360°F (182°C) and set time to 6 minutes. Press Start to begin preheating.
4. Once preheated, place the pan into the oven. Stir the skin halfway through.
5. When cooking is complete, the skin should be crispy.
6. Serve immediately.

Chicken Drumsticks with Cajun Seasoning

Prep time: 5 minutes | Cook time: 18 minutes | Serves 5

- 1 tablespoon olive oil
- 10 chicken drumsticks
- 1½ tablespoons Cajun seasoning
- Salt and ground black pepper, to taste

1. Grease the perforated pan with olive oil.
2. On a clean work surface, rub the chicken drumsticks with Cajun seasoning, salt, and ground black pepper.
3. Arrange the seasoned chicken drumsticks in the perforated pan.
4. Select Air Fry. Set temperature to 390°F (199°C) and set time to 18 minutes. Press Start to begin preheating.
5. Once preheated, place the pan into the oven. Flip the drumsticks halfway through.
6. When cooking is complete, the drumsticks should be lightly browned.
7. Remove the chicken drumsticks from the oven. Serve immediately.

Ginger Chicken Bites in Sherry

Prep time: 15 minutes | Cook time: 15 minutes | Serves 4

- ½ cup pineapple juice
- 2 tablespoons apple cider vinegar
- ½ tablespoon minced ginger
- ½ cup ketchup
- 2 garlic cloves, minced
- ½ cup brown sugar
- 2 tablespoons sherry

- ½ cup soy sauce
- 4 chicken breasts, cubed
- Cooking spray

1. Combine the pineapple juice, cider vinegar, ginger, ketchup, garlic, and sugar in a saucepan. Stir to mix well. Heat over low heat for 5 minutes or until thickened. Fold in the sherry and soy sauce.
2. Dunk the chicken cubes in the mixture. Press to submerge. Wrap the bowl in plastic and refrigerate to marinate for at least an hour.
3. Spritz the perforated pan with cooking spray.
4. Remove the chicken cubes from the marinade. Shake the excess off and put in the perforated pan. Spritz with cooking spray.
5. Select Air Fry. Set temperature to 360°F (182°C) and set time to 15 minutes. Press Start to begin preheating.
6. Once preheated, place the pan into the oven. Flip the chicken cubes at least three times during the air frying.
7. When cooking is complete, the chicken cubes should be glazed and well browned.
8. Serve immediately.

Honey-Ginger Chicken Breasts

Prep time: 5 minutes | Cook time: 10 minutes | Serves 4

- 4 (4-ounce / 113-g) boneless, skinless chicken breasts
- Chicken seasoning or rub, to taste
- Salt and ground black pepper, to taste
- ¼ cup honey
- 2 tablespoons soy sauce
- 2 teaspoons grated fresh ginger
- 2 garlic cloves, minced
- Cooking spray

1. Spritz the perforated pan with cooking spray.
2. Rub the chicken breasts with chicken seasoning, salt, and black pepper on a clean work surface.
3. Arrange the chicken breasts in the perforated pan and spritz with cooking spray.
4. Select Air Fry. Set temperature to 400°F (205°C) and set time to 10 minutes. Press Start to begin preheating.
5. Once preheated, place the pan into the oven. Flip the chicken breasts halfway through.
6. When cooking is complete, the internal temperature of the thickest part of the chicken should reach at least 165°F (74°C).
7. Meanwhile, combine the honey, soy sauce, ginger, and garlic in a saucepan and heat over medium-high heat for 3 minutes or until thickened. Stir constantly.
8. Remove the chicken from the oven and serve with the honey glaze.

Parmesan Chicken Cutlets

Prep time: 15 minutes | Cook time: 15 minutes | Serves 4

- 2 tablespoons panko bread crumbs
- ¼ cup grated Parmesan cheese
- ⅛ tablespoon paprika
- ½ tablespoon garlic powder
- 2 large eggs
- 4 chicken cutlets
- 1 tablespoon parsley
- Salt and ground black pepper, to taste
- Cooking spray

1. Spritz the perforated pan with cooking spray.
2. Combine the bread crumbs, Parmesan, paprika, garlic powder, salt, and ground black pepper in a large bowl. Stir to mix well. Beat the eggs in a separate bowl.
3. Dredge the chicken cutlets in the beaten eggs, then roll over the bread crumbs mixture to coat well. Shake the excess off.
4. Transfer the chicken cutlets in the perforated pan and spritz with cooking spray.
5. Select Air Fry. Set temperature to 400°F (205°C) and set time to 15 minutes. Press Start to begin preheating.
6. Once preheated, place the pan into the oven. Flip the cutlets halfway through.
7. When cooking is complete, the cutlets should be crispy and golden brown.
8. Serve with parsley on top.

Rosemary Chicken Breasts with Tomatoes

Prep time: 10 minutes | Cook time: 35 minutes | Serves 8

- 3 pounds (1.4 kg) chicken breasts, bone-in
- 1 teaspoon minced fresh basil
- 1 teaspoon minced fresh rosemary
- 2 tablespoons minced fresh parsley
- 1 teaspoon cayenne pepper
- ½ teaspoon salt
- ½ teaspoon freshly ground black pepper
- 4 medium Roma tomatoes, halved
- Cooking spray

1. Spritz the perforated pan with cooking spray.
2. Combine all the ingredients, except for the chicken breasts and tomatoes, in a large bowl. Stir to mix well.
3. Dunk the chicken breasts in the mixture and press to coat well.
4. Transfer the chicken breasts to the perforated pan.
5. Select Air Fry. Set temperature to 370°F (188°C) and set time to 20 minutes. Press Start to begin preheating.
6. Once preheated, place the pan into the oven. Flip the breasts halfway through the cooking time.
7. When cooking is complete, the internal temperature of the thickest part of the breasts should reach at least 165°F (74°C).

8. Remove the cooked chicken breasts from the oven and adjust the temperature to 350°F (180°C).
9. Place the tomatoes in the perforated pan and spritz with cooking spray. Sprinkle with a touch of salt.
10. Set time to 10 minutes. Stir the tomatoes halfway through the cooking time.
11. When cooking is complete, the tomatoes should be tender.
12. Serve the tomatoes with chicken breasts on a large serving plate.

Chicken Tacos with Lettuce

Prep time: 10 minutes | Cook time: 6 minutes | Serves 4

- 1 pound (454 g) ground chicken
- 2 cloves garlic, minced
- ¼ cup diced onions
- ¼ teaspoon sea salt
- Cooking spray

Peanut Sauce:
- ¼ cup creamy peanut butter, at room temperature
- 2 tablespoons tamari
- 1½ teaspoons hot sauce
- 2 tablespoons lime juice
- 2 tablespoons grated fresh ginger
- 2 tablespoons chicken broth
- 2 teaspoons sugar

For Serving:
- 2 small heads butter lettuce, leaves separated
- Lime slices (optional)

1. Spritz a baking pan with cooking spray.
2. Combine the ground chicken, garlic, and onions in the baking pan, then sprinkle with salt. Use a fork to break the ground chicken and combine them well.
3. Select Bake. Set temperature to 350°F (180°C) and set time to 5 minutes. Press Start to begin preheating.
4. Once preheated, place the pan into the oven. Stir them halfway through the cooking time.
5. When cooking is complete, the chicken should be lightly browned.
6. Meanwhile, combine the ingredients for the sauce in a small bowl. Stir to mix well.
7. Pour the sauce in the pan of chicken, then bake for 1 more minute or until heated through.
8. Unfold the lettuce leaves on a large serving plate, then divide the chicken mixture on the lettuce leaves. Drizzle with lime juice and serve immediately.

Buttermilk Chicken Drumsticks

Prep time: 10 minutes | Cook time: 14 minutes | Serves 4

- 8 (4- to 5-ounce / 113- to 142-g) skinless bone-in chicken drumsticks
- ½ cup plain full-fat or low-fat yogurt
- ¼ cup buttermilk
- 2 teaspoons minced garlic
- 2 teaspoons minced fresh ginger
- 2 teaspoons ground cinnamon
- 2 teaspoons ground coriander
- 2 teaspoons mild paprika
- 1 teaspoon salt
- 1 teaspoon Tabasco hot red pepper sauce

1. In a large bowl, stir together all the ingredients except for chicken drumsticks until well combined. Add the chicken drumsticks to the bowl and toss until well coated. Cover in plastic and set in the refrigerator to marinate for 1 hour, tossing once.
2. Arrange the marinated drumsticks in the perforated pan, leaving enough space between them.
3. Select Air Fry. Set temperature to 375°F (190°C) and set time to 14 minutes. Press Start to begin preheating.
4. Once preheated, place the pan into the oven. Flip the drumsticks once halfway through to ensure even cooking.
5. When cooking is complete, the internal temperature of the chicken drumsticks should reach 160°F (71°C) on a meat thermometer.
6. Transfer the drumsticks to plates. Rest for 5 minutes before serving.

Chicken Thighs with Cherry Tomatoes

Prep time: 10 minutes | Cook time: 18 minutes | Serves 4

- 1½ pounds (680 g) boneless, skinless chicken thighs
- 1¼ teaspoon kosher salt, divided
- 2 tablespoons plus 1 teaspoon olive oil, divided
- ⅔ cup plus 2 tablespoons plain Greek yogurt, divided
- 2 tablespoons freshly squeezed lemon juice (about 1 medium lemon)
- 4 garlic cloves, minced, divided
- 1 tablespoon Shawarma Seasoning
- 4 pita breads, cut in half
- 2 cups cherry tomatoes
- ½ small cucumber, peeled, deseeded, and chopped
- 1 tablespoon chopped fresh parsley

1. Sprinkle the chicken thighs on both sides with 1 teaspoon of kosher salt. Place in a resealable plastic bag and set aside while you make the marinade.
2. In a small bowl, mix 2 tablespoons of olive oil, 2 tablespoons of yogurt, the lemon juice, 3 garlic cloves, and Shawarma Seasoning until thoroughly combined. Pour the marinade over the chicken. Seal the bag, squeezing out as much air as possible. And massage the chicken to coat it with the sauce. Set aside.
3. Wrap 2 pita breads each in two pieces of aluminum foil and place on a baking pan.
4. Select Bake. Set temperature to 300°F (150°C) and set time to 6 minutes. Press Start to begin preheating.
5. Once the oven has preheated, place the pan into the oven. After 3 minutes, remove the pan from the oven and turn

over the foil packets. Return the pan to the oven and continue cooking. When cooking is complete, remove the pan from the oven and place the foil-wrapped pitas on the top of the oven to keep warm.

6. Remove the chicken from the marinade, letting the excess drip off into the bag. Place them on the baking pan. Arrange the tomatoes around the sides of the chicken. Discard the marinade.
7. Select Broil. Set temperature to High, and set time to 12 minutes.
8. Place the pan into the oven.
9. After 6 minutes, remove the pan from the oven and turn over the chicken. Return the pan to the oven and continue cooking.
10. Wrap the cucumber in a paper towel to remove as much moisture as possible. Place them in a small bowl. Add the remaining yogurt, kosher salt, olive oil, garlic clove, and parsley. Whisk until combined.
11. When cooking is complete, the chicken should be browned, crisp along its edges, and sizzling. Remove the pan from the oven and place the chicken on a cutting board. Cut each thigh into several pieces. Unwrap the pitas. Spread a tablespoon of sauce into a pita half. Add some chicken and add 2 roasted tomatoes. Serve.

Mozzarella Chicken Breasts with Basil

Prep time: 30 minutes | Cook time: 1 hour | Serves 2

- 1 large egg
- ¼ cup almond meal
- 2 (6-ounce / 170-g) boneless, skinless chicken breast halves
- 1 (8-ounce / 227-g) jar marinara sauce, divided
- 4 tablespoons shredded Mozzarella cheese, divided
- 4 tablespoons grated Parmesan cheese, divided
- 4 tablespoons chopped fresh basil, divided
- Salt and freshly ground black pepper, to taste
- Cooking spray

1. Spritz the perforated pan with cooking spray.
2. In a shallow bowl, beat the egg.
3. In a separate shallow bowl, place the almond meal.
4. Dip 1 chicken breast half into the egg, then into the almond meal to coat. Place the coated chicken in the perforated pan. Repeat with the remaining 1 chicken breast half.
5. Select Bake. Set temperature to 350°F (180°C) and set time to 40 minutes. Press Start to begin preheating.
6. Once preheated, place the pan into the oven.
7. After 20 minutes, remove the pan from the oven and flip the chicken. Return the pan to oven and continue cooking.
8. When cooking is complete, the chicken should no longer pink and the juices run clear.
9. In a baking pan, pour half of marinara sauce.
10. Place the cooked chicken in the sauce. Cover with the remaining marinara.
11. Sprinkle 2 tablespoons of Mozzarella cheese and 2 tablespoons of soy Parmesan cheese on each chicken breast. Top each with 2 tablespoons of basil.
12. Place the baking pan back in the oven and set the baking time to 20 minutes. Flip the chicken halfway through the cooking time.
13. When cooking is complete, an instant-read thermometer inserted into the center of the chicken should read at least 165°F (74°C).
14. Remove the pan from oven and divide between 2 plates. Season with salt and pepper and serve.

Chicken Thighs with Cabbage Slaw

Prep time: 10 minutes | Cook time: 27 minutes | Serves 4

- 4 bone-in, skin-on chicken thighs
- 1½ teaspoon kosher salt, divided
- 1 tablespoon smoked paprika
- ½ teaspoon granulated garlic
- ½ teaspoon dried oregano
- ¼ teaspoon freshly ground black pepper
- 3 cups shredded cabbage
- ½ small red onion, thinly sliced
- 4 large radishes, julienned
- 3 tablespoons red wine vinegar
- 2 tablespoons olive oil
- Cooking spray

1. Salt the chicken thighs on both sides with 1 teaspoon of kosher salt. In a small bowl, combine the paprika, garlic, oregano, and black pepper. Sprinkle half this mixture over the skin sides of the thighs. Spritz a baking pan with cooking spray and place the thighs skin-side down on the pan. Sprinkle the remaining spice mixture over the other sides of the chicken pieces.
2. Select Roast. Set temperature to 375°F (190°C) and set time to 27 minutes. Press Start to begin preheating.
3. Once preheated, place the pan into the oven.
4. After 10 minutes, remove the pan from the oven and turn over the chicken thighs. Return the pan to the oven and continue cooking.
5. While the chicken cooks, place the cabbage, onion, and radishes in a large bowl. Sprinkle with the remaining kosher salt, vinegar, and olive oil. Toss to coat.
6. After another 9 to 10 minutes, remove the pan from the oven and place the chicken thighs on a cutting board. Place the cabbage mixture in the pan and toss with the chicken fat and spices.
7. Spread the cabbage in an even layer on the pan and place the chicken on it, skin-side up. place the pan into the oven and continue cooking. Roast for another 7 to 8 minutes.
8. When cooking is complete, the cabbage is just becoming

tender. Remove the pan from the oven. Taste and adjust the seasoning if necessary. Serve.

Buttery Chicken with Corn

Prep time: 10 minutes | Cook time: 25 minutes | Serves 4

- 4 bone-in, skin-on chicken thighs
- 2 teaspoons kosher salt, divided
- 1 cup Bisquick baking mix
- ½ cup butter, melted, divided
- 1 pound (454 g) small red potatoes, quartered
- 3 ears corn, shucked and cut into rounds 1- to 1½-inches thick
- ⅓ cup heavy whipping cream
- ½ teaspoon freshly ground black pepper

1. Sprinkle the chicken on all sides with 1 teaspoon of kosher salt. Place the baking mix in a shallow dish. Brush the thighs on all sides with ¼ cup of butter, then dredge them in the baking mix, coating them all on sides. Place the chicken in the center of a baking pan.
2. Place the potatoes in a large bowl with 2 tablespoons of butter and toss to coat. Place them on one side of the chicken on the pan.
3. Place the corn in a medium bowl and drizzle with the remaining butter. Sprinkle with ¼ teaspoon of kosher salt and toss to coat. Place on the pan on the other side of the chicken.
4. Select Roast. Set temperature to 375°F (190°C) and set time to 25 minutes. Press Start to begin preheating.
5. Once preheated, place the pan into the oven.
6. After 20 minutes, remove the pan from the oven and transfer the potatoes back to the bowl. Return the pan to oven and continue cooking.
7. As the chicken continues cooking, add the cream, black pepper, and remaining kosher salt to the potatoes. Lightly mash the potatoes with a potato masher.
8. When cooking is complete, the corn should be tender and the chicken cooked through, reading 165°F (74°C) on a meat thermometer. Remove the pan from the oven and serve the chicken with the smashed potatoes and corn on the side.

Vinegary Chicken with Pineapple

Prep time: 10 minutes | Cook time: 10 minutes | Serves 6

- 1½ pounds (680 g) boneless, skinless chicken breasts, cut into 1-inch chunks
- ¾ cup soy sauce
- 2 tablespoons ketchup
- 2 tablespoons brown sugar
- 2 tablespoons rice vinegar
- 1 red bell pepper, cut into 1-inch chunks
- 1 green bell pepper, cut into 1-inch chunks
- 6 scallions, cut into 1-inch pieces
- 1 cup (¾-inch chunks) fresh pineapple, rinsed and drained
- Cooking spray

1. Place the chicken in a large bowl. Add the soy sauce, ketchup, brown sugar, vinegar, red and green peppers, and scallions. Toss to coat.
2. Spritz a baking pan with cooking spray and place the chicken and vegetables on the pan.
3. Select Roast. Set temperature to 375°F (190°C) and set time to 10 minutes. Press Start to begin preheating.
4. Once preheated, place the pan into the oven.
5. After 6 minutes, remove the pan from the oven. Add the pineapple chunks to the pan and stir. Return the pan to the oven and continue cooking.
6. When cooking is complete, remove the pan from the oven. Serve with steamed rice, if desired.

Chicken Gnocchi with Spinach

Prep time: 10 minutes | Cook time: 13 minutes | Serves 4

- 1 (1-pound / 454-g) package shelf-stable gnocchi
- 1¼ cups chicken stock
- ½ teaspoon kosher salt
- 1 pound (454 g) chicken breast, cut into 1-inch chunks
- 1 cup heavy whipping cream
- 2 tablespoons sun-dried tomato purée
- 1 garlic clove, minced
- 1 cup frozen spinach, thawed and drained
- 1 cup grated Parmesan cheese

1. Place the gnocchi in an even layer on a baking pan. Pour the chicken stock over the gnocchi.
2. Select Bake. Set temperature to 450°F (235°C) and set time to 7 minutes. Press Start to begin preheating.
3. Once preheated, place the pan into the oven.
4. While the gnocchi are cooking, sprinkle the salt over the chicken pieces. In a small bowl, mix the cream, tomato purée, and garlic.
5. When cooking is complete, blot off any remaining stock, or drain the gnocchi and return it to the pan. Top the gnocchi with the spinach and chicken. Pour the cream mixture over the ingredients in the pan.
6. Select Roast. Set temperature to 400°F (205°C) and set time to 6 minutes. Place the pan into the oven.
7. After 4 minutes, remove the pan from the oven and gently stir the ingredients. Return the pan to the oven and continue cooking.
8. When cooking is complete, the gnocchi should be tender and the chicken should be cooked through. Remove the pan from the oven. Stir in the Parmesan cheese until it's melted and serve.

Peach Chicken with Dark Cherry

Prep time: 8 minutes | Cook time: 15 minutes | Serves 4

- ⅓ cup peach preserves
- 1 teaspoon ground rosemary
- ½ teaspoon black pepper
- ½ teaspoon salt
- ½ teaspoon marjoram
- 1 teaspoon light olive oil
- 1 pound (454 g) boneless chicken breasts, cut in 1½-inch chunks
- 1 (10-ounce / 284-g) package frozen dark cherries, thawed and drained
- Cooking spray

1. In a medium bowl, mix peach preserves, rosemary, pepper, salt, marjoram, and olive oil.
2. Stir in chicken chunks and toss to coat well with the preserve mixture.
3. Spritz the perforated pan with cooking spray and lay chicken chunks in the perforated pan.
4. Select Bake. set temperature to 400°F (205°C) and set time to 15 minutes. Press Start to begin preheating.
5. Once preheated, place the pan into the oven.
6. After 7 minutes, remove the pan from the oven. Flip the chicken chunks. Return the pan to the oven and continue cooking.
7. When cooking is complete, the chicken should no longer pink and the juices should run clear.
8. Scatter the cherries over and cook for an additional minute to heat cherries.
9. Serve immediately.

Turkey Meatloaves with Onion

Prep time: 6 minutes | Cook time: 24 minutes | Serves 4

- ¼ cup grated carrot
- 2 garlic cloves, minced
- 2 tablespoons ground almonds
- ⅓ cup minced onion
- 2 teaspoons olive oil
- 1 teaspoon dried marjoram
- 1 egg white
- ¾ pound (340 g) ground turkey breast

1. In a medium bowl, stir together the carrot, garlic, almonds, onion, olive oil, marjoram, and egg white.
2. Add the ground turkey. Mix until combined.
3. Double 16 foil muffin cup liners to make 8 cups. Divide the turkey mixture evenly among the liners.
4. Select Bake. Set temperature to 400°F (205°C) and set time to 24 minutes. Press Start to begin preheating.
5. Once preheated, place the muffin cups into the oven.
6. When cooking is complete, the meatloaves should reach an internal temperature of 165°F (74°C) on a meat thermometer.
7. Serve immediately.

Paprika Hens with Creole Seasoning

Prep time: 10 minutes | Cook time: 40 minutes | Serves 4

- ½ tablespoon Creole seasoning
- ½ tablespoon garlic powder
- ½ tablespoon onion powder
- ½ tablespoon freshly ground black pepper
- ½ tablespoon paprika
- 2 tablespoons olive oil
- 2 Cornish hens
- Cooking spray

1. Spritz the perforated pan with cooking spray.
2. In a small bowl, mix the Creole seasoning, garlic powder, onion powder, pepper, and paprika.
3. Pat the Cornish hens dry and brush each hen all over with the olive oil. Rub each hen with the seasoning mixture. Place the Cornish hens in the perforated pan.
4. Select Air Fry. Set temperature to 375°F (190°C) and set time to 30 minutes. Press Start to begin preheating.
5. Once preheated, place the pan into the oven.
6. After 15 minutes, remove the pan from the oven. Flip the hens over and baste it with any drippings collected in the bottom drawer of the oven. Return the pan to the oven and continue cooking.
7. When cooking is complete, a thermometer inserted into the thickest part of the hens should reach at least 165°F (74°C).
8. Let the hens rest for 10 minutes before carving.

Paprika Hens in Wine

Prep time: 2 hours 15 minutes | Cook time: 30 minutes | Serves 8

- 4 (1¼-pound / 567-g) Cornish hens, giblets removed, split lengthwise
- 2 cups white wine, divided
- 2 garlic cloves, minced
- 1 small onion, minced
- ½ teaspoon celery seeds
- ½ teaspoon poultry seasoning
- ½ teaspoon paprika
- ½ teaspoon dried oregano
- ¼ teaspoon freshly ground black pepper

1. Place the hens, cavity side up, on a rack in a baking pan. Pour 1½ cups of the wine over the hens; set aside.
2. In a shallow bowl, combine the garlic, onion, celery seeds, poultry seasoning, paprika, oregano, and pepper. Sprinkle half of the combined seasonings over the cavity of each split half. Cover and refrigerate. Allow the hens to marinate for 2 hours.
3. Transfer the hens in the perforated pan.
4. Select Bake. Set temperature to 350°F (180°C) and set time to 90 minutes. Press Start to begin preheating.
5. Once preheated, place the pan into the oven.
6. Remove the panpan from the oven halfway through the baking, turn breast side up, and remove the skin. Pour the remaining ½ cup of wine over the top, and sprinkle with the

remaining seasonings.

7. When cooking is complete, the inner temperature of the hens should be at least 165°F (74°C). Transfer the hens to a serving platter and serve hot.

Chili Chicken Fries

Prep time: 20 minutes | Cook time: 6 minutes | Serves 4 to 6

- 1 pound (454 g) chicken tenders, cut into about ½-inch-wide strips
- Salt, to taste
- ¼ cup all-purpose flour
- 2 eggs
- ¾ cup panko bread crumbs
- ¾ cup crushed organic nacho cheese tortilla chips
- Cooking spray

Seasonings:
- ½ teaspoon garlic powder
- 1 tablespoon chili powder
- ½ teaspoon onion powder
- 1 teaspoon ground cumin

1. Stir together all seasonings in a small bowl and set aside.
2. Sprinkle the chicken with salt. Place strips in a large bowl and sprinkle with 1 tablespoon of the seasoning mix. Stir well to distribute seasonings.
3. Add flour to chicken and stir well to coat all sides.
4. Beat eggs in a separate bowl.
5. In a shallow dish, combine the panko, crushed chips, and the remaining 2 teaspoons of seasoning mix.
6. Dip chicken strips in eggs, then roll in crumbs. Mist with oil or cooking spray. Arrange the chicken strips in a single layer in the perforated pan.
7. Select Air Fry. Set temperature to 400°F (205°C) and set time to 6 minutes. Press Start to begin preheating.
8. Once preheated, place the pan into the oven.
9. After 4 minutes, remove the pan from the oven. Flip the strips with tongs. Return the pan to the oven and continue cooking.
10. When cooking is complete, the chicken should be crispy and its juices should be run clear.
11. Allow to cool under room temperature before serving.

Chapter 3 Fish and Seafood

Tuna Casserole with Basil

Prep time: 10 minutes | Cook time: 16 minutes | Serves 4

- ½ tablespoon sesame oil
- ⅓ cup yellow onions, chopped
- ½ bell pepper, seeded and chopped
- 2 cups canned tuna, chopped
- Cooking spray
- 5 eggs, beaten
- ½ chili pepper, deveined and finely minced
- 1½ tablespoons sour cream
- ⅓ teaspoon dried basil
- ⅓ teaspoon dried oregano
- Fine sea salt and ground black pepper, to taste

1. Heat the sesame oil in a nonstick skillet over medium heat until it shimmers.
2. Add the onions and bell pepper and sauté for 4 minutes, stirring occasionally, or until tender.
3. Add the canned tuna and keep stirring until the tuna is heated through.
4. Meanwhile, coat a baking dish lightly with cooking spray.
5. Transfer the tuna mixture to the baking dish, along with the beaten eggs, chili pepper, sour cream, basil, and oregano. Stir to combine well. Season with sea salt and black pepper.
6. Select Bake. Set temperature to 325°F (163°C) and set time to 12 minutes. Press Start to begin preheating.
7. Once preheated, place the baking dish into the oven.
8. When cooking is complete, the eggs should be completely set and the top lightly browned. Remove from the oven and serve on a plate.

Salmon Spring Rolls with Parsley

Prep time: 20 minutes | Cook time: 18 minutes | Serves 4

- ½ pound (227 g) salmon fillet
- 1 teaspoon toasted sesame oil
- 1 onion, sliced
- 1 carrot, shredded
- 1 yellow bell pepper, thinly sliced
- ⅓ cup chopped fresh flat-leaf parsley
- ¼ cup chopped fresh basil
- 8 rice paper wrappers

1. Arrange the salmon in the perforated pan. Drizzle the sesame oil all over the salmon and scatter the onion on top.
2. Select Air Fry. Set temperature to 370°F (188°C) and set time to 10 minutes. Press Start to begin preheating.
3. Once preheated, place the pan into the oven.
4. Meanwhile, fill a small shallow bowl with warm water. One by one, dip the rice paper wrappers into the water for a few seconds or just until moistened, then put them on a work surface.
5. When cooking is complete, the fish should flake apart with a fork. Remove from the oven to a plate.
6. Make the spring rolls: Place ⅛ of the salmon and onion mixture, carrot, bell pepper, parsley, and basil into the center of the rice wrapper and fold the sides over the filling. Roll up the wrapper carefully and tightly like you would a burrito. Repeat with the remaining wrappers and filling.
7. Transfer the rolls to the perforated pan.
8. Select Bake. Set temperature to 380°F (193°C) and set time to 8 minutes. Place the pan into the oven.
9. When cooking is complete, the rolls should be crispy and lightly browned. Remove from the oven and cut each roll in half and serve warm.

Cajun Tilapia Tacos

Prep time: 10 minutes | Cook time: 10 to 15 minutes | Serves 6

- 1 tablespoon avocado oil
- 1 tablespoon Cajun seasoning
- 4 (5 to 6 ounce / 142 to 170 g) tilapia fillets
- 1 (14-ounce / 397-g) package coleslaw mix
- 12 corn tortillas
- 2 limes, cut into wedges

1. Line a baking pan with parchment paper.
2. In a shallow bowl, stir together the avocado oil and Cajun seasoning to make a marinade. Place the tilapia fillets into the bowl, turning to coat evenly.
3. Put the fillets in the baking pan in a single layer.
4. Select Air Fry. Set temperature to 375°F (190°C) and set time to 10 minutes. Press Start to begin preheating.
5. Once preheated, slide the pan into the oven.
6. When cooked, the fish should be flaky. If necessary, continue cooking for 5 minutes more. Remove the fish from the oven to a plate.
7. Assemble the tacos: Spoon some of the coleslaw mix into each tortilla and top each with ⅓ of a tilapia fillet. Squeeze some lime juice over the top of each taco and serve immediately.

Hoisin Tuna with Lemongrass

Prep time: 15 minutes | Cook time: 5 minutes | Serves 4

- ½ cup hoisin sauce
- 2 tablespoons rice wine vinegar
- 2 teaspoons sesame oil
- 2 teaspoons dried lemongrass
- 1 teaspoon garlic powder
- ¼ teaspoon red pepper flakes
- ½ small onion, quartered and thinly sliced
- 8 ounces (227 g) fresh tuna, cut into 1-inch cubes
- Cooking spray
- 3 cups cooked jasmine rice

1. In a small bowl, whisk together the hoisin sauce, vinegar, sesame oil, lemongrass, garlic powder, and red pepper flakes.
2. Add the sliced onion and tuna cubes and gently toss until the fish is evenly coated.
3. Arrange the coated tuna cubes in the perforated pan in a single layer.
4. Select Air Fry. Set temperature to 390°F (199°C) and set time to 5 minutes. Press Start to begin preheating.
5. Once preheated, place the pan into the oven. Flip the fish halfway through the cooking time.
6. When cooking is complete, the fish should begin to flake. Continue cooking for 1 minute, if necessary. Remove from the oven and serve over hot jasmine rice.

Tilapia Meunière with Parsley

Prep time: 10 minutes | Cook time: 20 minutes | Serves 4

- 10 ounces (283 g) Yukon Gold potatoes, sliced ¼-inch thick
- 5 tablespoons unsalted butter, melted, divided
- 1 teaspoon kosher salt, divided
- 4 (8-ounce / 227-g) tilapia fillets
- ½ pound (227 g) green beans, trimmed
- Juice of 1 lemon
- 2 tablespoons chopped fresh parsley, for garnish

1. In a large bowl, drizzle the potatoes with 2 tablespoons of melted butter and ¼ teaspoon of kosher salt. Transfer the potatoes to the sheet pan.
2. Select Roast. Set temperature to 375°F (190°C) and set time to 20 minutes. Press Start to begin preheating.
3. Once the oven has preheated, place the pan into the oven.
4. Meanwhile, season both sides of the fillets with ½ teaspoon of kosher salt. Put the green beans in the medium bowl and sprinkle with the remaining ¼ teaspoon of kosher salt and 1 tablespoon of butter, tossing to coat.
5. After 10 minutes, remove the pan and push the potatoes to one side. Put the fillets in the middle of the pan and add the green beans on the other side. Drizzle the remaining 2 tablespoons of butter over the fillets. Return the pan to the oven and continue cooking, or until the fish flakes easily with a fork and the green beans are crisp-tender.
6. When cooked, remove the pan from the oven. Drizzle the lemon juice over the fillets and sprinkle the parsley on top for garnish. Serve hot.

Tuna and Fruit Kebabs with Honey Glaze

Prep time: 15 minutes | Cook time: 10 minutes | Serves 4

Kebabs:
- 1 pound (454 g) tuna steaks, cut into 1-inch cubes
- ½ cup canned pineapple chunks, drained, juice reserved
- ½ cup large red grapes

Marinade:
- 1 tablespoon honey
- 1 teaspoon olive oil
- 2 teaspoons grated fresh ginger
- Pinch cayenne pepper

Special Equipment:
- 4 metal skewers

1. Make the kebabs: Thread, alternating tuna cubes, pineapple chunks, and red grapes, onto the metal skewers.
2. Make the marinade: Whisk together the honey, olive oil, ginger, and cayenne pepper in a small bowl. Brush generously the marinade over the kebabs and allow to sit for 10 minutes.
3. When ready, transfer the kebabs to the perforated pan.
4. Select Air Fry. Set temperature to 370°F (188°C) and set time to 10 minutes. Press Start to begin preheating.
5. Once preheated, place the pan into the oven.
6. After 5 minutes, remove from the oven and flip the kebabs and brush with the remaining marinade. Return the pan to the oven and continue cooking for an additional 5 minutes.
7. When cooking is complete, the kebabs should reach an internal temperature of 145°F (63°C) on a meat thermometer. Remove from the oven and discard any remaining marinade. Serve hot.

Breaded Fish Fillets with Mustard

Prep time: 20 minutes | Cook time: 7 minutes | Serves 4

- 1 pound (454 g) fish fillets
- 1 tablespoon coarse brown mustard
- 1 teaspoon Worcestershire sauce
- ½ teaspoon hot sauce
- Salt, to taste
- Cooking spray

Crumb Coating:
- ¾ cup panko bread crumbs
- ¼ cup stone-ground cornmeal
- ¼ teaspoon salt

1. On your cutting board, cut the fish fillets crosswise into slices, about 1 inch wide.
2. In a small bowl, stir together the mustard, Worcestershire sauce, and hot sauce to make a paste and rub this paste on all sides of the fillets. Season with salt to taste.
3. In a shallow bowl, thoroughly combine all the ingredients for the crumb coating and spread them on a sheet of wax paper.
4. Roll the fish fillets in the crumb mixture until thickly coated. Spritz all sides of the fish with cooking spray, then arrange them in the perforated pan in a single layer.
5. Select Air Fry. Set temperature to 400°F (205°C) and set time to 7 minutes. Press Start to begin preheating.
6. Once preheated, place the perforated pan into the oven.
7. When cooking is complete, the fish should flake apart with a fork. Remove from the oven and serve warm.

Cayenne Cod Fillets with Garlic

Prep time: 10 minutes | Cook time: 12 minutes | Serves 4

- 1 teaspoon olive oil
- 4 cod fillets
- ¼ teaspoon fine sea salt
- ¼ teaspoon ground black pepper, or more to taste
- 1 teaspoon cayenne pepper
- ½ cup fresh Italian parsley, coarsely chopped
- ½ cup nondairy milk
- 1 Italian pepper, chopped
- 4 garlic cloves, minced
- 1 teaspoon dried basil
- ½ teaspoon dried oregano

1. Lightly coat the sides and bottom of a baking dish with the olive oil. Set aside.
2. In a large bowl, sprinkle the fillets with salt, black pepper, and cayenne pepper.
3. In a food processor, pulse the remaining ingredients until smoothly puréed.
4. Add the purée to the bowl of fillets and toss to coat, then transfer to the prepared baking dish.
5. Select Bake. Set temperature to 380°F (193°C) and set time to 12 minutes. Press Start to begin preheating.
6. Once preheated, place the baking dish into the oven.
7. When cooking is complete, the fish should flake when pressed lightly with a fork. Remove from the oven and serve warm.

Tuna and Veggie Salad

Prep time: 10 minutes | Cook time: 15 minutes | Serves 4

- 10 ounces (283 g) small red potatoes, quartered
- 8 tablespoons extra-virgin olive oil, divided
- 1 teaspoon kosher salt, divided
- ½ pound (227 g) green beans, trimmed
- 1 pint cherry tomatoes
- 1 teaspoon Dijon mustard
- 3 tablespoons red wine vinegar
- Freshly ground black pepper, to taste
- 1 (9-ounce / 255-g) bag spring greens, washed and dried if needed
- 2 (5-ounce / 142-g) cans oil-packed tuna, drained
- 2 hard-cooked eggs, peeled and quartered
- ⅓ cup kalamata olives, pitted

1. In a large bowl, drizzle the potatoes with 1 tablespoon of olive oil and season with ¼ teaspoon of kosher salt. Transfer to a sheet pan.
2. Select Roast. Set temperature to 375°F (190°C) and set time to 15 minutes. Press Start to begin preheating.
3. Once the oven has preheated, place the pan into the oven.
4. Meanwhile, in a mixing bowl, toss the green beans and cherry tomatoes with 1 tablespoon of olive oil and ¼ teaspoon of kosher salt until evenly coated.
5. After 10 minutes, remove the pan and fold in the green beans and cherry tomatoes. Return the pan to the oven and continue cooking.
6. Meanwhile, make the vinaigrette by whisking together the remaining 6 tablespoons of olive oil, mustard, vinegar, the remaining ½ teaspoon of kosher salt, and black pepper in a small bowl. Set aside.
7. When done, remove the pan from the oven. Allow the vegetables to cool for 5 minutes.
8. Spread out the spring greens on a plate and spoon the tuna into the center of the greens. Arrange the potatoes, green beans, cheery tomatoes, and eggs around the tuna. Serve drizzled with the vinaigrette and scattered with the olives.

Salmon with Roasted Asparagus

Prep time: 5 minutes | Cook time: 12 minutes | Serves 2

- 2 teaspoons olive oil, plus additional for drizzling
- 2 (5-ounce / 142-g) salmon fillets, with skin
- Salt and freshly ground black pepper, to taste
- 1 bunch asparagus, trimmed
- 1 teaspoon dried tarragon
- 1 teaspoon dried chives
- Fresh lemon wedges, for serving

1. Rub the olive oil all over the salmon fillets. Sprinkle with salt and pepper to taste.
2. Put the asparagus on a foil-lined baking sheet and place the salmon fillets on top, skin-side down.
3. Select Roast. Set temperature to 425°F (220°C) and set time to 12 minutes. Press Start to begin preheating.
4. Once preheated, place the pan into the oven.
5. When cooked, the fillets should register 145°F (63°C) on an instant-read thermometer. Remove from the oven and cut the salmon fillets in half crosswise, then use a metal spatula to lift flesh from skin and transfer to a serving plate. Discard the skin and drizzle the salmon fillets with additional olive oil. Scatter with the herbs.
6. Serve the salmon fillets with roasted asparagus spears and lemon wedges on the side.

Salmon with Cherry Tomatoes

Prep time: 10 minutes | Cook time: 15 minutes | Serves 4

- 4 (6-ounce / 170-g) salmon fillets, patted dry
- 1 teaspoon kosher salt, divided
- 2 pints cherry or grape tomatoes, halved if large, divided
- 3 tablespoons extra-virgin olive oil, divided
- 2 garlic cloves, minced
- 1 small red bell pepper, seeded and chopped
- 2 tablespoons chopped fresh basil, divided

1. Season both sides of the salmon with ½ teaspoon of kosher salt.
2. Put about half of the tomatoes in a large bowl, along with

the remaining ½ teaspoon of kosher salt, 2 tablespoons of olive oil, garlic, bell pepper, and 1 tablespoon of basil. Toss to coat and then transfer to the sheet pan.

3. Arrange the salmon fillets on the sheet pan, skin-side down. Brush them with the remaining 1 tablespoon of olive oil.
4. Select Roast. Set temperature to 375°F (190°C) and set time to 15 minutes. Press Start to begin preheating.
5. Once preheated, place the pan into the oven.
6. After 7 minutes, remove the pan and fold in the remaining tomatoes. Return the pan to the oven and continue cooking.
7. When cooked, remove the pan from the oven. Serve sprinkled with the remaining 1 tablespoon of basil.

Teriyaki Salmon and Bok Choy

Prep time: 15 minutes | Cook time: 15 minutes | Serves 4

- ¾ cup Teriyaki sauce, divided
- 4 (6-ounce / 170-g) skinless salmon fillets
- 4 heads baby bok choy, root ends trimmed off and cut in half lengthwise through the root
- 1 teaspoon sesame oil
- 1 tablespoon vegetable oil
- 1 tablespoon toasted sesame seeds

1. Set aside ¼ cup of Teriyaki sauce and pour the remaining sauce into a resealable plastic bag. Put the salmon into the bag and seal, squeezing as much air out as possible. Allow the salmon to marinate for at least 10 minutes.
2. Arrange the bok choy halves on the sheet pan. Drizzle the oils over the vegetables, tossing to coat. Drizzle about 1 tablespoon of the reserved Teriyaki sauce over the bok choy, then push them to the sides of the sheet pan.
3. Put the salmon fillets in the middle of the sheet pan.
4. Select Roast. Set temperature to 375°F (190°C) and set time to 15 minutes. Press Start to begin preheating.
5. Once the oven has preheated, place the pan into the oven.
6. When done, remove the pan and brush the salmon with the remaining Teriyaki sauce. Serve garnished with the sesame seeds.

Honey-Lemon Snapper with Grapes

Prep time: 15 minutes | Cook time: 12 minutes | Serves 4

- 4 (4-ounce / 113-g) red snapper fillets
- 2 teaspoons olive oil
- 3 plums, halved and pitted
- 3 nectarines, halved and pitted
- 1 cup red grapes
- 1 tablespoon freshly squeezed lemon juice
- 1 tablespoon honey
- ½ teaspoon dried thyme

1. Arrange the red snapper fillets in the perforated pan and drizzle the olive oil over the top.
2. Select Air Fry. Set temperature to 390°F (199°C) and set time to 12 minutes. Press Start to begin preheating.
3. Once preheated, place the pan into the oven.
4. After 4 minutes, remove the pan from the oven. Top the fillets with the plums and nectarines. Scatter the red grapes all over the fillets. Drizzle with the lemon juice and honey and sprinkle the thyme on top. Return the pan to the oven and continue cooking for 8 minutes, or until the fish is flaky.
5. When cooking is complete, remove from the oven and serve warm.

Ginger Swordfish Steaks with Jalapeño

Prep time: 10 minutes | Cook time: 8 minutes | Serves 4

- 4 (4-ounce / 113-g) swordfish steaks
- ½ teaspoon toasted sesame oil
- 1 jalapeño pepper, finely minced
- 2 garlic cloves, grated
- 2 tablespoons freshly squeezed lemon juice
- 1 tablespoon grated fresh ginger
- ½ teaspoon Chinese five-spice powder
- ⅛ teaspoon freshly ground black pepper

1. On a clean work surface, place the swordfish steaks and brush both sides of the fish with the sesame oil.
2. Combine the jalapeño, garlic, lemon juice, ginger, five-spice powder, and black pepper in a small bowl and stir to mix well. Rub the mixture all over the fish until completely coated. Allow to sit for 10 minutes.
3. When ready, arrange the swordfish steaks in the perforated pan.
4. Select Air Fry. Set temperature to 380°F (193°C) and set time to 8 minutes. Press Start to begin preheating.
5. Once preheated, place the pan into the oven. Flip the steaks halfway through.
6. When cooking is complete, remove from the oven and cool for 5 minutes before serving.

Baked Salmon in Wine

Prep time: 5 minutes | Cook time: 10 minutes | Serves 4

- 4 tablespoons butter, melted
- 2 cloves garlic, minced
- Sea salt and ground black pepper, to taste
- ¼ cup dry white wine
- 1 tablespoon lime juice
- 1 teaspoon smoked paprika
- ½ teaspoon onion powder
- 4 salmon steaks
- Cooking spray

1. Place all the ingredients except the salmon and oil in a shallow dish and stir to mix well.
2. Add the salmon steaks, turning to coat well on both sides.

Transfer the salmon to the refrigerator to marinate for 30 minutes.
3. When ready, put the salmon steaks in the perforated pan, discarding any excess marinade. Spray the salmon steaks with cooking spray.
4. Select Air Fry. Set temperature to 360°F (182°C) and set time to 10 minutes. Press Start to begin preheating.
5. Once preheated, place the pan into the oven. Flip the salmon steaks halfway through.
6. When cooking is complete, remove from the oven and divide the salmon steaks among four plates. Serve warm.

Fried Cod Fillets in Beer

Prep time: 5 minutes | Cook time: 15 minutes | Serves 4

- 2 eggs
- 1 cup malty beer
- 1 cup all-purpose flour
- ½ cup cornstarch
- 1 teaspoon garlic powder
- Salt and pepper, to taste
- 4 (4-ounce / 113-g) cod fillets
- Cooking spray

1. In a shallow bowl, beat together the eggs with the beer. In another shallow bowl, thoroughly combine the flour and cornstarch. Sprinkle with the garlic powder, salt, and pepper.
2. Dredge each cod fillet in the flour mixture, then in the egg mixture. Dip each piece of fish in the flour mixture a second time.
3. Spritz the perforated pan with cooking spray. Arrange the cod fillets in the pan in a single layer.
4. Select Air Fry. Set temperature to 400°F (205°C) and set time to 15 minutes. Press Start to begin preheating.
5. Once preheated, place the pan into the oven. Flip the fillets halfway through the cooking time.
6. When cooking is complete, the cod should reach an internal temperature of 145°F (63°C) on a meat thermometer and the outside should be crispy. Let the fish cool for 5 minutes and serve.

Parmesan Fish Fillets with Tarragon

Prep time: 8 minutes | Cook time: 17 minutes | Serves 4

- ⅓ cup grated Parmesan cheese
- ½ teaspoon fennel seed
- ½ teaspoon tarragon
- ⅓ teaspoon mixed peppercorns
- 2 eggs, beaten
- 4 (4-ounce / 113-g) fish fillets, halved
- 2 tablespoons dry white wine
- 1 teaspoon seasoned salt

1. Place the grated Parmesan cheese, fennel seed, tarragon, and mixed peppercorns in a food processor and pulse for about 20 seconds until well combined. Transfer the cheese mixture to a shallow dish.
2. Place the beaten eggs in another shallow dish.
3. Drizzle the dry white wine over the top of fish fillets. Dredge each fillet in the beaten eggs on both sides, shaking off any excess, then roll them in the cheese mixture until fully coated. Season with the salt.
4. Arrange the fillets in the perforated pan.
5. Select Air Fry. Set temperature to 345°F (174°C) and set time to 17 minutes. Press Start to begin preheating.
6. Once preheated, place the pan into the oven. Flip the fillets once halfway through the cooking time.
7. When cooking is complete, the fish should be cooked through no longer translucent. Remove from the oven and cool for 5 minutes before serving.

Cajun Catfish Cakes with Parmesan

Prep time: 5 minutes | Cook time: 15 minutes | Serves 4

- 2 catfish fillets
- 3 ounces (85 g) butter
- 1 cup shredded Parmesan cheese
- 1 cup shredded Swiss cheese
- ½ cup buttermilk
- 1 teaspoon baking powder
- 1 teaspoon baking soda
- 1 teaspoon Cajun seasoning

1. Bring a pot of salted water to a boil. Add the catfish fillets to the boiling water and let them boil for 5 minutes until they become opaque.
2. Remove the fillets from the pot to a mixing bowl and flake them into small pieces with a fork.
3. Add the remaining ingredients to the bowl of fish and stir until well incorporated.
4. Divide the fish mixture into 12 equal portions and shape each portion into a patty. Place the patties in the perforated pan.
5. Select Air Fry. Set temperature to 380°F (193°C) and set time to 15 minutes. Press Start to begin preheating.
6. Once preheated, place the pan into the oven. Flip the patties halfway through the cooking time.
7. When cooking is complete, the patties should be golden brown and cooked through. Remove from the oven. Let the patties sit for 5 minutes and serve.

Coconut Curried Fish with Chilies

Prep time: 10 minutes | Cook time: 22 minutes | Serves 4

- 2 tablespoons sunflower oil, divided
- 1 pound (454 g) fish, chopped
- 1 ripe tomato, puréed
- 2 red chilies, chopped
- 1 shallot, minced
- 1 garlic clove, minced
- 1 cup coconut milk
- 1 tablespoon coriander powder
- 1 teaspoon red curry paste

- ½ teaspoon fenugreek seeds
- Salt and white pepper, to taste

1. Coat the perforated pan with 1 tablespoon of sunflower oil. Place the fish in the perforated pan.
2. Select Air Fry. Set temperature to 380°F (193°C) and set time to 10 minutes. Press Start to begin preheating.
3. Once preheated, place the pan into the oven. Flip the fish halfway through the cooking time.
4. When cooking is complete, transfer the cooked fish to a baking pan greased with the remaining 1 tablespoon of sunflower oil. Stir in the remaining ingredients.
5. Select Air Fry. Set temperature to 350°F (180°C) and set time to 12 minutes. Place the pan into the oven.
6. When cooking is complete, they should be heated through. Cool for 5 to 8 minutes before serving.

Shrimp and Veggie Spring Rolls

Prep time: 10 minutes | Cook time: 20 minutes | Serves 4

- 1 tablespoon olive oil
- 2 teaspoons minced garlic
- 1 cup matchstick cut carrots
- 2 cups finely sliced cabbage
- 2 (4-ounce / 113-g) cans tiny shrimp, drained
- 4 teaspoons soy sauce
- Salt and freshly ground black pepper, to taste
- 16 square spring roll wrappers
- Cooking spray

1. Spray the perforated pan with cooking spray. Set aside.
2. Heat the olive oil in a medium skillet over medium heat until it shimmers.
3. Add the garlic to the skillet and cook for 30 seconds. Stir in the cabbage and carrots and sauté for about 5 minutes, stirring occasionally, or until the vegetables are lightly tender.
4. Fold in the shrimp and soy sauce and sprinkle with salt and pepper, then stir to combine. Sauté for another 2 minutes, or until the moisture is evaporated. Remove from the heat and set aside to cool.
5. Put a spring roll wrapper on a work surface and spoon 1 tablespoon of the shrimp mixture onto the lower end of the wrapper.
6. Roll the wrapper away from you halfway, and then fold in the right and left sides, like an envelope. Continue to roll to the very end, using a little water to seal the edge. Repeat with the remaining wrappers and filling.
7. Place the spring rolls in the perforated pan in a single layer, leaving space between each spring roll. Mist them lightly with cooking spray.
8. Select Air Fry. Set temperature to 375°F (190°C) and set time to 10 minutes. Press Start to begin preheating.
9. Once preheated, place the pan into the oven. Flip the rolls halfway through the cooking time.
10. When cooking is complete, the spring rolls will be heated through and start to brown. If necessary, continue cooking for 5 minutes more. Remove from the oven and cool for a few minutes before serving.

Orange Shrimp with Cayenne

Prep time: 40 minutes | Cook time: 12 minutes | Serves 4

- ⅓ cup orange juice
- 3 teaspoons minced garlic
- 1 teaspoon Old Bay seasoning
- ¼ to ½ teaspoon cayenne pepper
- 1 pound (454 g) medium shrimp, thawed, deveined, peeled, with tails off, and patted dry
- Cooking spray

1. Stir together the orange juice, garlic, Old Bay seasoning, and cayenne pepper in a medium bowl. Add the shrimp to the bowl and toss to coat well.
2. Cover the bowl with plastic wrap and marinate in the refrigerator for 30 minutes.
3. Spritz the perforated pan with cooking spray. Place the shrimp in the pan and spray with cooking spray.
4. Select Air Fry. Set temperature to 400°F (205°C) and set time to 12 minutes. Press Start to begin preheating.
5. Once preheated, place the pan into the oven. Flip the shrimp halfway through the cooking time.
6. When cooked, the shrimp should be opaque and crisp. Remove from the oven and serve hot.

Flounder Fillets with Lemon Pepper

Prep time: 8 minutes | Cook time: 12 minutes | Serves 2

- 2 flounder fillets, patted dry
- 1 egg
- ½ teaspoon Worcestershire sauce
- ¼ cup almond flour
- ¼ cup coconut flour
- ½ teaspoon coarse sea salt
- ½ teaspoon lemon pepper
- ¼ teaspoon chili powder
- Cooking spray

1. In a shallow bowl, beat together the egg with Worcestershire sauce until well incorporated.
2. In another bowl, thoroughly combine the almond flour, coconut flour, sea salt, lemon pepper, and chili powder.
3. Dredge the fillets in the egg mixture, shaking off any excess, then roll in the flour mixture to coat well.
4. Spritz the perforated pan with cooking spray. Place the fillets in the pan.
5. Select Bake. Set temperature to 390°F (199°C) and set time to 12 minutes. Press Start to begin preheating.
6. Once preheated, place the pan into the oven.

7. After 7 minutes, remove from the oven and flip the fillets and spray with cooking spray. Return the pan to the oven and continue cooking for 5 minutes, or until the fish is flaky.
8. When cooking is complete, remove from the oven and serve warm.

Paprika Tiger Shrimp

Prep time: 5 minutes | Cook time: 10 minutes | Serves 4

- 1 pound (454 g) tiger shrimp
- 2 tablespoons olive oil
- ½ tablespoon Old Bay seasoning
- ¼ tablespoon smoked paprika
- ¼ teaspoon cayenne pepper
- A pinch of sea salt

1. Toss all the ingredients in a large bowl until the shrimp are evenly coated.
2. Arrange the shrimp in the perforated pan.
3. Select Air Fry. Set temperature to 380°F (193°C) and set time to 10 minutes. Press Start to begin preheating.
4. Once preheated, place the pan into the oven.
5. When cooking is complete, the shrimp should be pink and cooked through. Remove from the oven and serve hot.

Chapter 4 Casseroles, Quiches, and Frittatas

Mushroom and Beef Casserole

Prep time: 10 minutes | Cook time: 25 minutes | Serves 4

- 1½ pounds (680 g) beef steak
- 1 ounce (28 g) dry onion soup mix
- 2 cups sliced mushrooms
- 1 (14.5-ounce / 411-g) can cream of mushroom soup
- ½ cup beef broth
- ¼ cup red wine
- 3 garlic cloves, minced
- 1 whole onion, chopped

1. Put the beef steak in a large bowl, then sprinkle with dry onion soup mix. Toss to coat well.
2. Combine the mushrooms with mushroom soup, beef broth, red wine, garlic, and onion in a large bowl. Stir to mix well.
3. Transfer the beef steak in a baking pan, then pour in the mushroom mixture.
4. Select Bake. Set temperature to 360°F (182°C) and set time to 25 minutes. Press Start to begin preheating.
5. Once preheated, place the pan into the oven.
6. When cooking is complete, the mushrooms should be soft and the beef should be well browned.
7. Remove the baking pan from the oven and serve immediately.

Cauliflower Casserole with Pecan Butter

Prep time: 15 minutes | Cook time: 50 minutes | Serves 6

- 1 cup chicken broth
- 2 cups cauliflower florets
- 1 cup canned pumpkin purée
- ¼ cup heavy cream
- 1 teaspoon vanilla extract
- 2 large eggs, beaten
- ⅓ cup unsalted butter, melted, plus more for greasing the pan
- ¼ cup sugar
- 1 teaspoon fine sea salt
- Chopped fresh parsley leaves, for garnish

Topping:
- ½ cup blanched almond flour
- 1 cup chopped pecans
- ⅓ cup unsalted butter, melted
- ½ cup sugar

1. Pour the chicken broth in a baking pan, then add the cauliflower.
2. Select Bake. Set temperature to 350°F (180°C) and set time to 20 minutes. Press Start to begin preheating.
3. Once preheated, place the pan into the oven.
4. When cooking is complete, the cauliflower should be soft.
5. Meanwhile, combine the ingredients for the topping in a large bowl. Stir to mix well.
6. Pat the cauliflower dry with paper towels, then place in a food processor and pulse with pumpkin purée, heavy cream, vanilla extract, eggs, butter, sugar, and salt until smooth.
7. Clean the baking pan and grease with more butter, then pour the purée mixture in the pan. Spread the topping over the mixture.
8. Place the baking pan back to the oven. Select Bake and set time to 30 minutes.
9. When baking is complete, the topping of the casserole should be lightly browned.
10. Remove the casserole from the oven and serve with fresh parsley on top.

Cheddar Chicken Sausage Casserole

Prep time: 10 minutes | Cook time: 20 minutes | Serves 8

- 10 eggs
- 1 cup Cheddar cheese, shredded and divided
- ¾ cup heavy whipping cream
- 1 (12-ounce / 340-g) package cooked chicken sausage
- 1 cup broccoli, chopped
- 2 cloves garlic, minced
- ½ tablespoon salt
- ¼ tablespoon ground black pepper
- Cooking spray

1. Spritz a baking pan with cooking spray.
2. Whisk the eggs with Cheddar and cream in a large bowl to mix well.
3. Combine the cooked sausage, broccoli, garlic, salt, and ground black pepper in a separate bowl. Stir to mix well.
4. Pour the sausage mixture into the baking pan, then spread the egg mixture over to cover.
5. Select Bake. Set temperature to 400°F (205°C) and set time to 20 minutes. Press Start to begin preheating.
6. Once preheated, place the pan into the oven.
7. When cooking is complete, the egg should be set and a toothpick inserted in the center should come out clean.
8. Serve immediately.

Corn Casserole with Bell Pepper

Prep time: 10 minutes | Cook time: 20 minutes | Serves 4

- 1 cup corn kernels
- ¼ cup bell pepper, finely chopped
- ½ cup low-fat milk
- 1 large egg, beaten
- ½ cup yellow cornmeal
- ½ cup all-purpose flour
- ½ teaspoon baking powder
- 2 tablespoons melted unsalted butter
- 1 tablespoon granulated sugar
- Pinch of cayenne pepper
- ¼ teaspoon kosher salt

- Cooking spray
1. Spritz a baking pan with cooking spray.
2. Combine all the ingredients in a large bowl. Stir to mix well. Pour the mixture into the baking pan.
3. Select Bake. Set temperature to 330°F (166°C) and set time to 20 minutes. Press Start to begin preheating.
4. Once preheated, place the pan into the oven.
5. When cooking is complete, the casserole should be lightly browned and set.
6. Remove the baking pan from the oven and serve immediately.

Asparagus Casserole with Grits

Prep time: 5 minutes | Cook time: 30 minutes | Serves 4

- 10 fresh asparagus spears, cut into 1-inch pieces
- 2 cups cooked grits, cooled to room temperature
- 2 teaspoons Worcestershire sauce
- 1 egg, beaten
- ½ teaspoon garlic powder
- ¼ teaspoon salt
- 2 slices provolone cheese, crushed
- Cooking spray

1. Spritz a baking pan with cooking spray.
2. Set the asparagus in the perforated pan. Spritz the asparagus with cooking spray.
3. Select Air Fry. Set temperature to 390°F (199°C) and set time to 5 minutes. Press Start to begin preheating.
4. Once preheated, place the pan into the oven. Flip the asparagus halfway through.
5. When cooking is complete, the asparagus should be lightly browned and crispy.
6. Meanwhile, combine the grits, Worcestershire sauce, egg, garlic powder, and salt in a bowl. Stir to mix well.
7. Pour half of the grits mixture in the prepared baking pan, then spread with fried asparagus.
8. Spread the cheese over the asparagus and pour the remaining grits over.
9. Select Bake. Set time to 25 minutes. Place the pan into the oven.
10. When cooking is complete, the egg should be set.
11. Serve immediately.

Cheddar Broccoli Casserole

Prep time: 5 minutes | Cook time: 30 minutes | Serves 6

- 4 cups broccoli florets
- ¼ cup heavy whipping cream
- ½ cup sharp Cheddar cheese, shredded
- ¼ cup ranch dressing
- Kosher salt and ground black pepper, to taste

1. Combine all the ingredients in a large bowl. Toss to coat well broccoli well.
2. Pour the mixture into a baking pan.
3. Select Bake. Set temperature to 375°F (190°C) and set time to 30 minutes. Press Start to begin preheating.
4. Once preheated, place the pan into the oven.
5. When cooking is complete, the broccoli should be tender.
6. Remove the baking pan from the oven and serve immediately.

Tilapia and Rockfish Casserole

Prep time: 8 minutes | Cook time: 22 minutes | Serves 2

- 1 tablespoon olive oil
- 1 small yellow onion, chopped
- 2 garlic cloves, minced
- 4 ounces (113 g) tilapia pieces
- 4 ounces (113 g) rockfish pieces
- ½ teaspoon dried basil
- Salt and ground white pepper, to taste
- 4 eggs, lightly beaten
- 1 tablespoon dry sherry
- 4 tablespoons cheese, shredded

1. Heat the olive oil in a nonstick skillet over medium-high heat until shimmering.
2. Add the onion and garlic and sauté for 2 minutes or until fragrant.
3. Add the tilapia, rockfish, basil, salt, and white pepper to the skillet. Sauté to combine well and transfer them on a baking pan.
4. Combine the eggs, sherry and cheese in a large bowl. Stir to mix well. Pour the mixture in the baking pan over the fish mixture.
5. Select Bake. Set temperature to 360°F (182°C) and set time to 20 minutes. Press Start to begin preheating.
6. Once preheated, place the pan into the oven.
7. When cooking is complete, the eggs should be set and the casserole edges should be lightly browned.
8. Serve immediately.

Parmesan Green Bean Casserole

Prep time: 4 minutes | Cook time: 6 minutes | Serves 4

- 1 tablespoon melted butter
- 1 cup green beans
- 6 ounces (170 g) Cheddar cheese, shredded
- 7 ounces (198 g) Parmesan cheese, shredded
- ¼ cup heavy cream
- Sea salt, to taste

1. Grease a baking pan with the melted butter.
2. Add the green beans, Cheddar, salt, and black pepper to the prepared baking pan. Stir to mix well, then spread the Parmesan and cream on top.

3. Select Bake. Set temperature to 400°F (205°C) and set time to 6 minutes. Press Start to begin preheating.
4. Once preheated, place the pan into the oven.
5. When cooking is complete, the beans should be tender and the cheese should be melted.
6. Serve immediately.

Cheddar Pastrami Casserole

Prep time: 10 minutes | Cook time: 8 minutes | Serves 2

- 1 cup pastrami, sliced
- 1 bell pepper, chopped
- ¼ cup Greek yogurt
- 2 spring onions, chopped
- ½ cup Cheddar cheese, grated
- 4 eggs
- ¼ teaspoon ground black pepper
- Sea salt, to taste
- Cooking spray

1. Spritz a baking pan with cooking spray.
2. Whisk together all the ingredients in a large bowl. Stir to mix well. Pour the mixture into the baking pan.
3. Select Bake. Set temperature to 330°F (166°C) and set time to 8 minutes. Press Start to begin preheating.
4. Once preheated, place the pan into the oven.
5. When cooking is complete, the eggs should be set and the casserole edges should be lightly browned.
6. Remove the baking pan from the oven and allow to cool for 10 minutes before serving.

Swiss Chicken and Ham Casserole

Prep time: 15 minutes | Cook time: 15 minutes | Serves 4 to 6

- 2 cups diced cooked chicken
- 1 cup diced ham
- ¼ teaspoon ground nutmeg
- ½ cup half-and-half
- ½ teaspoon ground black pepper
- 6 slices Swiss cheese
- Cooking spray

1. Spritz a baking pan with cooking spray.
2. Combine the chicken, ham, nutmeg, half-and-half, and ground black pepper in a large bowl. Stir to mix well.
3. Pour half of the mixture into the baking pan, then top the mixture with 3 slices of Swiss cheese, then pour in the remaining mixture and top with remaining cheese slices.
4. Select Bake. Set temperature to 350°F (180°C) and set time to 15 minutes. Press Start to begin preheating.
5. Once preheated, place the pan into the oven.
6. When cooking is complete, the egg should be set and the cheese should be melted.
7. Serve immediately.

Spinach and Mushroom Frittata

Prep time: 7 minutes | Cook time: 8 minutes | Serves 2

- 1 cup chopped mushrooms
- 2 cups spinach, chopped
- 4 eggs, lightly beaten
- 3 ounces (85 g) feta cheese, crumbled
- 2 tablespoons heavy cream
- A handful of fresh parsley, chopped
- Salt and ground black pepper, to taste
- Cooking spray

1. Spritz a baking pan with cooking spray.
2. Whisk together all the ingredients in a large bowl. Stir to mix well.
3. Pour the mixture in the prepared baking pan.
4. Select Bake. Set temperature to 350°F (180°C) and set time to 8 minutes. Press Start to begin preheating.
5. Once preheated, place the pan into the oven. Stir the mixture halfway through.
6. When cooking is complete, the eggs should be set.
7. Serve immediately.

Cauliflower and Okra Casserole

Prep time: 8 minutes | Cook time: 12 minutes | Serves 4

- 1 head cauliflower, cut into florets
- 1 cup okra, chopped
- 1 yellow bell pepper, chopped
- 2 eggs, beaten
- ½ cup chopped onion
- 1 tablespoon soy sauce
- 2 tablespoons olive oil
- Salt and ground black pepper, to taste

1. Spritz a baking pan with cooking spray.
2. Put the cauliflower in a food processor and pulse to rice the cauliflower.
3. Pour the cauliflower rice in the baking pan and add the remaining ingredients. Stir to mix well.
4. Select Bake. Set temperature to 380°F (193°C) and set time to 12 minutes. Press Start to begin preheating.
5. Once preheated, place the pan into the oven.
6. When cooking is complete, the eggs should be set.
7. Remove the baking pan from the oven and serve immediately.

Turkey Casserole with Almond Mayo

Prep time: 5 minutes | Cook time: 32 minutes | Serves 4

- 1 pound (454 g) turkey breasts
- 1 tablespoon olive oil
- 2 boiled eggs, chopped
- 2 tablespoons chopped pimentos
- ¼ cup slivered almonds, chopped

- ¼ cup mayonnaise
- ½ cup diced celery
- 2 tablespoons chopped green onion
- ¼ cup cream of chicken soup
- ¼ cup bread crumbs
- Salt and ground black pepper, to taste

1. Put the turkey breasts in a large bowl. Sprinkle with salt and ground black pepper and drizzle with olive oil. Toss to coat well.
2. Transfer the turkey in the perforated pan.
3. Select Air Fry. Set temperature to 390°F (199°C) and set time to 12 minutes. Press Start to begin preheating.
4. Once preheated, place the pan into the oven. Flip the turkey halfway through.
5. When cooking is complete, the turkey should be well browned.
6. Remove the turkey breasts from the oven and cut into cubes, then combine the chicken cubes with eggs, pimentos, almonds, mayo, celery, green onions, and chicken soup in a large bowl. Stir to mix.
7. Pour the mixture into a baking pan, then spread with bread crumbs.
8. Select Bake. Set time to 20 minutes. Place the pan into the oven.
9. When cooking is complete, the eggs should be set.
10. Remove the baking pan from the oven and serve immediately.

Peppery Sausage Casserole with Cheddar

Prep time: 15 minutes | Cook time: 25 minutes | Serves 6

- 1 pound (454 g) minced breakfast sausage
- 1 yellow pepper, diced
- 1 red pepper, diced
- 1 green pepper, diced
- 1 sweet onion, diced
- 2 cups Cheddar cheese, shredded
- 6 eggs
- Salt and freshly ground black pepper, to taste
- Fresh parsley, for garnish

1. Cook the sausage in a nonstick skillet over medium heat for 10 minutes or until well browned. Stir constantly.
2. When the cooking is finished, transfer the cooked sausage to a baking pan and add the peppers and onion. Scatter with Cheddar cheese.
3. Whisk the eggs with salt and ground black pepper in a large bowl, then pour the mixture into the baking pan.
4. Select Bake. Set temperature to 360°F (182°C) and set time to 15 minutes. Press Start to begin preheating.
5. Once preheated, place the pan into the oven.
6. When cooking is complete, the egg should be set and the edges of the casserole should be lightly browned.
7. Remove the baking pan from the oven and top with fresh parsley before serving.

Chickpea and Spinach Casserole

Prep time: 10 minutes | Cook time: 21 to 22 minutes | Serves 4

- 2 tablespoons olive oil
- 2 garlic cloves, minced
- 1 tablespoon ginger, minced
- 1 onion, chopped
- 1 chili pepper, minced
- Salt and ground black pepper, to taste
- 1 pound (454 g) spinach
- 1 can coconut milk
- ½ cup dried tomatoes, chopped
- 1 (14-ounce / 397-g) can chickpeas, drained

1. Heat the olive oil in a saucepan over medium heat. Sauté the garlic and ginger in the olive oil for 1 minute, or until fragrant.
2. Add the onion, chili pepper, salt and pepper to the saucepan. Sauté for 3 minutes.
3. Mix in the spinach and sauté for 3 to 4 minutes or until the vegetables become soft. Remove from heat.
4. Pour the vegetable mixture into a baking pan. Stir in coconut milk, dried tomatoes and chickpeas until well blended.
5. Select Bake. Set temperature to 370°F (188°C) and set time to 15 minutes. Press Start to begin preheating.
6. Once preheated, place the pan into the oven.
7. When cooking is complete, transfer the casserole to a serving dish. Let cool for 5 minutes before serving.

Beef and Bean Casserole

Prep time: 15 minutes | Cook time: 31 minutes | Serves 4

- 1 tablespoon olive oil
- ½ cup finely chopped bell pepper
- ½ cup chopped celery
- 1 onion, chopped
- 2 garlic cloves, minced
- 1 pound (454 g) ground beef
- 1 can diced tomatoes
- ½ teaspoon parsley
- ½ tablespoon chili powder
- 1 teaspoon chopped cilantro
- 1½ cups vegetable broth
- 1 (8-ounce / 227-g) can cannellini beans
- Salt and ground black pepper, to taste

1. Heat the olive oil in a nonstick skillet over medium heat until shimmering.
2. Add the bell pepper, celery, onion, and garlic to the skillet and sauté for 5 minutes or until the onion is translucent.
3. Add the ground beef and sauté for an additional 6 minutes or until lightly browned.
4. Mix in the tomatoes, parsley, chili powder, cilantro and vegetable broth, then cook for 10 more minutes. Stir constantly.
5. Pour them in a baking pan, then mix in the beans and sprin-

kle with salt and ground black pepper.

6. Select Bake. Set temperature to 350°F (180°C) and set time to 10 minutes. Press Start to begin preheating.
7. Once preheated, place the pan into the oven.
8. When cooking is complete, the vegetables should be tender and the beef should be well browned.
9. Remove the baking pan from the oven and serve immediately.

Cheddar Chicken and Broccoli Divan

Prep time: 5 minutes | Cook time: 24 minutes | Serves 4

- 4 chicken breasts
- Salt and ground black pepper, to taste
- 1 head broccoli, cut into florets
- ½ cup cream of mushroom soup
- 1 cup shredded Cheddar cheese
- ½ cup croutons
- Cooking spray

1. Spritz the perforated pan with cooking spray.
2. Put the chicken breasts in the perforated pan and sprinkle with salt and ground black pepper.
3. Select Air Fry. Set temperature to 390°F (199°C) and set time to 14 minutes. Press Start to begin preheating.
4. Once preheated, place the pan into the oven. Flip the breasts halfway through the cooking time.
5. When cooking is complete, the breasts should be well browned and tender.
6. Remove the breasts from the oven and allow to cool for a few minutes on a plate, then cut the breasts into bite-size pieces.
7. Combine the chicken, broccoli, mushroom soup, and Cheddar cheese in a large bowl. Stir to mix well.
8. Spritz a baking pan with cooking spray. Pour the chicken mixture into the pan. Spread the croutons over the mixture.
9. Select Bake. Set time to 10 minutes. Place the pan into the oven.
10. When cooking is complete, the croutons should be lightly browned and the mixture should be set.
11. Remove the baking pan from the oven and serve immediately.

Smoked Trout Frittata with Dill

Prep time: 8 minutes | Cook time: 17 minutes | Serves 4

- 2 tablespoons olive oil
- 1 onion, sliced
- 1 egg, beaten
- ½ tablespoon horseradish sauce
- 6 tablespoons crème fraiche
- 1 cup diced smoked trout
- 2 tablespoons chopped fresh dill
- Cooking spray

1. Spritz a baking pan with cooking spray.
2. Heat the olive oil in a nonstick skillet over medium heat until shimmering.
3. Add the onion and sauté for 3 minutes or until translucent.
4. Combine the egg, horseradish sauce, and crème fraiche in a large bowl. Stir to mix well, then mix in the sautéed onion, smoked trout, and dill.
5. Pour the mixture in the prepared baking pan.
6. Select Bake. Set temperature to 350°F (180°C) and set time to 14 minutes. Press Start to begin preheating.
7. Once preheated, place the pan into the oven. Stir the mixture halfway through.
8. When cooking is complete, the egg should be set and the edges should be lightly browned.
9. Serve immediately.

Cheddar and Egg Frittata with Parsley

Prep time: 10 minutes | Cook time: 20 minutes | Serves 4

- ½ cup shredded Cheddar cheese
- ½ cup half-and-half
- 4 large eggs
- 2 tablespoons chopped scallion greens
- 2 tablespoons chopped fresh parsley
- ½ teaspoon kosher salt
- ½ teaspoon ground black pepper
- Cooking spray

1. Spritz a baking pan with cooking spray.
2. Whisk together all the ingredients in a large bowl, then pour the mixture into the prepared baking pan.
3. Select Bake. Set temperature to 300°F (150°C) and set time to 20 minutes. Press Start to begin preheating.
4. Once preheated, place the pan into the oven. Stir the mixture halfway through.
5. When cooking is complete, the eggs should be set.
6. Serve immediately.

Cheddar Broccoli and Carrot Quiche

Prep time: 6 minutes | Cook time: 14 minutes | Serves 4

- 4 eggs
- 1 teaspoon dried thyme
- 1 cup whole milk
- 1 steamed carrots, diced
- 2 cups steamed broccoli florets
- 2 medium tomatoes, diced
- ¼ cup crumbled feta cheese
- 1 cup grated Cheddar cheese
- 1 teaspoon chopped parsley
- Salt and ground black pepper, to taste
- Cooking spray

1. Spritz a baking pan with cooking spray.

2. Whisk together the eggs, thyme, salt, and ground black pepper in a bowl and fold in the milk while mixing.
3. Put the carrots, broccoli, and tomatoes in the prepared baking pan, then spread with feta cheese and ½ cup Cheddar cheese. Pour the egg mixture over, then scatter with remaining Cheddar on top.
4. Select Bake. Set temperature to 350°F (180°C) and set time to 14 minutes. Press Start to begin preheating.
5. Once preheated, place the pan into the oven.
6. When cooking is complete, the egg should be set and the quiche should be puffed.
7. Remove the quiche from the oven and top with chopped parsley, then slice to serve.

Chapter 5 Wraps and Sandwiches

Nugget and Veggie Taco Wraps

Prep time: 5 minutes | Cook time: 15 minutes | Serves 4

- 1 tablespoon water
- 4 pieces commercial vegan nuggets, chopped
- 1 small yellow onion, diced
- 1 small red bell pepper, chopped
- 2 cobs grilled corn kernels
- 4 large corn tortillas
- Mixed greens, for garnish

1. Preheat the air fryer to 400°F (204°C).
2. Over a medium heat, sauté the nuggets in the water with the onion, corn kernels and bell pepper in a skillet, then remove from the heat.
3. Fill the tortillas with the nuggets and vegetables and fold them up. Transfer to the inside of the fryer and air fry for 15 minutes.
4. Once crispy, serve immediately, garnished with the mixed greens.

Veggie Salsa Wraps

Prep time: 5 minutes | Cook time: 7 minutes | Serves 4

- 1 cup red onion, sliced
- 1 zucchini, chopped
- 1 poblano pepper, deseeded and finely chopped
- 1 head lettuce
- ½ cup salsa
- 8 ounces (227 g) Mozzarella cheese

1. Preheat the air fryer to 390°F (199°C).
2. Place the red onion, zucchini, and poblano pepper in the air fryer basket and air fry for 7 minutes, or until they are tender and fragrant.
3. Divide the veggie mixture among the lettuce leaves and spoon the salsa over the top. Finish off with Mozzarella cheese. Wrap the lettuce leaves around the filling.
4. Serve immediately.

Tuna and Lettuce Wraps

Prep time: 10 minutes | Cook time: 4 to 7 minutes | Serves 4

- 1 pound (454 g) fresh tuna steak, cut into 1-inch cubes
- 1 tablespoon grated fresh ginger
- 2 garlic cloves, minced
- ½ teaspoon toasted sesame oil
- 4 low-sodium whole-wheat tortillas
- ¼ cup low-fat mayonnaise
- 2 cups shredded romaine lettuce
- 1 red bell pepper, thinly sliced

1. Preheat the air fryer to 390°F (199°C).
2. In a medium bowl, mix the tuna, ginger, garlic, and sesame oil. Let it stand for 10 minutes.
3. Air fry the tuna in the air fryer basket for 4 to 7 minutes, or until lightly browned.
4. Make the wraps with the tuna, tortillas, mayonnaise, lettuce, and bell pepper.
5. Serve immediately.

Lettuce Fajita Meatball Wraps

Prep time: 10 minutes | Cook time: 10 minutes | Serves 4

- 1 pound (454 g) 85% lean ground beef
- ½ cup salsa, plus more for serving
- ¼ cup chopped onions
- ¼ cup diced green or red bell peppers
- 1 large egg, beaten
- 1 teaspoon fine sea salt
- ½ teaspoon chili powder
- ½ teaspoon ground cumin
- 1 clove garlic, minced
- Cooking spray

For Serving:
- 8 leaves Boston lettuce
- Pico de gallo or salsa
- Lime slices

1. Preheat the air fryer to 350°F (177°C). Spray the air fryer basket with cooking spray.
2. In a large bowl, mix together all the ingredients until well combined.
3. Shape the meat mixture into eight 1-inch balls. Place the meatballs in the air fryer basket, leaving a little space between them. Air fry for 10 minutes, or until cooked through and no longer pink inside and the internal temperature reaches 145°F (63°C).
4. Serve each meatball on a lettuce leaf, topped with pico de gallo or salsa. Serve with lime slices.

Chicken-Lettuce Wraps

Prep time: 15 minutes | Cook time: 12 to 16 minutes | Serves 2 to 4

- 1 pound (454 g) boneless, skinless chicken thighs, trimmed
- 1 teaspoon vegetable oil
- 2 tablespoons lime juice
- 1 shallot, minced
- 1 tablespoon fish sauce, plus extra for serving
- 2 teaspoons packed brown sugar
- 1 garlic clove, minced
- ⅛ teaspoon red pepper flakes
- 1 mango, peeled, pitted, and cut into ¼-inch pieces
- ⅓ cup chopped fresh mint
- ⅓ cup chopped fresh cilantro
- ⅓ cup chopped fresh Thai basil
- 1 head Bibb lettuce, leaves separated (8 ounces / 227 g)
- ¼ cup chopped dry-roasted peanuts
- 2 Thai chiles, stemmed and sliced thin

1. Preheat the air fryer to 400°F (204°C).

2. Pat the chicken dry with paper towels and rub with oil. Place the chicken in air fryer basket and air fry for 12 to 16 minutes, or until the chicken registers 175°F (79°C), flipping and rotating chicken halfway through cooking.
3. Meanwhile, whisk lime juice, shallot, fish sauce, sugar, garlic, and pepper flakes together in large bowl; set aside.
4. Transfer chicken to cutting board, let cool slightly, then shred into bite-size pieces using 2 forks. Add the shredded chicken, mango, mint, cilantro, and basil to bowl with dressing and toss to coat.
5. Serve the chicken in the lettuce leaves, passing peanuts, Thai chiles, and extra fish sauce separately.

Cheesy Chicken Sandwich

Prep time: 10 minutes | Cook time: 5 to 7 minutes | Serves 1

- ⅓ cup chicken, cooked and shredded
- 2 Mozzarella slices
- 1 hamburger bun
- ¼ cup shredded cabbage
- 1 teaspoon mayonnaise
- 2 teaspoons butter, melted
- 1 teaspoon olive oil
- ½ teaspoon balsamic vinegar
- ¼ teaspoon smoked paprika
- ¼ teaspoon black pepper
- ¼ teaspoon garlic powder
- Pinch of salt

1. Preheat the air fryer to 370°F (188°C).
2. Brush some butter onto the outside of the hamburger bun.
3. In a bowl, coat the chicken with the garlic powder, salt, pepper, and paprika.
4. In a separate bowl, stir together the mayonnaise, olive oil, cabbage, and balsamic vinegar to make coleslaw.
5. Slice the bun in two. Start building the sandwich, starting with the chicken, followed by the Mozzarella, the coleslaw, and finally the top bun.
6. Transfer the sandwich to the air fryer and bake for 5 to 7 minutes.
7. Serve immediately.

Smoky Chicken Sandwich

Prep time: 10 minutes | Cook time: 11 minutes | Serves 2

- 2 boneless, skinless chicken breasts (8 ounces / 227 g each), sliced horizontally in half and separated into 4 thinner cutlets
- Kosher salt and freshly ground black pepper, to taste
- ½ cup all-purpose flour
- 3 large eggs, lightly beaten
- ½ cup dried bread crumbs
- 1 tablespoon smoked paprika
- Cooking spray
- ½ cup marinara sauce
- 6 ounces (170 g) smoked Mozzarella cheese, grated
- 2 store-bought soft, sesame-seed hamburger or Italian buns, split

1. Preheat the air fryer to 350°F (177°C).
2. Season the chicken cutlets all over with salt and pepper. Set up three shallow bowls: Place the flour in the first bowl, the eggs in the second, and stir together the bread crumbs and smoked paprika in the third. Coat the chicken pieces in the flour, then dip fully in the egg. Dredge in the paprika bread crumbs, then transfer to a wire rack set over a baking sheet and spray both sides liberally with cooking spray.
3. Transfer 2 of the chicken cutlets to the air fryer and air fry for 6 minutes, or until beginning to brown. Spread each cutlet with 2 tablespoons of the marinara sauce and sprinkle with one-quarter of the smoked Mozzarella. Increase the temperature to 400°F (204°C) and air fry for 5 minutes more, or until the chicken is cooked through and crisp and the cheese is melted and golden brown.
4. Transfer the cutlets to a plate, stack on top of each other, and place inside a bun. Repeat with the remaining chicken cutlets, marinara, smoked Mozzarella, and bun.
5. Serve the sandwiches warm.

Cheesy Potato Taquitos

Prep time: 5 minutes | Cook time: 6 minutes per batch | Makes 12 taquitos

- 2 cups mashed potatoes
- ½ cup shredded Mexican cheese
- 12 corn tortillas
- Cooking spray

1. Preheat the air fryer to 400°F (204°C). Line the baking pan with parchment paper.
2. In a bowl, combine the potatoes and cheese until well mixed. Microwave the tortillas on high heat for 30 seconds, or until softened. Add some water to another bowl and set alongside.
3. On a clean work surface, lay the tortillas. Scoop 3 tablespoons of the potato mixture in the center of each tortilla. Roll up tightly and secure with toothpicks if necessary.
4. Arrange the filled tortillas, seam side down, in the prepared baking pan. Spritz the tortillas with cooking spray. Air fry for 6 minutes, or until crispy and golden brown, flipping once halfway through the cooking time. You may need to work in batches to avoid overcrowding.
5. Serve hot.

Chicken and Yogurt Taquitos

Prep time: 15 minutes | Cook time: 12 minutes | Serves 4

- 1 cup cooked chicken, shredded
- ¼ cup Greek yogurt
- ¼ cup salsa
- 1 cup shredded Mozzarella cheese
- Salt and ground black pepper, to taste
- 4 flour tortillas
- Cooking spray

1. Preheat the air fryer to 380°F (193°C) and spritz with cooking spray.

2. Combine all the ingredients, except for the tortillas, in a large bowl. Stir to mix well.
3. Make the taquitos: Unfold the tortillas on a clean work surface, then scoop up 2 tablespoons of the chicken mixture in the middle of each tortilla. Roll the tortillas up to wrap the filling.
4. Arrange the taquitos in the preheated air fryer and spritz with cooking spray.
5. Air fry for 12 minutes or until golden brown and the cheese melts. Flip the taquitos halfway through.
6. Serve immediately.

Pork Momos

Prep time: 20 minutes | Cook time: 10 minutes per batch | Serves 4

- 2 tablespoons olive oil
- 1 pound (454 g) ground pork
- 1 shredded carrot
- 1 onion, chopped
- 1 teaspoon soy sauce
- 16 wonton wrappers
- Salt and ground black pepper, to taste

1. Preheat the air fryer to 320°F (160°C).
2. Heat the olive oil in a nonstick skillet over medium heat until shimmering.
3. Add the ground pork, carrot, onion, soy sauce, salt, and ground black pepper and sauté for 10 minutes or until the pork is well browned and carrots are tender.
4. Unfold the wrappers on a clean work surface, then divide the cooked pork and vegetables on the wrappers. Fold the edges around the filling to form momos. Nip the top to seal the momos.
5. Arrange the momos in the preheated air fryer and spritz with cooking spray. Air fry for 10 minutes or until the wrappers are lightly browned. Work in batches to avoid overcrowding.
6. Serve immediately.

Air Fried Cream Cheese Wontons

Prep time: 5 minutes | Cook time: 6 minutes | Serves 4

- 2 ounces (57 g) cream cheese, softened
- 1 tablespoon sugar
- 16 square wonton wrappers
- Cooking spray

1. Preheat the air fryer to 350°F (177°C). Spritz the air fryer basket with cooking spray.
2. In a mixing bowl, stir together the cream cheese and sugar until well mixed. Prepare a small bowl of water alongside.
3. On a clean work surface, lay the wonton wrappers. Scoop ¼ teaspoon of cream cheese in the center of each wonton wrapper. Dab the water over the wrapper edges. Fold each wonton wrapper diagonally in half over the filling to form a triangle.
4. Arrange the wontons in the air fryer basket. Spritz the wontons with cooking spray. Air fry for 6 minutes, or until golden brown and crispy. Flip once halfway through to ensure even cooking.
5. Divide the wontons among four plates. Let rest for 5 minutes before serving.

Crispy Crab and Cream Cheese Wontons

Prep time: 10 minutes | Cook time: 10 minutes per batch | Serves 6 to 8

- 24 wonton wrappers, thawed if frozen
- Cooking spray

For the Filling:
- 5 ounces (142 g) lump crabmeat, drained and patted dry
- 4 ounces (113 g) cream cheese, at room temperature
- 2 scallions, sliced
- 1½ teaspoons toasted sesame oil
- 1 teaspoon Worcestershire sauce
- Kosher salt and ground black pepper, to taste

1. Preheat the air fryer to 350°F (177°C). Spritz the air fryer basket with cooking spray.
2. In a medium-size bowl, place all the ingredients for the filling and stir until well mixed. Prepare a small bowl of water alongside.
3. On a clean work surface, lay the wonton wrappers. Scoop 1 teaspoon of the filling in the center of each wrapper. Wet the edges with a touch of water. Fold each wonton wrapper diagonally in half over the filling to form a triangle.
4. Arrange the wontons in the air fryer basket. Spritz the wontons with cooking spray. Work in batches, 6 to 8 at a time. Air fry for 10 minutes, or until crispy and golden brown. Flip once halfway through.
5. Serve immediately.

Cabbage and Pork Gyoza

Prep time: 10 minutes | Cook time: 10 minutes per batch | Makes 48 gyozas

- 1 pound (454 g) ground pork
- 1 small head Napa cabbage (about 1 pound / 454 g), sliced thinly and minced
- ½ cup minced scallions
- 1 teaspoon minced fresh chives
- 1 teaspoon soy sauce
- 1 teaspoon minced fresh ginger
- 1 tablespoon minced garlic
- 1 teaspoon granulated sugar
- 2 teaspoons kosher salt
- 48 to 50 wonton or dumpling wrappers
- Cooking spray

1. Make the filling: Combine all the ingredients, except for the wrappers in a large bowl. Stir to mix well.

2. Unfold a wrapper on a clean work surface, then dab the edges with a little water. Scoop up 2 teaspoons of the filling mixture in the center.
3. Make the gyoza: Fold the wrapper over to filling and press the edges to seal. Pleat the edges if desired. Repeat with remaining wrappers and fillings.
4. Preheat the air fryer to 360°F (182°C) and spritz with cooking spray.
5. Arrange the gyozas in the preheated air fryer and spritz with cooking spray. Air fry for 10 minutes or until golden brown. Flip the gyozas halfway through. Work in batches to avoid overcrowding.
6. Serve immediately.

Pea and Potato Samosas with Chutney

Prep time: 30 minutes | Cook time: 1 hour 10 minutes | Makes 16 samosas

Dough:
- 4 cups all-purpose flour, plus more for flouring the work surface
- ¼ cup plain yogurt
- ½ cup cold unsalted butter, cut into cubes
- 2 teaspoons kosher salt
- 1 cup ice water

Filling:
- 2 tablespoons vegetable oil
- 1 onion, diced
- 1½ teaspoons coriander
- 1½ teaspoons cumin
- 1 clove garlic, minced
- 1 teaspoon turmeric
- 1 teaspoon kosher salt
- ½ cup peas, thawed if frozen
- 2 cups mashed potatoes
- 2 tablespoons yogurt
- Cooking spray

Chutney:
- 1 cup mint leaves, lightly packed
- 2 cups cilantro leaves, lightly packed
- 1 green chile pepper, deseeded and minced
- ½ cup minced onion
- Juice of 1 lime
- 1 teaspoon granulated sugar
- 1 teaspoon kosher salt
- 2 tablespoons vegetable oil

1. Put the flour, yogurt, butter, and salt in a food processor. Pulse to combine until grainy. Pour in the water and pulse until a smooth and firm dough forms.
2. Transfer the dough on a clean and lightly floured working surface. Knead the dough and shape it into a ball. Cut in half and flatten the halves into 2 discs. Wrap them in plastic and let sit in refrigerator until ready to use.
3. Meanwhile, make the filling: Heat the vegetable oil in a saucepan over medium heat.
4. Add the onion and sauté for 5 minutes or until lightly browned.
5. Add the coriander, cumin, garlic, turmeric, and salt and sauté for 2 minutes or until fragrant.
6. Add the peas, potatoes, and yogurt and stir to combine well. Turn off the heat and allow to cool.
7. Meanwhile, combine the ingredients for the chutney in a food processor. Pulse to mix well until glossy. Pour the chutney in a bowl and refrigerate until ready to use.
8. Make the samosas: Remove the dough discs from the refrigerator and cut each disc into 8 parts. Shape each part into a ball, then roll the ball into a 6-inch circle. Cut the circle in half and roll each half into a cone.
9. Scoop up 2 tablespoons of the filling into the cone, press the edges of the cone to seal and form into a triangle. Repeat with remaining dough and filling.
10. Preheat the air fryer to 360°F (182°C) and spritz with cooking spray.
11. Arrange four samosas each batch in the preheated air fryer and spritz with cooking spray. Air fry for 15 minutes or until golden brown and crispy. Flip the samosas halfway through.
12. Serve the samosas with the chutney.

Bulgogi Burgers

Prep time: 15 minutes | Cook time: 10 minutes | Serves 4

For the Burgers:
- 1 pound (454 g) 85% lean ground beef
- 2 tablespoons gochujang
- ¼ cup chopped scallions
- 2 teaspoons minced garlic
- 2 teaspoons minced fresh ginger
- 1 tablespoon soy sauce
- 1 tablespoon toasted sesame oil
- 2 teaspoons sugar
- ½ teaspoon kosher salt
- 4 hamburger buns
- Cooking spray

For the Korean Mayo:
- 1 tablespoon gochujang
- ¼ cup mayonnaise
- 2 teaspoons sesame seeds
- ¼ cup chopped scallions
- 1 tablespoon toasted sesame oil

1. Combine the ingredients for the burgers, except for the buns, in a large bowl. Stir to mix well, then wrap the bowl in plastic and refrigerate to marinate for at least an hour.
2. Preheat the air fryer to 350°F (177°C) and spritz with cooking spray.
3. Divide the meat mixture into four portions and form into four balls. Bash the balls into patties.
4. Arrange the patties in the preheated air fryer and spritz with cooking spray. Air fry for 10 minutes or until golden brown. Flip the patties halfway through.
5. Meanwhile, combine the ingredients for the Korean mayo in a small bowl. Stir to mix well.
6. Remove the patties from the air fryer and assemble with the buns, then spread the Korean mayo over the patties to make the burgers. Serve immediately.

Eggplant Hoagies

Prep time: 15 minutes | Cook time: 12 minutes | Makes 3 hoagies

- 6 peeled eggplant slices (about ½ inch thick and 3 inches in diameter)
- ¼ cup jarred pizza sauce
- 6 tablespoons grated Parmesan cheese
- 3 Italian sub rolls, split open lengthwise, warmed
- Cooking spray

1. Preheat the air fryer to 350°F (177°C) and spritz with cooking spray.
2. Arrange the eggplant slices in the preheated air fryer and spritz with cooking spray.
3. Air fry for 10 minutes or until lightly wilted and tender. Flip the slices halfway through.
4. Divide and spread the pizza sauce and cheese on top of the eggplant slice and air fry over 375°F (191°C) for 2 more minutes or until the cheese melts.
5. Assemble each sub roll with two slices of eggplant and serve immediately.

Lamb and Feta Hamburgers

Prep time: 15 minutes | Cook time: 16 minutes | Makes 4 burgers

- 1½ pounds (680 g) ground lamb
- ¼ cup crumbled feta
- 1½ teaspoons tomato paste
- 1½ teaspoons minced garlic
- 1 teaspoon ground dried ginger
- 1 teaspoon ground coriander
- ¼ teaspoon salt
- ¼ teaspoon cayenne pepper
- 4 kaiser rolls or hamburger buns, split open lengthwise, warmed
- Cooking spray

1. Preheat the air fryer to 375°F (191°C) and spritz with cooking spray.
2. Combine all the ingredients, except for the buns, in a large bowl. Coarsely stir to mix well.
3. Shape the mixture into four balls, then pound the balls into four 5-inch diameter patties.
4. Arrange the patties in the preheated air fryer and spritz with cooking spray. Air fry for 16 minutes or until well browned. Flip the patties halfway through.
5. Assemble the buns with patties to make the burgers and serve immediately.

Chapter 6 Vegan and Vegetarian

Roasted Veggie and Tofu

Prep time: 10 minutes | Cook time: 10 minutes | Serves 4

- ⅓ cup Asian-Style sauce
- 1 teaspoon cornstarch
- ½ teaspoon red pepper flakes, or more to taste
- 1 pound (454 g) firm or extra-firm tofu, cut into 1-inch cubes
- 1 small carrot, peeled and cut into ¼-inch-thick coins
- 1 small green bell pepper, cut into bite-size pieces
- 3 scallions, sliced, whites and green parts separated
- 3 tablespoons roasted unsalted peanuts

1. In a large bowl, whisk together the sauce, cornstarch, and red pepper flakes. Fold in the tofu, carrot, pepper, and the white parts of the scallions and toss to coat. Spread the mixture evenly on the sheet pan.
2. Select Roast. Set temperature to 375°F (190°C) and set time to 10 minutes. Press Start to begin preheating.
3. Once preheated, place the pan into the oven. Stir the ingredients once halfway through the cooking time.
4. When done, remove the pan from the oven. Serve sprinkled with the peanuts and scallion greens.

Black Bean and Salsa Tacos

Prep time: 12 minutes | Cook time: 7 minutes | Serves 4

- 1 (15-ounce / 425-g) can black beans, drained and rinsed
- ½ cup prepared salsa
- 1½ teaspoons chili powder
- 4 ounces (113 g) grated Monterey Jack cheese
- 2 tablespoons minced onion
- 8 (6-inch) flour tortillas
- 2 tablespoons vegetable or extra-virgin olive oil
- Shredded lettuce, for serving

1. In a medium bowl, add the beans, salsa and chili powder. Coarsely mash them with a potato masher. Fold in the cheese and onion and stir until combined.
2. Arrange the flour tortillas on a cutting board and spoon 2 to 3 tablespoons of the filling into each tortilla. Fold the tortillas over, pressing lightly to even out the filling. Brush the tacos on one side with half the olive oil and put them, oiled side down, on the sheet pan. Brush the top side with the remaining olive oil.
3. Select Air Fry. Set temperature to 400°F (205°C) and set time to 7 minutes. Press Start to begin preheating.
4. Once preheated, place the pan into the oven. Flip the tacos halfway through the cooking time.
5. Remove the pan from the oven and allow to cool for 5 minutes. Serve with the shredded lettuce on the side.

Thai Curried Veggies

Prep time: 10 minutes | Cook time: 8 minutes | Serves 4

- 1 small head Napa cabbage, shredded, divided
- 1 medium carrot, cut into thin coins
- 8 ounces (227 g) snow peas
- 1 red or green bell pepper, sliced into thin strips
- 1 tablespoon vegetable oil
- 2 tablespoons soy sauce
- 1 tablespoon sesame oil
- 2 tablespoons brown sugar
- 2 tablespoons freshly squeezed lime juice
- 2 teaspoons red or green Thai curry paste
- 1 serrano chile, deseeded and minced
- 1 cup frozen mango slices, thawed
- ½ cup chopped roasted peanuts or cashews

1. Put half the Napa cabbage in a large bowl, along with the carrot, snow peas, and bell pepper. Drizzle with the vegetable oil and toss to coat. Spread them evenly on the sheet pan.
2. Select Roast. Set temperature to 375°F (190°C) and set time to 8 minutes. Press Start to begin preheating.
3. Once preheated, place the pan into the oven.
4. Meanwhile, whisk together the soy sauce, sesame oil, brown sugar, lime juice, and curry paste in a small bowl.
5. When done, the vegetables should be tender and crisp. Remove the pan and put the vegetables back into the bowl. Add the chile, mango slices, and the remaining cabbage. Pour over the dressing and toss to coat. Top with the roasted nuts and serve.

Eggplant and Bell Peppers with Basil

Prep time: 15 minutes | Cook time: 20 minutes | Serves 2

- 1 small eggplant, halved and sliced
- 1 yellow bell pepper, cut into thick strips
- 1 red bell pepper, cut into thick strips
- 2 garlic cloves, quartered
- 1 red onion, sliced
- 1 tablespoon extra-virgin olive oil
- Salt and freshly ground black pepper, to taste
- ½ cup chopped fresh basil, for garnish
- Cooking spray

1. Grease a nonstick baking dish with cooking spray.
2. Place the eggplant, bell peppers, garlic, and red onion in the greased baking dish. Drizzle with the olive oil and toss to coat well. Spritz any uncoated surfaces with cooking spray.
3. Select Bake. Set temperature to 350°F (180°C) and set time to 20 minutes. Press Start to begin preheating.
4. Once preheated, place the baking dish into the oven. Flip the vegetables halfway through the cooking time.
5. When done, remove from the oven and sprinkle with salt and pepper.
6. Sprinkle the basil on top for garnish and serve.

Vinegary Asparagus

Prep time: 15 minutes | Cook time: 10 minutes | Serves 4

- 4 tablespoons olive oil, plus more for greasing
- 4 tablespoons balsamic vinegar
- 1½ pounds (680 g) asparagus spears, trimmed
- Salt and freshly ground black pepper, to taste

1. Grease the perforated pan with olive oil.
2. In a shallow bowl, stir together the 4 tablespoons of olive oil and balsamic vinegar to make a marinade.
3. Put the asparagus spears in the bowl so they are thoroughly covered by the marinade and allow to marinate for 5 minutes.
4. Put the asparagus in the greased pan in a single layer and season with salt and pepper.
5. Select Air Fry. Set temperature to 350°F (180°C) and set time to 10 minutes. Press Start to begin preheating.
6. Once preheated, place the pan into the oven. Flip the asparagus halfway through the cooking time.
7. When done, the asparagus should be tender and lightly browned. Cool for 5 minutes before serving.

Baked Eggs with Spinach and Basil

Prep time: 10 minutes | Cook time: 10 minutes | Serves 2

- 2 tablespoons olive oil
- 4 eggs, whisked
- 5 ounces (142 g) fresh spinach, chopped
- 1 medium-sized tomato, chopped
- 1 teaspoon fresh lemon juice
- ½ teaspoon ground black pepper
- ½ teaspoon coarse salt
- ½ cup roughly chopped fresh basil leaves, for garnish

1. Generously grease a baking pan with olive oil.
2. Stir together the remaining ingredients except the basil leaves in the greased baking pan until well incorporated.
3. Select Bake. Set temperature to 280°F (137°C) and set time to 10 minutes. Press Start to begin preheating.
4. Once preheated, place the pan into the oven.
5. When cooking is complete, the eggs should be completely set and the vegetables should be tender. Remove from the oven and serve garnished with the fresh basil leaves.

Cheesy Broccoli with Rosemary

Prep time: 5 minutes | Cook time: 18 minutes | Serves 4

- 1 large-sized head broccoli, stemmed and cut into small florets
- 2½ tablespoons canola oil
- 2 teaspoons dried basil
- 2 teaspoons dried rosemary
- Salt and ground black pepper, to taste
- ⅓ cup grated yellow cheese

1. Bring a pot of lightly salted water to a boil. Add the broccoli florets to the boiling water and let boil for about 3 minutes.
2. Drain the broccoli florets well and transfer to a large bowl. Add the canola oil, basil, rosemary, salt, and black pepper to the bowl and toss until the broccoli is fully coated. Place the broccoli in the perforated pan.
3. Select Air Fry. Set temperature to 390°F (199°C) and set time to 15 minutes. Press Start to begin preheating.
4. Once preheated, place the pan into the oven. Stir the broccoli halfway through the cooking time.
5. When cooking is complete, the broccoli should be crisp. Remove the pan from the oven. Serve the broccoli warm with grated cheese sprinkled on top.

Kale with Tahini-Lemon Dressing

Prep time: 5 minutes | Cook time: 15 minutes | Serves 2 to 4

Dressing:
- ¼ cup tahini
- ¼ cup fresh lemon juice
- 2 tablespoons olive oil
- 1 teaspoon sesame seeds
- ½ teaspoon garlic powder
- ¼ teaspoon cayenne pepper

Kale:
- 4 cups packed torn kale leaves (stems and ribs removed and leaves torn into palm-size pieces)
- Kosher salt and freshly ground black pepper, to taste

1. Make the dressing: Whisk together the tahini, lemon juice, olive oil, sesame seeds, garlic powder, and cayenne pepper in a large bowl until well mixed.
2. Add the kale and massage the dressing thoroughly all over the leaves. Sprinkle the salt and pepper to season.
3. Place the kale in the perforated pan in a single layer.
4. Select Air Fry. Set temperature to 350°F (180°C) and set time to 15 minutes. Press Start to begin preheating.
5. Once preheated, place the pan into the oven.
6. When cooking is complete, the leaves should be slightly wilted and crispy. Remove from the oven and serve on a plate.

Vegetable Mélange with Garlic

Prep time: 10 minutes | Cook time: 16 minutes | Serves 4

- 1 (8-ounce / 227-g) package sliced mushrooms
- 1 yellow summer squash, sliced
- 1 red bell pepper, sliced
- 3 cloves garlic, sliced
- 1 tablespoon olive oil
- ½ teaspoon dried basil
- ½ teaspoon dried thyme
- ½ teaspoon dried tarragon

1. Toss the mushrooms, squash, and bell pepper with the

garlic and olive oil in a large bowl until well coated. Mix in the basil, thyme, and tarragon and toss again.

2. Spread the vegetables evenly in the perforated pan.
3. Select Roast. Set temperature to 350°F (180°C) and set time to 16 minutes. Press Start to begin preheating.
4. Once preheated, place the pan into the oven.
5. When cooking is complete, the vegetables should be fork-tender. Remove the pan from the oven. Cool for 5 minutes before serving.

Garlic Carrots with Sesame Seeds

Prep time: 5 minutes | Cook time: 16 minutes | Serves 4 to 6

- 1 pound (454 g) baby carrots
- 1 tablespoon sesame oil
- ½ teaspoon dried dill
- Pinch salt
- Freshly ground black pepper, to taste
- 6 cloves garlic, peeled
- 3 tablespoons sesame seeds

1. In a medium bowl, drizzle the baby carrots with the sesame oil. Sprinkle with the dill, salt, and pepper and toss to coat well.
2. Place the baby carrots in the perforated pan.
3. Select Roast. Set temperature to 380°F (193°C) and set time to 16 minutes. Press Start to begin preheating.
4. Once preheated, place the pan into the oven.
5. After 8 minutes, remove the pan from the oven and stir in the garlic. Return the pan to the oven and continue roasting for 8 minutes more.
6. When cooking is complete, the carrots should be lightly browned. Remove the pan from the oven and serve sprinkled with the sesame seeds.

Thai-Flavored Brussels Sprouts

Prep time: 5 minutes | Cook time: 20 minutes | Serves 2

- ¼ cup Thai sweet chili sauce
- 2 tablespoons black vinegar or balsamic vinegar
- ½ teaspoon hot sauce
- 2 small shallots, cut into ¼-inch-thick slices
- 8 ounces (227 g) Brussels sprouts, trimmed (large sprouts halved)
- Kosher salt and freshly ground black pepper, to taste
- 2 teaspoons lightly packed fresh cilantro leaves, for garnish

1. Place the chili sauce, vinegar, and hot sauce in a large bowl and whisk to combine.
2. Add the shallots and Brussels sprouts and toss to coat. Sprinkle with the salt and pepper. Transfer the Brussels sprouts and sauce to a baking pan.
3. Select Roast. Set temperature to 390°F (199°C) and set time to 20 minutes. Press Start to begin preheating.
4. Once preheated, place the pan into the oven. Stir the Brussels sprouts twice during cooking.
5. When cooking is complete, the Brussels sprouts should be crisp-tender. Remove from the oven. Sprinkle the cilantro on top for garnish and serve warm.

Honey Eggplant with Yogurt Sauce

Prep time: 5 minutes | Cook time: 15 minutes | Serves 2

- 1 medium eggplant, quartered and cut crosswise into ½-inch-thick slices
- 2 tablespoons vegetable oil
- Kosher salt and freshly ground black pepper, to taste
- ½ cup plain yogurt (not Greek)
- 2 tablespoons harissa paste
- 1 garlic clove, grated
- 2 teaspoons honey

1. Toss the eggplant slices with the vegetable oil, salt, and pepper in a large bowl until well coated.
2. Lay the eggplant slices in the perforated pan.
3. Select Air Fry. Set temperature to 400°F (205°C) and set time to 15 minutes. Press Start to begin preheating.
4. Once preheated, place the pan into the oven. Stir the slices two to three times during cooking.
5. Meanwhile, make the yogurt sauce by whisking together the yogurt, harissa paste, and garlic in a small bowl.
6. When cooking is complete, the eggplant slices should be golden brown. Spread the yogurt sauce on a platter, and pile the eggplant slices over the top. Serve drizzled with the honey.

Parmesan Cabbage Wedges

Prep time: 5 minutes | Cook time: 20 minutes | Serves 4

- 4 tablespoons melted butter
- 1 head cabbage, cut into wedges
- 1 cup shredded Parmesan cheese
- Salt and black pepper, to taste
- ½ cup shredded Mozzarella cheese

1. Brush the melted butter over the cut sides of cabbage wedges and sprinkle both sides with the Parmesan cheese. Season with salt and pepper to taste.
2. Place the cabbage wedges in the perforated pan.
3. Select Air Fry. Set temperature to 380°F (193°C) and set time to 20 minutes. Press Start to begin preheating.
4. Once preheated, place the pan into the oven. Flip the cabbage halfway through the cooking time.
5. When cooking is complete, the cabbage wedges should be lightly browned. Transfer the cabbage wedges to a plate and serve with the Mozzarella cheese sprinkled on top.

Sesame Mushrooms with Thyme

Prep time: 5 minutes | Cook time: 15 minutes | Serves 2

- 1 tablespoon soy sauce
- 2 teaspoons toasted sesame oil
- 3 teaspoons vegetable oil, divided
- 1 garlic clove, minced
- 7 ounces (198 g) maitake (hen of the woods) mushrooms
- ½ teaspoon flaky sea salt
- ½ teaspoon sesame seeds
- ½ teaspoon finely chopped fresh thyme leaves

1. Whisk together the soy sauce, sesame oil, 1 teaspoon of vegetable oil, and garlic in a small bowl.
2. Arrange the mushrooms in the perforated pan in a single layer. Drizzle the soy sauce mixture over the mushrooms.
3. Select Roast. Set temperature to 300°F (150°C) and set time to 15 minutes. Press Start to begin preheating.
4. Once preheated, place the pan into the oven.
5. After 10 minutes, remove the pan from the oven. Flip the mushrooms and sprinkle the sea salt, sesame seeds, and thyme leaves on top. Drizzle the remaining 2 teaspoons of vegetable oil all over. Return to the oven and continue roasting for an additional 5 minutes.
6. When cooking is complete, remove the mushrooms from the oven to a plate and serve hot.

Ratatouille with Bread Crumb Topping

Prep time: 10 minutes | Cook time: 12 minutes | Serves 6

- 1 medium zucchini, sliced ½-inch thick
- 1 small eggplant, peeled and sliced ½-inch thick
- 2 teaspoons kosher salt, divided
- 4 tablespoons extra-virgin olive oil, divided
- 3 garlic cloves, minced
- 1 small onion, chopped
- 1 small red bell pepper, cut into ½-inch chunks
- 1 small green bell pepper, cut into ½-inch chunks
- ½ teaspoon dried oregano
- ¼ teaspoon freshly ground black pepper
- 1 pint cherry tomatoes
- 2 tablespoons minced fresh basil
- 1 cup panko bread crumbs
- ½ cup grated Parmesan cheese (optional)

1. Season one side of the zucchini and eggplant slices with ¾ teaspoon of salt. Put the slices, salted side down, on a rack set over a baking sheet. Sprinkle the other sides with ¾ teaspoon of salt. Allow to sit for 10 minutes, or until the slices begin to exude water. When ready, rinse and dry them. Cut the zucchini slices into quarters and the eggplant slices into eighths.
2. Pour the zucchini and eggplant into a large bowl, along with 2 tablespoons of olive oil, garlic, onion, bell peppers, oregano, and black pepper. Toss to coat well. Arrange the vegetables on the sheet pan.
3. Select Roast. Set temperature to 375°F (190°C) and set time to 12 minutes. Press Start to begin preheating.
4. Once preheated, place the pan into the oven.
5. Meanwhile, add the tomatoes and basil to the large bowl. Sprinkle with the remaining ½ teaspoon of salt and 1 tablespoon of olive oil. Toss well and set aside.
6. Stir together the remaining 1 tablespoon of olive oil, panko, and Parmesan cheese (if desired) in a small bowl.
7. After 6 minutes, remove the pan and add the tomato mixture to the sheet pan and stir to mix well. Scatter the panko mixture on top. Return the pan to the oven and continue cooking for 6 minutes, or until the vegetables are softened and the topping is golden brown.
8. Cool for 5 minutes before serving.

Butternut Squash and Parsnip with Thyme

Prep time: 5 minutes | Cook time: 16 minutes | Serves 2

- 1 parsnip, sliced
- 1 cup sliced butternut squash
- 1 small red onion, cut into wedges
- ½ chopped celery stalk
- 1 tablespoon chopped fresh thyme
- 2 teaspoons olive oil
- Salt and black pepper, to taste

1. Toss all the ingredients in a large bowl until the vegetables are well coated.
2. Transfer the vegetables to the perforated pan.
3. Select Air Fry. Set temperature to 380°F (193°C) and set time to 16 minutes. Press Start to begin preheating.
4. Once preheated, place the pan into the oven. Stir the vegetables halfway through the cooking time.
5. When cooking is complete, the vegetables should be golden brown and tender. Remove from the oven and serve warm.

Butternut Squash with Goat Cheese

Prep time: 5 minutes | Cook time: 20 minutes | Serves 2

- 1 pound (454 g) butternut squash, cut into wedges
- 2 tablespoons olive oil
- 1 tablespoon dried rosemary
- Salt, to salt
- 1 cup crumbled goat cheese
- 1 tablespoon maple syrup

1. Toss the squash wedges with the olive oil, rosemary, and salt in a large bowl until well coated.
2. Transfer the squash wedges to the perforated pan, spreading them out in as even a layer as possible.
3. Select Air Fry. Set temperature to 350°F (180°C) and set time to 20 minutes. Press Start to begin preheating.
4. Once preheated, place the pan into the oven.
5. After 10 minutes, remove from the oven and flip the squash.

Return the pan to the oven and continue cooking for 10 minutes.

6. When cooking is complete, the squash should be golden brown. Remove the pan from the oven. Sprinkle the goat cheese on top and serve drizzled with the maple syrup.

Ginger-Pepper Broccoli

Prep time: 5 minutes | Cook time: 10 minutes | Serves 2

- 12 ounces (340 g) broccoli florets
- 2 tablespoons Asian hot chili oil
- 1 teaspoon ground Sichuan peppercorns (or black pepper)
- 2 garlic cloves, finely chopped
- 1 (2-inch) piece fresh ginger, peeled and finely chopped
- Kosher salt and freshly ground black pepper

1. Toss the broccoli florets with the chili oil, Sichuan peppercorns, garlic, ginger, salt, and pepper in a mixing bowl until thoroughly coated.
2. Transfer the broccoli florets to the perforated pan.
3. Select Air Fry. Set temperature to 375°F (190°C) and set time to 10 minutes. Press Start to begin preheating.
4. Once preheated, place the pan into the oven. Stir the broccoli florets halfway through the cooking time.
5. When cooking is complete, the broccoli florets should be lightly browned and tender. Remove the broccoli from the oven and serve on a plate.

Parmesan Brussels Sprouts

Prep time: 10 minutes | Cook time: 20 minutes | Serves 4

- 1 pound (454 g) fresh Brussels sprouts, trimmed
- 1 tablespoon olive oil
- ½ teaspoon salt
- ⅛ teaspoon pepper
- ¼ cup grated Parmesan cheese

1. In a large bowl, combine the Brussels sprouts with olive oil, salt, and pepper and toss until evenly coated.
2. Spread the Brussels sprouts evenly in the perforated pan.
3. Select Air Fry. Set temperature to 330°F (166°C) and set time to 20 minutes. Press Start to begin preheating.
4. Once preheated, place the pan into the oven. Stir the Brussels sprouts twice during cooking.
5. When cooking is complete, the Brussels sprouts should be golden brown and crisp. Remove the pan from the oven. Sprinkle the grated Parmesan cheese on top and serve warm.

Chapter 7 Appetizers and Snacks

Cheddar Baked Potatoes with Chives

Prep time: 5 minutes | Cook time: 20 minutes | Serves 6

- 12 small red potatoes
- 1 teaspoon kosher salt, divided
- 1 tablespoon extra-virgin olive oil
- ¼ cup grated sharp Cheddar cheese
- ¼ cup sour cream
- 2 tablespoons chopped chives
- 2 tablespoons grated Parmesan cheese

1. Add the potatoes to a large bowl. Sprinkle with the ½ teaspoon of the salt and drizzle with the olive oil. Toss to coat. Place the potatoes in the sheet pan.
2. Select Roast. Set temperature to 375°F (190°C) and set time to 15 minutes. Press Start to begin preheating.
3. When the unit has preheated, place the pan into the oven.
4. After 10 minutes, rotate the pan and continue cooking.
5. When cooking is complete, remove the pan and let the potatoes rest for 5 minutes. Halve the potatoes lengthwise. Using a spoon, scoop the flesh into a bowl, leaving a thin shell of skin. Arrange the potato halves on the sheet pan.
6. Mash the potato flesh until smooth. Stir in the remaining ½ teaspoon of the salt, Cheddar cheese, sour cream and chives. Transfer the filling into a pastry bag with one corner snipped off. Pipe the filling into the potato shells, mounding up slightly. Sprinkle with the Parmesan cheese.
7. Select Roast. Set temperature to 375°F (190°C) and set time to 5 minutes. Place the pan into the oven.
8. When cooking is complete, the tops should be browning slightly. Remove the pan from the oven and let the potatoes cool slightly before serving.

Sausage and Onion Rolls with Mustard

Prep time: 15 minutes | Cook time: 15 minutes | Serves 12

- 1 pound (454 g) bulk breakfast sausage
- ½ cup finely chopped onion
- ½ cup fresh bread crumbs
- ½ teaspoon dried mustard
- ½ teaspoon dried sage
- ¼ teaspoon cayenne pepper
- 1 large egg, beaten
- 1 garlic clove, minced
- 2 sheets (1 package) frozen puff pastry, thawed
- All-purpose flour, for dusting

1. In a medium bowl, break up the sausage. Stir in the onion, bread crumbs, mustard, sage, cayenne pepper, egg and garlic. Divide the sausage mixture in half and tightly wrap each half in plastic wrap. Refrigerate for 5 to 10 minutes.
2. Lay the pastry sheets on a lightly floured work surface. Using a rolling pin, lightly roll out the pastry to smooth out the dough. Take out one of the sausage packages and form the sausage into a long roll. Remove the plastic wrap and place the sausage on top of the puff pastry about 1 inch from one of the long edges. Roll the pastry around the sausage and pinch the edges of the dough together to seal. Repeat with the other pastry sheet and sausage.
3. Slice the logs into lengths about 1½ inches long. Place the sausage rolls on the sheet pan, cut-side down.
4. Select Roast. Set temperature to 350°F (180°C) and set time to 15 minutes. Press Start to begin preheating.
5. Once the unit has preheated, place the pan into the oven.
6. After 7 or 8 minutes, rotate the pan and continue cooking.
7. When cooking is complete, the rolls will be golden brown and sizzling. Remove the pan from the oven and let cool for 5 minutes.

Honey Roasted Grapes with Basil

Prep time: 5 minutes | Cook time: 10 minutes | Serves 6

- 2 cups seedless red grapes, rinsed and patted dry
- 1 tablespoon apple cider vinegar
- 1 tablespoon honey
- 1 cup low-fat Greek yogurt
- 2 tablespoons 2 percent milk
- 2 tablespoons minced fresh basil

1. Spread the red grapes in the perforated pan and drizzle with the cider vinegar and honey. Lightly toss to coat.
2. Select Roast. Set temperature to 380°F (193°C) and set time to 10 minutes. Press Start to begin preheating.
3. Once the unit has preheated, place the pan into the oven.
4. When cooking is complete, the grapes will be wilted but still soft. Remove the pan from the oven.
5. In a medium bowl, whisk together the yogurt and milk. Gently fold in the grapes and basil.
6. Serve immediately.

Parmesan Cauliflower with Turmeric

Prep time: 15 minutes | Cook time: 15 minutes | Makes 5 cups

- 8 cups small cauliflower florets (about 1¼ pounds / 567 g)
- 3 tablespoons olive oil
- 1 teaspoon garlic powder
- ½ teaspoon salt
- ½ teaspoon turmeric
- ¼ cup shredded Parmesan cheese

1. In a bowl, combine the cauliflower florets, olive oil, garlic powder, salt, and turmeric and toss to coat. Transfer to the perforated pan.
2. Select Air Fry. Set temperature to 390°F (199°C) and set time to 15 minutes. Press Start to begin preheating.
3. Once preheated, place the pan into the oven.

4. After 5 minutes, remove from the oven and stir the cauliflower florets. Return the pan to the oven and continue cooking.
5. After 6 minutes, remove from the oven and stir the cauliflower. Return the pan to the oven and continue cooking for 4 minutes. The cauliflower florets should be crisp-tender.
6. When cooking is complete, remove from the oven to a plate. Sprinkle with the shredded Parmesan cheese and toss well. Serve warm.

Cheddar Mushrooms with Pimientos

Prep time: 10 minutes | Cook time: 18 minutes | Serves 12

- 24 medium raw white button mushrooms, rinsed and drained
- 4 ounces (113 g) shredded extra-sharp Cheddar cheese
- 2 ounces (57 g) cream cheese, at room temperature
- 1 ounce (28 g) chopped jarred pimientos
- 2 tablespoons grated onion
- ⅛ teaspoon smoked paprika
- ⅛ teaspoon hot sauce
- 2 tablespoons butter, melted, divided
- ⅓ cup panko bread crumbs
- 2 tablespoons grated Parmesan cheese

1. Gently pull out the stems of the mushrooms and discard. Set aside.
2. In a medium bowl, stir together the Cheddar cheese, cream cheese, pimientos, onion, paprika and hot sauce.
3. Brush the sheet pan with 1 tablespoon of the melted butter. Arrange the mushrooms evenly on the pan, hollow-side up.
4. Place the cheese mixture into a large heavy plastic bag and cut off the end. Fill the mushrooms with the cheese mixture.
5. In a small bowl, whisk together the remaining 1 tablespoon of the melted butter, bread crumbs and Parmesan cheese. Sprinkle the panko mixture over each mushroom.
6. Select Roast. Set temperature to 350°F (180°C) and set time to 18 minutes. Press Start to begin preheating.
7. When the unit has preheated, place the pan into the oven.
8. After about 9 minutes, rotate the pan and continue cooking.
9. When cooking is complete, let the stuffed mushrooms rest for 2 minutes before serving.

Roasted Mushrooms with Garlic

Prep time: 5 minutes | Cook time: 27 minutes | Serves 4

- 16 garlic cloves, peeled
- 2 teaspoons olive oil, divided
- 16 button mushrooms
- ½ teaspoon dried marjoram
- ⅛ teaspoon freshly ground black pepper
- 1 tablespoon white wine

1. Place the garlic cloves on the sheet pan and drizzle with 1 teaspoon of the olive oil. Toss to coat well.
2. Select Roast. Set temperature to 350°F (180°C) and set time to 12 minutes. Press Start to begin preheating.
3. Once the unit has preheated, place the pan into the oven.
4. When cooking is complete, remove the pan from the oven. Stir in the mushrooms, marjoram and pepper. Drizzle with the remaining 1 teaspoon of the olive oil and the white wine. Toss to coat well. Return the pan to the oven.
5. Select Roast. Set temperature to 350°F (180°C) and set time to 15 minutes. place the pan into the oven.
6. Once done, the mushrooms and garlic cloves will be softened. Remove the pan from the oven.
7. Serve warm.

Jalapeño Poppers with Cheddar

Prep time: 10 minutes | Cook time: 15 minutes | Serves 8

- 6 ounces (170 g) cream cheese, at room temperature
- 4 ounces (113 g) shredded Cheddar cheese
- 1 teaspoon chili powder
- 12 large jalapeño peppers, deseeded and sliced in half lengthwise
- 2 slices cooked bacon, chopped
- ¼ cup panko bread crumbs
- 1 tablespoon butter, melted

1. In a medium bowl, whisk together the cream cheese, Cheddar cheese and chili powder. Spoon the cheese mixture into the jalapeño halves and arrange them on the sheet pan.
2. In a small bowl, stir together the bacon, bread crumbs and butter. Sprinkle the mixture over the jalapeño halves.
3. Select Roast. Set temperature to 375°F (190°C) and set time to 15 minutes. Press Start to begin preheating.
4. When the unit has preheated, place the pan into the oven.
5. After 7 or 8 minutes, rotate the pan and continue cooking until the peppers are softened, the filling is bubbling and the bread crumbs are browned.
6. When cooking is complete, remove the pan from the oven. Let the poppers cool for 5 minutes before serving.

Green Chiles and Cheese Nachos

Prep time: 10 minutes | Cook time: 10 minutes | Serves 6

- 8 ounces (227 g) tortilla chips
- 3 cups shredded Monterey Jack cheese, divided
- 2 (7-ounce / 198-g) cans chopped green chiles, drained
- 1 (8-ounce / 227-g) can tomato sauce
- ¼ teaspoon dried oregano
- ¼ teaspoon granulated garlic
- ¼ teaspoon freshly ground black pepper
- Pinch cinnamon
- Pinch cayenne pepper

1. Arrange the tortilla chips close together in a single layer on the sheet pan. Sprinkle 1½ cups of the cheese over the chips. Arrange the green chiles over the cheese as evenly as possible. Top with the remaining 1½ cups of the cheese.
2. Select Roast. Set temperature to 375°F (190°C) and set time to 10 minutes. Press Start to begin preheating.
3. When the unit has preheated, place the pan into the oven.
4. After 5 minutes, rotate the pan and continue cooking.
5. Meanwhile, stir together the remaining ingredients in a bowl.
6. When cooking is complete, the cheese will be melted and starting to crisp around the edges of the pan. Remove the pan from the oven. Drizzle the sauce over the nachos and serve warm.

Pepperoni Pizza Bites with Marinara

Prep time: 5 minutes | Cook time: 12 minutes | Serves 8

- 1 cup finely shredded Mozzarella cheese
- ½ cup chopped pepperoni
- ¼ cup Marinara sauce
- 1 (8-ounce / 227-g) can crescent roll dough
- All-purpose flour, for dusting

1. In a small bowl, stir together the cheese, pepperoni and Marinara sauce.
2. Lay the dough on a lightly floured work surface. Separate it into 4 rectangles. Firmly pinch the perforations together and pat the dough pieces flat.
3. Divide the cheese mixture evenly between the rectangles and spread it out over the dough, leaving a ¼-inch border. Roll a rectangle up tightly, starting with the short end. Pinch the edge down to seal the roll. Repeat with the remaining rolls.
4. Slice the rolls into 4 or 5 even slices. Place the slices on the sheet pan, leaving a few inches between each slice.
5. Select Roast. Set temperature to 350°F (180°C) and set time to 12 minutes. Press Start to begin preheating.
6. Once the unit has preheated, place the pan into the oven.
7. After 6 minutes, rotate the pan and continue cooking.
8. When cooking is complete, the rolls will be golden brown with crisp edges. Remove the pan from the oven. Serve hot.

Cheddar Sausage Balls

Prep time: 10 minutes | Cook time: 10 minutes | Serves 8

- 12 ounces (340 g) mild ground sausage
- 1½ cups baking mix
- 1 cup shredded mild Cheddar cheese
- 3 ounces (85 g) cream cheese, at room temperature
- 1 to 2 tablespoons olive oil

1. Line the perforated pan with parchment paper. Set aside.
2. Mix together the ground sausage, baking mix, Cheddar cheese, and cream cheese in a large bowl and stir to incorporate.
3. Divide the sausage mixture into 16 equal portions and roll them into 1-inch balls with your hands. Arrange the sausage balls on the parchment, leaving space between each ball. Brush the sausage balls with the olive oil.
4. Select Air Fry. Set temperature to 325°F (163°C) and set time to 10 minutes. Press Start to begin preheating.
5. Once preheated, place the pan into the oven. Flip the balls halfway through the cooking time.
6. When cooking is complete, the balls should be firm and lightly browned on both sides. Remove from the oven to a plate and serve warm.

Tuna Melts with Mayo

Prep time: 10 minutes | Cook time: 6 minutes | Serves 6

- 2 (5- to 6-ounce / 142- to 170-g) cans oil-packed tuna, drained
- 1 large scallion, chopped
- 1 small stalk celery, chopped
- ⅓ cup mayonnaise
- 1 tablespoon chopped fresh dill
- 1 tablespoon capers, drained
- ¼ teaspoon celery salt
- 12 slices cocktail rye bread
- 2 tablespoons butter, melted
- 6 slices sharp Cheddar cheese

1. In a medium bowl, stir together the tuna, scallion, celery, mayonnaise, dill, capers and celery salt.
2. Brush one side of the bread slices with the butter. Arrange the bread slices on the sheet pan, buttered-side down. Scoop a heaping tablespoon of the tuna mixture on each slice of bread, spreading it out evenly to the edges.
3. Cut the cheese slices to fit the dimensions of the bread and place a cheese slice on each piece.
4. Select Roast. Set temperature to 375°F (190°C) and set time to 6 minutes. Press Start to begin preheating.
5. Once the unit has preheated, place the pan into the oven.
6. After 4 minutes, remove the pan from the oven and check the tuna melts. The tuna melts are done when the cheese has melted and the tuna is heated through. If needed, continue cooking.
7. When cooking is complete, remove the pan from the oven. Use a spatula to transfer the tuna melts to a clean work surface and slice each one in half diagonally. Serve warm.

Sugar Roasted Walnuts

Prep time: 5 minutes | Cook time: 15 minutes | Makes 4 cups

- 1 pound (454 g) walnut halves and pieces
- ½ cup granulated sugar
- 3 tablespoons vegetable oil
- 1 teaspoon cayenne pepper

- ½ teaspoon fine salt

1. Soak the walnuts in a large bowl with boiling water for a minute or two. Drain the walnuts. Stir in the sugar, oil and cayenne pepper to coat well. Spread the walnuts in a single layer on the sheet pan.
2. Select Roast. Set temperature to 325°F (163°C) and set time to 15 minutes. Press Start to begin preheating.
3. When the unit has preheated, place the pan into the oven.
4. After 7 or 8 minutes, remove the pan from the oven. Stir the nuts. Return the pan to the oven and continue cooking, check frequently.
5. When cooking is complete, the walnuts should be dark golden brown. Remove the pan from the oven. Sprinkle the nuts with the salt and let cool. Serve.

Balsamic Prosciutto-Wrapped Pears

Prep time: 12 minutes | Cook time: 6 minutes | Serves 8

- 2 large, ripe Anjou pears
- 4 thin slices Parma prosciutto
- 2 teaspoons aged balsamic vinegar

1. Peel the pears. Slice into 8 wedges and cut out the core from each wedge.
2. Cut the prosciutto into 8 long strips. Wrap each pear wedge with a strip of prosciutto. Place the wrapped pears in the sheet pan.
3. Select Broil. Set temperature to High and set time to 6 minutes. Press Start to begin preheating.
4. When the unit has preheated, place the pan into the oven.
5. After 2 or 3 minutes, check the pears. The pears should be turned over if the prosciutto is beginning to crisp up and brown. Return the pan to the oven and continue cooking.
6. When cooking is complete, remove the pan from the oven. Drizzle the pears with the balsamic vinegar and serve warm.

Breaded Zucchini Tots

Prep time: 15 minutes | Cook time: 6 minutes | Serves 8

- 2 medium zucchini (about 12 ounces / 340 g) shredded
- 1 large egg, whisked
- ½ cup grated pecorino romano cheese
- ½ cup panko bread crumbs
- ¼ teaspoon black pepper
- 1 clove garlic, minced
- Cooking spray

1. Using your hands, squeeze out as much liquid from the zucchini as possible. In a large bowl, mix the zucchini with the remaining ingredients except the oil until well incorporated.
2. Make the zucchini tots: Use a spoon or cookie scoop to place tablespoonfuls of the zucchini mixture onto a lightly floured cutting board and form into 1-inch logs.
3. Spritz the perforated pan with cooking spray. Place the zucchini tots in the pan.
4. Select Air Fry. Set temperature to 375°F (190°C) and set time to 6 minutes. Press Start to begin preheating.
5. Once preheated, place the pan into the oven.
6. When cooking is complete, the tots should be golden brown. Remove from the oven to a serving plate and serve warm.

Ginger Shrimp with Sesame Seeds

Prep time: 15 minutes | Cook time: 8 minutes | Serves 4 to 6

- ½ pound (227 g) raw shrimp, peeled and deveined
- 1 egg, beaten
- 2 scallions, chopped, plus more for garnish
- 2 tablespoons chopped fresh cilantro
- 2 teaspoons grated fresh ginger
- 1 to 2 teaspoons sriracha sauce
- 1 teaspoon soy sauce
- ½ teaspoon toasted sesame oil
- 6 slices thinly sliced white sandwich bread
- ½ cup sesame seeds
- Cooking spray
- Thai chili sauce, for serving

1. In a food processor, add the shrimp, egg, scallions, cilantro, ginger, sriracha sauce, soy sauce and sesame oil, and pulse until chopped finely. You'll need to stop the food processor occasionally to scrape down the sides. Transfer the shrimp mixture to a bowl.
2. On a clean work surface, cut the crusts off the sandwich bread. Using a brush, generously brush one side of each slice of bread with shrimp mixture.
3. Place the sesame seeds on a plate. Press bread slices, shrimp-side down, into sesame seeds to coat evenly. Cut each slice diagonally into quarters.
4. Spritz the perforated pan with cooking spray. Spread the coated slices in a single layer in the perforated pan.
5. Select Air Fry. Set temperature to 400°F (205°C) and set time to 8 minutes. Press Start to begin preheating.
6. Once preheated, place the pan into the oven. Flip the bread slices halfway through.
7. When cooking is complete, they should be golden and crispy. Remove from the oven to a plate and let cool for 5 minutes. Top with the chopped scallions and serve warm with Thai chili sauce.

Paprika Polenta Fries with Chili-Lime Mayo

Prep time: 10 minutes | Cook time: 28 minutes | Serves 4

Polenta Fries:

- 2 teaspoons vegetable or olive oil
- ¼ teaspoon paprika
- 1 pound (454 g) prepared polenta, cut into 3-inch × ½-inch strips

- Salt and freshly ground black pepper, to taste

Chili-Lime Mayo:
- ½ cup mayonnaise
- 1 teaspoon chili powder
- 1 teaspoon chopped fresh cilantro
- ¼ teaspoon ground cumin
- Juice of ½ lime
- Salt and freshly ground black pepper, to taste

1. Mix the oil and paprika in a bowl. Add the polenta strips and toss until evenly coated. Transfer the polenta strips to the perforated pan.
2. Select Air Fry. Set temperature to 400°F (205°C) and set time to 28 minutes. Press Start to begin preheating.
3. Once preheated, place the pan into the oven. Stir the polenta strips halfway through the cooking time.
4. Meanwhile, whisk together all the ingredients for the chili-lime mayo in a small bowl.
5. When cooking is complete, remove the polenta fries from the oven to a plate. Season as desired with salt and pepper. Serve alongside the chili-lime mayo as a dipping sauce.

Lemon Ricotta with Capers

Prep time: 10 minutes | Cook time: 8 minutes | Serves 4 to 6

- 1½ cups whole milk ricotta cheese
- 2 tablespoons extra-virgin olive oil
- 2 tablespoons capers, rinsed
- Zest of 1 lemon, plus more for garnish
- 1 teaspoon finely chopped fresh rosemary
- Pinch crushed red pepper flakes
- Salt and freshly ground black pepper, to taste
- 1 tablespoon grated Parmesan cheese

1. In a mixing bowl, stir together the ricotta cheese, olive oil, capers, lemon zest, rosemary, red pepper flakes, salt, and pepper until well combined.
2. Spread the mixture evenly in a baking dish.
3. Select Air Fry. Set temperature to 380°F (193°C) and set time to 8 minutes. Press Start to begin preheating.
4. Once preheated, place the baking dish in the oven.
5. When cooking is complete, the top should be nicely browned. Remove from the oven and top with a sprinkle of grated Parmesan cheese. Garnish with the lemon zest and serve warm.

Deviled Eggs with Mayo

Prep time: 20 minutes | Cook time: 16 minutes | Serves 12

- 3 cups ice
- 12 large eggs
- ½ cup mayonnaise
- 10 hamburger dill pickle chips, diced
- ¼ cup diced onion
- 2 teaspoons salt
- 2 teaspoons yellow mustard
- 1 teaspoon freshly ground black pepper
- ½ teaspoon paprika

1. Put the ice in a large bowl and set aside. Carefully place the eggs in the perforated pan.
2. Select Bake. Set temperature to 250°F (121°C) and set time to 16 minutes. Press Start to begin preheating.
3. Once preheated, place the pan into the oven.
4. When cooking is complete, transfer the eggs to the large bowl of ice to cool.
5. When cool enough to handle, peel the eggs. Slice them in half lengthwise and scoop out yolks into a small bowl. Stir in the mayonnaise, pickles, onion, salt, mustard, and pepper. Mash the mixture with a fork until well combined.
6. Fill each egg white half with 1 to 2 teaspoons of the egg yolk mixture.
7. Sprinkle the paprika on top and serve immediately.

Honey Snack Mix

Prep time: 5 minutes | Cook time: 10 minutes | Makes about 10 cups

- 3 tablespoons butter, melted
- ½ cup honey
- 1 teaspoon salt
- 2 cups granola
- 2 cups sesame sticks
- 2 cups crispy corn puff cereal
- 2 cups mini pretzel crisps
- 1 cup cashews
- 1 cup pepitas
- 1 cup dried cherries

1. In a small mixing bowl, mix together the butter, honey, and salt until well incorporated.
2. In a large bowl, combine the granola, sesame sticks, corn puff cereal and pretzel crisps, cashews, and pepitas. Drizzle with the butter mixture and toss until evenly coated. Transfer the snack mix to a sheet pan.
3. Select Air Fry. Set temperature to 370°F (188°C) and set time to 10 minutes. Press Start to begin preheating.
4. Once preheated, slide the pan into the oven. Stir the snack mix halfway through the cooking time.
5. When cooking is complete, they should be lightly toasted. Remove from the oven and allow to cool completely. Scatter with the dried cherries and mix well. Serve immediately.

Parmesan Snack Mix

Prep time: 5 minutes | Cook time: 6 minutes | Makes 6 cups

- 2 cups oyster crackers
- 2 cups Chex rice
- 1 cup sesame sticks
- ⅔ cup finely grated Parmesan cheese
- 8 tablespoons unsalted butter, melted
- 1½ teaspoons granulated garlic
- ½ teaspoon kosher salt

1. Toss together all the ingredients in a large bowl until well coated. Spread the mixture on the sheet pan in an even

layer.

2. Select Roast. Set temperature to 350°F (180°C) and set time to 6 minutes. Press Start to begin preheating.
3. When the unit has preheated, place the pan into the oven.
4. After 3 minutes, remove the pan and stir the mixture. Return the pan to the oven and continue cooking.
5. When cooking is complete, the mixture should be lightly browned and fragrant. Let cool before serving.

Paprika Potato Chips

Prep time: 5 minutes | Cook time: 22 minutes | Serves 3

- 2 medium potatoes, preferably Yukon Gold, scrubbed
- Cooking spray
- 2 teaspoons olive oil
- ½ teaspoon garlic granules
- ¼ teaspoon paprika
- ¼ teaspoon plus ⅛ teaspoon sea salt
- ¼ teaspoon freshly ground black pepper
- Ketchup or hot sauce, for serving

1. Spritz the perforated pan with cooking spray.
2. On a flat work surface, cut the potatoes into ¼-inch-thick slices. Transfer the potato slices to a medium bowl, along with the olive oil, garlic granules, paprika, salt, and pepper and toss to coat well. Transfer the potato slices to the perforated pan.
3. Select Air Fry. Set temperature to 392°F (200°C) and set time to 22 minutes. Press Start to begin preheating.
4. Once preheated, place the pan into the oven. Stir the potato slices twice during the cooking process.
5. When cooking is complete, the potato chips should be tender and nicely browned. Remove from the oven and serve alongside the ketchup for dipping.

Hush Puppies with Jalapeño

Prep time: 45 minutes | Cook time: 10 minutes | Serves 12

- 1 cup self-rising yellow cornmeal
- ½ cup all-purpose flour
- 1 teaspoon sugar
- 1 teaspoon salt
- 1 teaspoon freshly ground black pepper
- 1 large egg
- ⅓ cup canned creamed corn
- 1 cup minced onion
- 2 teaspoons minced jalapeño pepper
- 2 tablespoons olive oil, divided

1. Thoroughly combine the cornmeal, flour, sugar, salt, and pepper in a large bowl.
2. Whisk together the egg and corn in a small bowl. Pour the egg mixture into the bowl of cornmeal mixture and stir to combine. Stir in the minced onion and jalapeño. Cover the bowl with plastic wrap and place in the refrigerator for 30 minutes.
3. Line the perforated pan with parchment paper and lightly brush it with 1 tablespoon of olive oil.
4. Scoop out the cornmeal mixture and form into 24 balls, about 1 inch.
5. Arrange the balls on the parchment, leaving space between each ball.
6. Select Air Fry. Set temperature to 375°F (190°C) and set time to 10 minutes. Press Start to begin preheating.
7. Once preheated, place the pan into the oven.
8. After 5 minutes, remove the pan from the oven. Flip the balls and brush them with the remaining 1 tablespoon of olive oil. Return to the oven and continue cooking for 5 minutes until golden brown.
9. When cooking is complete, remove the balls (hush puppies) from the oven and serve on a plate.

Fried Pickle Spears with Chili

Prep time: 5 minutes | Cook time: 15 minutes | Serves 6

- 2 jars sweet and sour pickle spears, patted dry
- 2 medium-sized eggs
- ⅓ cup milk
- 1 teaspoon garlic powder
- 1 teaspoon sea salt
- ½ teaspoon shallot powder
- ⅓ teaspoon chili powder
- ⅓ cup all-purpose flour
- Cooking spray

1. Spritz the perforated pan with cooking spray.
2. In a bowl, beat together the eggs with milk. In another bowl, combine garlic powder, sea salt, shallot powder, chili powder and all-purpose flour until well blended.
3. One by one, roll the pickle spears in the powder mixture, then dredge them in the egg mixture. Dip them in the powder mixture a second time for additional coating.
4. Place the coated pickles in the perforated pan.
5. Select Air Fry. Set temperature to 385°F (196°C) and set time to 15 minutes. Press Start to begin preheating.
6. Once preheated, place the pan into the oven. Stir the pickles halfway through the cooking time.
7. When cooking is complete, they should be golden and crispy. Transfer to a plate and let cool for 5 minutes before serving.

Cinnamon Apple Chips

Prep time: 10 minutes | Cook time: 10 minutes | Serves 4

- 2 apples, cored and cut into thin slices
- 2 heaped teaspoons
- ground cinnamon
- Cooking spray

1. Spritz the perforated pan with cooking spray.

2. In a medium bowl, sprinkle the apple slices with the cinnamon. Toss until evenly coated. Spread the coated apple slices on the pan in a single layer.
3. Select Air Fry. Set temperature to 350°F (180°C) and set time to 10 minutes. Press Start to begin preheating.
4. Once preheated, place the pan into the oven.
5. After 5 minutes, remove the pan from the oven. Stir the apple slices and return the pan to the oven to continue cooking.
6. When cooking is complete, the slices should be until crispy Remove the pan from the oven and let rest for 5 minutes before serving.

Avocado Chips with Lime

Prep time: 15 minutes | Cook time: 10 minutes | Serves 4

- 1 egg
- 1 tablespoon lime juice
- ⅛ teaspoon hot sauce
- 2 tablespoons flour
- ¾ cup panko bread crumbs
- ¼ cup cornmeal
- ¼ teaspoon salt
- 1 large avocado, pitted, peeled, and cut into ½-inch slices
- Cooking spray

1. Whisk together the egg, lime juice, and hot sauce in a small bowl.
2. On a sheet of wax paper, place the flour. In a separate sheet of wax paper, combine the bread crumbs, cornmeal, and salt.
3. Dredge the avocado slices one at a time in the flour, then in the egg mixture, finally roll them in the bread crumb mixture to coat well.
4. Place the breaded avocado slices in the perforated pan and mist them with cooking spray.
5. Select Air Fry. Set temperature to 390°F (199°C) and set time to 10 minutes. Press Start to begin preheating.
6. Once preheated, place the pan into the oven.
7. When cooking is complete, the slices should be nicely browned and crispy. Transfer the avocado slices to a plate and serve.

Brie Pear Sandwiches

Prep time: 10 minutes | Cook time: 6 minutes | Serves 4 to 8

- 8 ounces (227 g) Brie
- 8 slices oat nut bread
- 1 large ripe pear, cored and cut into ½-inch-thick slices
- 2 tablespoons butter, melted

1. Make the sandwiches: Spread each of 4 slices of bread with ¼ of the Brie. Top the Brie with the pear slices and remaining 4 bread slices.
2. Brush the melted butter lightly on both sides of each sandwich.
3. Arrange the sandwiches in the perforated pan.
4. Select Bake. Set temperature to 360°F (182°C) and set time to 6 minutes. Press Start to begin preheating.
5. Once preheated, place the pan into the oven.
6. When cooking is complete, the cheese should be melted. Remove the pan from the oven and serve warm.

Parmesan Crab Toasts

Prep time: 10 minutes | Cook time: 5 minutes | Makes 15 to 18 toasts

- 1 (6-ounce / 170-g) can flaked crab meat, well drained
- 3 tablespoons light mayonnaise
- ¼ cup shredded Parmesan cheese
- ¼ cup shredded Cheddar cheese
- 1 teaspoon Worcestershire sauce
- ½ teaspoon lemon juice
- 1 loaf artisan bread, French bread, or baguette, cut into ⅜-inch-thick slices

1. In a large bowl, stir together all the ingredients except the bread slices.
2. On a clean work surface, lay the bread slices. Spread ½ tablespoon of crab mixture onto each slice of bread.
3. Arrange the bread slices in the perforated pan in a single layer.
4. Select Bake. Set temperature to 360°F (182°C) and set time to 5 minutes. Press Start to begin preheating.
5. Once preheated, place the pan into the oven.
6. When cooking is complete, the tops should be lightly browned. Remove the pan from the oven. Serve warm.

Buttermilk-Marinated Chicken Wings

Prep time: 20 minutes | Cook time: 18 minutes | Serves 4

- 2 pounds (907 g) chicken wings
- Cooking spray

Marinade:
- 1 cup buttermilk
- ½ teaspoon salt
- ½ teaspoon black pepper

Coating:
- 1 cup flour
- 1 cup panko bread crumbs
- 2 tablespoons poultry seasoning
- 2 teaspoons salt

1. Whisk together all the ingredients for the marinade in a large bowl.
2. Add the chicken wings to the marinade and toss well. Transfer to the refrigerator to marinate for at least an hour.
3. Spritz the perforated pan with cooking spray. Set aside.
4. Thoroughly combine all the ingredients for the coating in a shallow bowl.

5. Remove the chicken wings from the marinade and shake off any excess. Roll them in the coating mixture.
6. Place the chicken wings in the perforated pan in a single layer. Mist the wings with cooking spray.
7. Select Air Fry. Set temperature to 360°F (182°C) and set time to 18 minutes. Press Start to begin preheating.
8. Once preheated, place the pan into the oven. Flip the wings halfway through the cooking time.
9. When cooking is complete, the wings should be crisp and golden brown on the outside. Remove from the oven to a plate and serve hot.

Pork and Turkey Sandwiches

Prep time: 20 minutes | Cook time: 8 minutes | Makes 4 sandwiches

- 8 slices ciabatta bread, about ¼-inch thick
- Cooking spray
- 1 tablespoon brown mustard

Toppings:

- 6 to 8 ounces (170 to 227 g) thinly sliced leftover roast pork
- 4 ounces (113 g) thinly sliced deli turkey
- ⅓ cup bread and butter pickle slices
- 2 to 3 ounces (57 to 85 g) Pepper Jack cheese slices

1. On a clean work surface, spray one side of each slice of bread with cooking spray. Spread the other side of each slice of bread evenly with brown mustard.
2. Top 4 of the bread slices with the roast pork, turkey, pickle slices, cheese, and finish with remaining bread slices. Transfer to the perforated pan.
3. Select Air Fry. Set temperature to 390°F (199°C) and set time to 8 minutes. Press Start to begin preheating.
4. Once preheated, place the pan into the oven.
5. When cooking is complete, remove the pan from the oven. Cool for 5 minutes and serve warm.

Horseradish Green Tomatoes

Prep time: 18 minutes | Cook time: 13 minutes | Serves 4

- 2 eggs
- ¼ cup buttermilk
- ½ cup bread crumbs
- ½ cup cornmeal
- ¼ teaspoon salt
- 1½ pounds (680 g) firm green tomatoes, cut into ¼-inch slices
- Cooking spray

Horseradish Sauce:

- ¼ cup sour cream
- ¼ cup mayonnaise
- 2 teaspoons prepared horseradish
- ½ teaspoon lemon juice
- ½ teaspoon Worcestershire sauce
- ⅛ teaspoon black pepper

1. Spritz the perforated pan with cooking spray. Set aside.
2. In a small bowl, whisk together all the ingredients for the horseradish sauce until smooth. Set aside.
3. In a shallow dish, beat the eggs and buttermilk.
4. In a separate shallow dish, thoroughly combine the bread crumbs, cornmeal, and salt.
5. Dredge the tomato slices, one at a time, in the egg mixture, then roll in the bread crumb mixture until evenly coated.
6. Place the tomato slices in the perforated pan in a single layer. Spray them with cooking spray.
7. Select Air Fry. Set temperature to 390°F (199°C) and set time to 13 minutes. Press Start to begin preheating.
8. Once preheated, place the pan into the oven. Flip the tomato slices halfway through the cooking time.
9. When cooking is complete, the tomato slices should be nicely browned and crisp. Remove from the oven to a platter and serve drizzled with the prepared horseradish sauce.

Turkey-Wrapped Dates and Almonds

Prep time: 10 minutes | Cook time: 6 minutes | Makes 16 appetizers

- 16 whole dates, pitted
- 16 whole almonds
- 6 to 8 strips turkey bacon, cut in half

Special Equipment:

- 16 toothpicks, soaked in water for at least 30 minutes

1. On a flat work surface, stuff each pitted date with a whole almond.
2. Wrap half slice of bacon around each date and secure it with a toothpick.
3. Place the bacon-wrapped dates in the perforated pan.
4. Select Air Fry. Set temperature to 390°F (199°C) and set time to 6 minutes. Press Start to begin preheating.
5. Once preheated, place the pan into the oven.
6. When cooking is complete, transfer the dates to a paper towel-lined plate to drain. Serve hot.

Italian Rice Balls with Olives

Prep time: 20 minutes | Cook time: 10 minutes | Makes 8 rice balls

- 1½ cups cooked sticky rice
- ½ teaspoon Italian seasoning blend
- ¾ teaspoon salt, divided
- 8 black olives, pitted
- 1 ounce (28 g) Mozzarella cheese, cut into tiny pieces (small enough to stuff into olives)
- 2 eggs
- ⅓ cup Italian bread crumbs
- ¾ cup panko bread crumbs
- Cooking spray

1. Stuff each black olive with a piece of Mozzarella cheese.
2. In a bowl, combine the cooked sticky rice, Italian seasoning blend, and ½ teaspoon of salt and stir to mix well. Form the

rice mixture into a log with your hands and divide it into 8 equal portions. Mold each portion around a black olive and roll into a ball.

3. Transfer to the freezer to chill for 10 to 15 minutes until firm.
4. In a shallow dish, place the Italian bread crumbs. In a separate shallow dish, whisk the eggs. In a third shallow dish, combine the panko bread crumbs and remaining salt.
5. One by one, roll the rice balls in the Italian bread crumbs, then dip in the whisked eggs, finally coat them with the panko bread crumbs.
6. Arrange the rice balls in the perforated pan and spritz both sides with cooking spray.
7. Select Air Fry. Set temperature to 390°F (199°C) and set time to 10 minutes. Press Start to begin preheating.
8. Once preheated, place the pan into the oven. Flip the balls halfway through the cooking time.
9. When cooking is complete, the rice balls should be golden brown. Remove from the oven and serve warm.

Muffuletta Sliders with Olive Mix

Prep time: 10 minutes | Cook time: 6 minutes | Makes 8 sliders

- ¼ pound (113 g) thinly sliced deli ham
- ¼ pound (113 g) thinly sliced pastrami
- 4 ounces (113 g) low-fat Mozzarella cheese, grated
- 8 slider buns, split in half
- Cooking spray
- 1 tablespoon sesame seeds

Olive Mix:

- ½ cup sliced green olives with pimentos
- ¼ cup sliced black olives
- ¼ cup chopped kalamata olives
- 1 teaspoon red wine vinegar
- ¼ teaspoon basil
- ⅛ teaspoon garlic powder

1. Combine all the ingredients for the olive mix in a small bowl and stir well.
2. Stir together the ham, pastrami, and cheese in a medium bowl and divide the mixture into 8 equal portions.
3. Assemble the sliders: Top each bottom bun with 1 portion of meat and cheese, 2 tablespoons of olive mix, finished by the remaining buns. Lightly spritz the tops with cooking spray. Scatter the sesame seeds on top.
4. Arrange the sliders in the perforated pan.
5. Select Bake. Set temperature to 360°F (182°C) and set time to 6 minutes. Press Start to begin preheating.
6. Once preheated, place the pan into the oven.
7. When cooking is complete, the cheese should be melted. Remove the pan from the oven and serve.

Chapter 8 Desserts

Lemon Caramelized Pear Tart

Prep time: 15 minutes | Cook time: 25 minutes | Serves 8

- Juice of 1 lemon
- 4 cups water
- 3 medium or 2 large ripe or almost ripe pears (preferably Bosc or Anjou) peeled, stemmed, and halved lengthwise
- 1 sheet (½ package) frozen puff pastry, thawed
- All-purpose flour, for dusting
- 4 tablespoons caramel sauce such as Smucker's Salted Caramel, divided

1. Combine the lemon juice and water in a large bowl.
2. Remove the seeds from the pears with a melon baller and cut out the blossom end. Remove any tough fibers between the stem end and the center. As you work, place the pear halves in the acidulated water.
3. On a lightly floured cutting board, unwrap and unfold the puff pastry, roll it very lightly with a rolling pin so as to press the folds together. Place it on the sheet pan.
4. Roll about ½ inch of the pastry edges up to form a ridge around the perimeter. Crimp the corners together so as to create a solid rim around the pastry to hold in the liquid as the tart cooks.
5. Brush 2 tablespoons of caramel sauce over the bottom of the pastry.
6. Remove the pear halves from the water and blot off any remaining water with paper towels.
7. Place one of the halves on the board cut-side down and cut ¼-inch-thick slices radially. Repeat with the remaining halves. Arrange the pear slices over the pastry. Drizzle the remaining 2 tablespoons of caramel sauce over the top.
8. Select Bake. Set temperature to 350°F (180°C) and set time to 25 minutes. Press Start to begin preheating.
9. Once the unit has preheated, place the pan into the oven.
10. After 15 minutes, check the tart, rotating the pan if the crust is not browning evenly. Continue cooking for another 10 minutes, or until the pastry is golden brown, the pears are soft, and the caramel is bubbling.
11. When done, remove the pan from the oven and allow to cool for about 10 minutes.
12. Served warm.

Honey Walnut and Pistachios Baklava

Prep time: 10 minutes | Cook time: 16 minutes | Serves 10

- 1 cup walnut pieces
- 1 cup shelled raw pistachios
- ½ cup unsalted butter, melted
- ¼ cup plus 2 tablespoons honey, divided
- 3 tablespoons granulated sugar
- 1 teaspoon ground cinnamon
- 2 (1.9-ounce / 54-g) packages frozen miniature phyllo tart shells

1. Place the walnuts and pistachios in the perforated pan in an even layer.
2. Select Air Fry. Set temperature to 350°F (180°C) and set time to 4 minutes. Press Start to begin preheating.
3. Once the unit has preheated, place the pan into the oven.
4. After 2 minutes, remove the pan and stir the nuts. Transfer the pan back to the oven and cook for another 1 to 2 minutes until the nuts are golden brown and fragrant.
5. Meanwhile, stir together the butter, ¼ cup of honey, sugar, and cinnamon in a medium bowl.
6. When done, remove the pan from the oven and place the nuts on a cutting board and allow to cool for 5 minutes. Finely chop the nuts. Add the chopped nuts and all the "nut dust" to the butter mixture and stir well.
7. Arrange the phyllo cups on the pan. Evenly fill the phyllo cups with the nut mixture, mounding it up. As you work, stir the nuts in the bowl frequently so that the syrup is evenly distributed throughout the filling.
8. Select Bake. Set temperature to 350°F (180°C) and set time to 12 minutes.
9. Place the pan into the oven. After about 8 minutes, check the cups. Continue cooking until the cups are golden brown and the syrup is bubbling.
10. When cooking is complete, remove the baklava from the oven, drizzle each cup with about ⅛ teaspoon of the remaining honey over the top.
11. Allow to cool for 5 minutes before serving.

Monk Fruit and Hazelnut Cake

Prep time: 5 minutes | Cook time: 20 minutes | Serves 6

- 1 stick butter, at room temperature
- 5 tablespoons liquid monk fruit
- 2 eggs plus 1 egg yolk, beaten
- ⅓ cup hazelnuts, roughly chopped
- 3 tablespoons sugar-free orange marmalade
- 6 ounces (170 g) unbleached almond flour
- 1 teaspoon baking soda
- ½ teaspoon baking powder
- ½ teaspoon ground cinnamon
- ½ teaspoon ground allspice
- ½ ground anise seed
- Cooking spray

1. Lightly spritz a baking pan with cooking spray.
2. In a mixing bowl, whisk the butter and liquid monk fruit until the mixture is pale and smooth. Mix in the beaten eggs, hazelnuts, and marmalade and whisk again until well incorporated.

3. Add the almond flour, baking soda, baking powder, cinnamon, allspice, anise seed and stir to mix well.
4. Scrape the batter into the prepared baking pan.
5. Select Bake. Set temperature to 310°F (154°C) and set time to 20 minutes. Press Start to begin preheating.
6. Once the oven has preheated, place the pan into the oven.
7. When cooking is complete, the top of the cake should spring back when gently pressed with your fingers.
8. Transfer to a wire rack and let the cake cool to room temperature. Serve immediately.

Blueberry and Peach Tart

Prep time: 10 minutes | Cook time: 30 minutes | Serves 6 to 8

- 4 peaches, pitted and sliced
- 1 cup fresh blueberries
- 2 tablespoons cornstarch
- 3 tablespoons sugar
- 1 tablespoon freshly squeezed lemon juice
- Cooking spray
- 1 sheet frozen puff pastry, thawed
- 1 tablespoon nonfat or low-fat milk
- Confectioners' sugar, for dusting

1. Add the peaches, blueberries, cornstarch, sugar, and lemon juice to a large bowl and toss to coat.
2. Spritz a round baking pan with cooking spray.
3. Unfold the pastry and put on the prepared baking pan.
4. Lay the peach slices on the pan, slightly overlapping them. Scatter the blueberries over the peach.
5. Drape the pastry over the outside of the fruit and press pleats firmly together. Brush the milk over the pastry.
6. Select Bake. Set temperature to 400°F (205°C) and set time to 30 minutes. Press Start to begin preheating.
7. Once the unit has preheated, place the pan into the oven.
8. Bake until the crust is golden brown and the fruit is bubbling.
9. When cooking is complete, remove the pan from the oven and allow to cool for 10 minutes.
10. Serve the tart with the confectioners' sugar sprinkled on top.

Butter Shortbread with Lemon

Prep time: 10 minutes | Cook time: 36 to 40 minutes | Makes 4 dozen cookies

- 1 tablespoon grated lemon zest
- 1 cup granulated sugar
- 1 pound (454 g) unsalted butter, at room temperature
- ¼ teaspoon fine salt
- 4 cups all-purpose flour
- ⅓ cup cornstarch
- Cooking spray

1. Add the lemon zest and sugar to a stand mixer fitted with the paddle attachment and beat on medium speed for 1 to 2 minute. Let stand for about 5 minutes. Fold in the butter and salt and blend until fluffy.
2. Mix together the flour and cornstarch in a large bowl. Add to the butter mixture and mix to combine.
3. Spritz the sheet pan with cooking spray and spread a piece of parchment paper onto the pan. Scrape the dough into the pan until even and smooth.
4. Select Bake. Set temperature to 325°F (163°C) and set time to 36 minutes. Press Start to begin preheating.
5. Once the unit has preheated, place the pan into the oven.
6. After 20 minutes, check the shortbread, rotating the pan if it is not browning evenly. Continue cooking for another 16 minutes until lightly browned.
7. When done, remove the pan from the oven. Slice and allow to cool for 5 minutes before serving.

Chocolate Coconut Cake

Prep time: 5 minutes | Cook time: 15 minutes | Serves 10

- 1¼ cups unsweetened bakers' chocolate
- 1 stick butter
- 1 teaspoon liquid stevia
- ⅓ cup shredded coconut
- 2 tablespoons coconut milk
- 2 eggs, beaten
- Cooking spray

1. Lightly spritz a baking pan with cooking spray.
2. Place the chocolate, butter, and stevia in a microwave-safe bowl. Microwave for about 30 seconds until melted. Let the chocolate mixture cool to room temperature.
3. Add the remaining ingredients to the chocolate mixture and stir until well incorporated. Pour the batter into the prepared baking pan.
4. Select Bake. Set temperature to 330°F (166°C) and set time to 15 minutes. Press Start to begin preheating.
5. Once the oven has preheated, place the pan into the oven.
6. When cooking is complete, a toothpick inserted in the center should come out clean.
7. Remove from the oven and allow to cool for about 10 minutes before serving.

Coffee Chocolate Cake with Cinnamon

Prep time: 5 minutes | Cook time: 30 minutes | Serves 8

Dry Ingredients:

- 1½ cups almond flour
- ½ cup coconut meal
- ⅔ cup Swerve
- 1 teaspoon baking powder
- ¼ teaspoon salt

Wet Ingredients:

- 1 egg
- 1 stick butter, melted
- ½ cup hot strongly brewed coffee

Topping:

- ½ cup confectioner's Swerve
- ¼ cup coconut flour
- 3 tablespoons coconut oil
- 1 teaspoon ground cinnamon
- ½ teaspoon ground cardamom

1. In a medium bowl, combine the almond flour, coconut meal, Swerve, baking powder, and salt.
2. In a large bowl, whisk the egg, melted butter, and coffee until smooth.
3. Add the dry mixture to the wet and stir until well incorporated. Transfer the batter to a greased baking pan.
4. Stir together all the ingredients for the topping in a small bowl. Spread the topping over the batter and smooth the top with a spatula.
5. Select Bake. Set temperature to 330°F (166°C) and set time to 30 minutes. Press Start to begin preheating.
6. Once the oven has preheated, place the pan into the oven.
7. When cooking is complete, the cake should spring back when gently pressed with your fingers.
8. Rest for 10 minutes before serving.

Vanilla Cookies with Chocolate Chips

Prep time: 10 minutes | Cook time: 22 minutes | Makes 30 cookies

- ⅓ cup (80g) organic brown sugar
- ⅓ cup (80g) organic cane sugar
- 4 ounces (112g) cashew-based vegan butter
- ½ cup coconut cream
- 1 teaspoon vanilla extract
- 2 tablespoons ground flaxseed
- 1 teaspoon baking powder
- 1 teaspoon baking soda
- Pinch of salt
- 2¼ cups (220g) almond flour
- ½ cup (90g) dairy-free dark chocolate chips

1. Line a baking sheet with parchment paper.
2. Mix together the brown sugar, cane sugar, and butter in a medium bowl or the bowl of a stand mixer. Cream together with a mixer.
3. Fold in the coconut cream, vanilla, flaxseed, baking powder, baking soda, and salt. Stir well.
4. Add the almond flour, a little at a time, mixing after each addition until fully incorporated. Stir in the chocolate chips with a spatula.
5. Scoop the dough onto the prepared baking sheet.
6. Select Bake. Set temperature to 325°F (163°C) and set time to 22 minutes. Press Start to begin preheating.
7. Once the unit has preheated, place the baking sheet into the oven.
8. Bake until the cookies are golden brown.
9. When cooking is complete, transfer the baking sheet onto a wire rack to cool completely before serving.

Chocolate Vanilla Cheesecake

Prep time: 5 minutes | Cook time: 18 minutes | Serves 6

Crust:

- ½ cup butter, melted
- ½ cup coconut flour
- 2 tablespoons stevia
- Cooking spray

Topping:

- 4 ounces (113 g) unsweetened baker's chocolate
- 1 cup mascarpone cheese, at room temperature
- 1 teaspoon vanilla extract
- 2 drops peppermint extract

1. Lightly coat a baking pan with cooking spray.
2. In a mixing bowl, whisk together the butter, flour, and stevia until well combined. Transfer the mixture to the prepared baking pan.
3. Select Bake. Set temperature to 350°F (180°C) and set time to 18 minutes. Press Start to begin preheating.
4. Once the oven has preheated, place the pan into the oven.
5. When done, a toothpick inserted in the center should come out clean.
6. Remove the crust from the oven to a wire rack to cool.
7. Once cooled completely, place it in the freezer for 20 minutes.
8. When ready, combine all the ingredients for the topping in a small bowl and stir to incorporate.
9. Spread this topping over the crust and let it sit for another 15 minutes in the freezer.
10. Serve chilled.

Strawberry Crumble with Rhubarb

Prep time: 10 minutes | Cook time: 12 to 17 minutes | Serves 6

- 1½ cups sliced fresh strawberries
- ⅓ cup sugar
- ¾ cup sliced rhubarb
- ⅔ cup quick-cooking oatmeal
- ¼ cup packed brown sugar
- ½ cup whole-wheat pastry flour
- ½ teaspoon ground cinnamon
- 3 tablespoons unsalted butter, melted

1. Place the strawberries, sugar, and rhubarb in a baking pan and toss to coat.
2. Combine the oatmeal, brown sugar, pastry flour, and cinnamon in a medium bowl.
3. Add the melted butter to the oatmeal mixture and stir until crumbly. Sprinkle this generously on top of the strawberries and rhubarb.

4. Select Bake. Set temperature to 370°F (188°C) and set time to 12 minutes. Press Start to begin preheating.
5. Once the unit has preheated, place the pan into the oven.
6. Bake until the fruit is bubbly and the topping is golden brown. Continue cooking for an additional 2 to 5 minutes if needed.
7. When cooking is complete, remove from the oven and serve warm.

Raspberry Muffins

Prep time: 5 minutes | Cook time: 15 minutes | Serves 6

- 2 cups almond flour
- ¾ cup Swerve
- 1¼ teaspoons baking powder
- ⅓ teaspoon ground allspice
- ⅓ teaspoon ground anise star
- ½ teaspoon grated lemon zest
- ¼ teaspoon salt
- 2 eggs
- 1 cup sour cream
- ½ cup coconut oil
- ½ cup raspberries

1. Line a muffin pan with 6 paper liners.
2. In a mixing bowl, mix the almond flour, Swerve, baking powder, allspice, anise, lemon zest, and salt.
3. In another mixing bowl, beat the eggs, sour cream, and coconut oil until well mixed. Add the egg mixture to the flour mixture and stir to combine. Mix in the raspberries.
4. Scrape the batter into the prepared muffin cups, filling each about three-quarters full.
5. Select Bake. Set temperature to 345°F (174°C) and set time to 15 minutes. Press Start to begin preheating.
6. Once the oven has preheated, place the muffin pan into the oven.
7. When cooking is complete, the tops should be golden and a toothpick inserted in the middle should come out clean.
8. Allow the muffins to cool for 10 minutes in the muffin pan before removing and serving.

Peach and Apple Crisp with Oatmeal

Prep time: 10 minutes | Cook time: 10 to 12 minutes | Serves 4

- 2 peaches, peeled, pitted, and chopped
- 1 apple, peeled and chopped
- 2 tablespoons honey
- 3 tablespoons packed brown sugar
- 2 tablespoons unsalted butter, at room temperature
- ½ cup quick-cooking oatmeal
- ⅓ cup whole-wheat pastry flour
- ½ teaspoon ground cinnamon

1. Place the peaches, apple, and honey in a baking pan and toss until thoroughly combined.
2. Mix together the brown sugar, butter, oatmeal, pastry flour, and cinnamon in a medium bowl and stir until crumbly. Sprinkle this mixture generously on top of the peaches and apples.
3. Select Bake. Set temperature to 380°F (193°C) and set time to 10 minutes. Press Start to begin preheating.
4. Once the unit has preheated, place the pan into the oven.
5. Bake until the fruit is bubbling and the topping is golden brown.
6. Once cooking is complete, remove the pan from the oven and allow to cool for 5 minutes before serving.

Vanilla Walnuts Tart with Cloves

Prep time: 5 minutes | Cook time: 13 minutes | Serves 6

- 1 cup coconut milk
- ½ cup walnuts, ground
- ½ cup Swerve
- ½ cup almond flour
- ½ stick butter, at room temperature
- 2 eggs
- 1 teaspoon vanilla essence
- ¼ teaspoon ground cardamom
- ¼ teaspoon ground cloves
- Cooking spray

1. Coat a baking pan with cooking spray.
2. Combine all the ingredients except the oil in a large bowl and stir until well blended. Spoon the batter mixture into the baking pan.
3. Select Bake. Set temperature to 360°F (182°C) and set time to 13 minutes. Press Start to begin preheating.
4. Once the oven has preheated, place the pan into the oven.
5. When cooking is complete, a toothpick inserted into the center of the tart should come out clean.
6. Remove from the oven and place on a wire rack to cool. Serve immediately.

Mixed Berry Bake with Almond Topping

Prep time: 5 minutes | Cook time: 17 minutes | Serves 3

- ½ cup mixed berries
- Cooking spray

Topping:

- 1 egg, beaten
- 3 tablespoons almonds, slivered
- 3 tablespoons chopped pecans
- 2 tablespoons chopped walnuts
- 3 tablespoons granulated Swerve
- 2 tablespoons cold salted butter, cut into pieces
- ½ teaspoon ground cinnamon

1. Lightly spray a baking dish with cooking spray.
2. Make the topping: In a medium bowl, stir together the beaten egg, nuts, Swerve, butter, and cinnamon until well blended.
3. Put the mixed berries in the bottom of the baking dish and

spread the topping over the top.

4. Select Bake. Set temperature to 340°F (171°C) and set time to 17 minutes. Press Start to begin preheating.
5. Once the oven has preheated, place the baking dish into the oven.
6. When cooking is complete, the fruit should be bubbly and topping should be golden brown.
7. Allow to cool for 5 to 10 minutes before serving.

Vanilla Coconut Cookies with Pecans

Prep time: 10 minutes | Cook time: 25 minutes | Serves 10

- 1½ cups coconut flour
- 1½ cups extra-fine almond flour
- ½ teaspoon baking powder
- ⅓ teaspoon baking soda
- 3 eggs plus an egg yolk, beaten
- ¾ cup coconut oil, at room temperature
- 1 cup unsalted pecan nuts, roughly chopped
- ¾ cup monk fruit
- ¼ teaspoon freshly grated nutmeg
- ⅓ teaspoon ground cloves
- ½ teaspoon pure vanilla extract
- ½ teaspoon pure coconut extract
- ⅛ teaspoon fine sea salt

1. Line the perforated pan with parchment paper.
2. Mix the coconut flour, almond flour, baking powder, and baking soda in a large mixing bowl.
3. In another mixing bowl, stir together the eggs and coconut oil. Add the wet mixture to the dry mixture.
4. Mix in the remaining ingredients and stir until a soft dough forms.
5. Drop about 2 tablespoons of dough on the parchment paper for each cookie and flatten each biscuit until it's 1 inch thick.
6. Select Bake. Set temperature to 370°F (188°C) and set time to 25 minutes. Press Start to begin preheating.
7. Once the oven has preheated, place the pan into the oven.
8. When cooking is complete, the cookies should be golden and firm to the touch.
9. Remove from the oven to a plate. Let the cookies cool to room temperature and serve.

Cinnamon Apple Fritters

Prep time: 30 minutes | Cook time: 7 minutes | Serves 6

- 1 cup chopped, peeled Granny Smith apple
- ½ cup granulated sugar
- 1 teaspoon ground cinnamon
- 1 cup all-purpose flour
- 1 teaspoon baking powder
- 1 teaspoon salt
- 2 tablespoons milk
- 2 tablespoons butter, melted
- 1 large egg, beaten
- Cooking spray
- ¼ cup confectioners' sugar (optional)

1. Mix together the apple, granulated sugar, and cinnamon in a small bowl. Allow to sit for 30 minutes.
2. Combine the flour, baking powder, and salt in a medium bowl. Add the milk, butter, and egg and stir to incorporate.
3. Pour the apple mixture into the bowl of flour mixture and stir with a spatula until a dough forms.
4. Make the fritters: On a clean work surface, divide the dough into 12 equal portions and shape into 1-inch balls. Flatten them into patties with your hands.
5. Line the perforated pan with parchment paper and spray it with cooking spray.
6. Transfer the apple fritters onto the parchment paper, evenly spaced but not too close together. Spray the fritters with cooking spray.
7. Select Bake. Set temperature to 350°F (180°C) and set time to 7 minutes. Press Start to begin preheating.
8. Once the oven has preheated, place the pan into the oven. Flip the fritters halfway through the cooking time.
9. When cooking is complete, the fritters should be lightly browned.
10. Remove from the oven to a plate and serve with the confectioners' sugar sprinkled on top, if desired.

Chocolate Blueberry Cupcakes

Prep time: 5 minutes | Cook time: 15 minutes | Serves 6

- ¾ cup granulated erythritol
- 1¼ cups almond flour
- 1 teaspoon unsweetened baking powder
- 3 teaspoons cocoa powder
- ½ teaspoon baking soda
- ½ teaspoon ground cinnamon
- ¼ teaspoon grated nutmeg
- ⅛ teaspoon salt
- ½ cup milk
- 1 stick butter, at room temperature
- 3 eggs, whisked
- 1 teaspoon pure rum extract
- ½ cup blueberries
- Cooking spray

1. Spray a 6-cup muffin tin with cooking spray.
2. In a mixing bowl, combine the erythritol, almond flour, baking powder, cocoa powder, baking soda, cinnamon, nutmeg, and salt and stir until well blended.
3. In another mixing bowl, mix together the milk, butter, egg, and rum extract until thoroughly combined. Slowly and carefully pour this mixture into the bowl of dry mixture. Stir in the blueberries.
4. Spoon the batter into the greased muffin cups, filling each about three-quarters full.
5. Select Bake. Set temperature to 345°F (174°C) and set time

to 15 minutes. Press Start to begin preheating.

6. Once the oven has preheated, place the muffin tin into the oven.
7. When done, the center should be springy and a toothpick inserted in the middle should come out clean.
8. Remove from the oven and place on a wire rack to cool. Serve immediately.

Vanilla Chocolate Chip Cookies

Prep time: 10 minutes | Cook time: 20 minutes | Makes 4 dozen (1-by-1½-inch) cookies

- 1 cup unsalted butter, at room temperature
- 1 cup dark brown sugar
- ½ cup granulated sugar
- 2 large eggs
- 1 tablespoon vanilla extract
- Pinch salt
- 2 cups old-fashioned rolled oats
- 1½ cups all-purpose flour
- 1 teaspoon baking powder
- 1 teaspoon baking soda
- 2 cups chocolate chips

1. Stir together the butter, brown sugar, and granulated sugar in a large mixing bowl until smooth and light in color.
2. Crack the eggs into the bowl, one at a time, mixing after each addition. Stir in the vanilla and salt.
3. Mix together the oats, flour, baking powder, and baking soda in a separate bowl. Add the mixture to the butter mixture and stir until mixed. Stir in the chocolate chips.
4. Spread the dough onto the sheet pan in an even layer.
5. Select Bake. Set temperature to 350°F (180°C) and set time to 20 minutes. Press Start to begin preheating.
6. Once the unit has preheated, place the pan into the oven.
7. After 15 minutes, check the cookie, rotating the pan if the crust is not browning evenly. Continue cooking for a total of 18 to 20 minutes or until golden brown.
8. When cooking is complete, remove the pan from the oven and allow to cool completely before slicing and serving.

Vanilla Chocolate Cake

Prep time: 5 minutes | Cook time: 15 minutes | Serves 6

- ½ cup unsweetened chocolate, chopped
- ½ stick butter, at room temperature
- 1 tablespoon liquid stevia
- 1½ cups coconut flour
- 2 eggs, whisked
- ½ teaspoon vanilla extract
- A pinch of fine sea salt
- Cooking spray

1. Place the chocolate, butter, and stevia in a microwave-safe bowl. Microwave for about 30 seconds until melted.
2. Let the chocolate mixture cool for 5 to 10 minutes.
3. Add the remaining ingredients to the bowl of chocolate mixture and whisk to incorporate.
4. Lightly spray a baking pan with cooking spray.
5. Scrape the chocolate mixture into the prepared baking pan.
6. Select Bake. Set temperature to 330°F (166°C) and set time to 15 minutes. Press Start to begin preheating.
7. Once the oven has preheated, place the pan into the oven.
8. When cooking is complete, the top should spring back lightly when gently pressed with your fingers.
9. Let the cake cool for 5 minutes and serve.

Coconut Orange Cake

Prep time: 5 minutes | Cook time: 17 minutes | Serves 6

- 1 stick butter, melted
- ¾ cup granulated Swerve
- 2 eggs, beaten
- ¾ cup coconut flour
- ¼ teaspoon salt
- ⅓ teaspoon grated nutmeg
- ⅓ cup coconut milk
- 1¼ cups almond flour
- ½ teaspoon baking powder
- 2 tablespoons unsweetened orange jam
- Cooking spray

1. Coat a baking pan with cooking spray. Set aside.
2. In a large mixing bowl, whisk together the melted butter and granulated Swerve until fluffy.
3. Mix in the beaten eggs and whisk again until smooth. Stir in the coconut flour, salt, and nutmeg and gradually pour in the coconut milk. Add the remaining ingredients and stir until well incorporated.
4. Scrape the batter into the baking pan.
5. Select Bake. Set temperature to 355°F (179°C) and set time to 17 minutes. Press Start to begin preheating.
6. Once the oven has preheated, place the pan into the oven.
7. When cooking is complete, the top of the cake should spring back when gently pressed with your fingers.
8. Remove from the oven to a wire rack to cool. Serve chilled.

Peach and Blueberry Galette

Prep time: 10 minutes | Cook time: 20 minutes | Serves 6

- 1 pint blueberries, rinsed and picked through (about 2 cups)
- 2 large peaches or nectarines, peeled and cut into ½-inch slices (about 2 cups)
- ⅓ cup plus 2 tablespoons granulated sugar, divided
- 2 tablespoons unbleached all-purpose flour
- ½ teaspoon grated lemon zest (optional)
- ¼ teaspoon ground allspice or cinnamon
- Pinch kosher or fine salt
- 1 (9-inch) refrigerated piecrust (or use homemade)
- 2 teaspoons unsalted butter, cut into pea-size pieces
- 1 large egg, beaten

1. Mix together the blueberries, peaches, ⅓ cup of sugar, flour, lemon zest (if desired) allspice, and salt in a medium bowl.
2. Unroll the crust on the sheet pan, patching any tears if needed. Place the fruit in the center of the crust, leaving about 1½ inches of space around the edges. Scatter the butter pieces over the fruit. Fold the outside edge of the crust over the outer circle of the fruit, making pleats as needed.
3. Brush the egg over the crust. Sprinkle the crust and fruit with the remaining 2 tablespoons of sugar.
4. Select Bake. Set temperature to 350°F (180°C) and set time to 20 minutes. Press Start to begin preheating.
5. Once the unit has preheated, place the pan into the oven.
6. After about 15 minutes, check the galette, rotating the pan if the crust is not browning evenly. Continue cooking until the crust is deep golden brown and the fruit is bubbling.
7. When cooking is complete, remove the pan from the oven and allow to cool for 10 minutes before slicing and serving.

Honey Apple-Peach Crumble

Prep time: 10 minutes | Cook time: 11 minutes | Serves 4

- 1 apple, peeled and chopped
- 2 peaches, peeled, pitted, and chopped
- 2 tablespoons honey
- ½ cup quick-cooking oatmeal
- ⅓ cup whole-wheat pastry flour
- 2 tablespoons unsalted butter, at room temperature
- 3 tablespoons packed brown sugar
- ½ teaspoon ground cinnamon

1. Mix together the apple, peaches, and honey in a baking pan until well incorporated.
2. In a bowl, combine the oatmeal, pastry flour, butter, brown sugar, and cinnamon and stir to mix well. Spread this mixture evenly over the fruit.
3. Select Bake. Set temperature to 380°F (193°C) and set time to 11 minutes. Press Start to begin preheating.
4. Once the oven has preheated, place the pan into the oven.
5. When cooking is complete, the fruit should be bubbling around the edges and the topping should be golden brown.
6. Remove from the oven and serve warm.

Cinnamon Apple with Apricots

Prep time: 5 minutes | Cook time: 15 to 18 minutes | Serves 4

- 4 large apples, peeled and sliced into 8 wedges
- 2 tablespoons olive oil
- ½ cup dried apricots, chopped
- 1 to 2 tablespoons sugar
- ½ teaspoon ground cinnamon

1. Toss the apple wedges with the olive oil in a mixing bowl until well coated.
2. Place the apple wedges in the perforated pan.
3. Select Air Fry. Set temperature to 350°F (180°C) and set time to 15 minutes. Press Start to begin preheating.
4. Once the oven has preheated, place the pan into the oven.
5. After about 12 minutes, remove from the oven. Sprinkle with the dried apricots and air fry for another 3 minutes.
6. Meanwhile, thoroughly combine the sugar and cinnamon in a small bowl.
7. Remove the apple wedges from the oven to a plate. Serve sprinkled with the sugar mixture.

Honey-Glazed Peach and Plum Kebabs

Prep time: 10 minutes | Cook time: 4 minutes | Serves 4

- 2 peaches, peeled, pitted, and thickly sliced
- 3 plums, halved and pitted
- 3 nectarines, halved and pitted
- 1 tablespoon honey
- ½ teaspoon ground cinnamon
- ¼ teaspoon ground allspice
- Pinch cayenne pepper

Special Equipment:

- 8 metal skewers

1. Thread, alternating peaches, plums, and nectarines onto the metal skewers that fit into the oven.
2. Thoroughly combine the honey, cinnamon, allspice, and cayenne in a small bowl. Brush generously the glaze over the fruit skewers.
3. Transfer the fruit skewers to the perforated pan.
4. Select Air Fry. Set temperature to 400°F (205°C) and set time to 4 minutes. Press Start to begin preheating.
5. Once the oven has preheated, place the pan into the oven.
6. When cooking is complete, the fruit should be caramelized.
7. Remove the fruit skewers from the oven and let rest for 5 minutes before serving.

Vanilla Pound Cake

Prep time: 5 minutes | Cook time: 30 minutes | Serves 8

- 1 stick butter, at room temperature
- 1 cup Swerve
- 4 eggs
- 1½ cups coconut flour
- ½ cup buttermilk
- ½ teaspoon baking soda
- ½ teaspoon baking powder
- ¼ teaspoon salt
- 1 teaspoon vanilla essence
- A pinch of ground star anise
- A pinch of freshly grated nutmeg
- Cooking spray

1. Spray a baking pan with cooking spray.
2. With an electric mixer or hand mixer, beat the butter and

Swerve until creamy. One at a time, mix in the eggs and whisk until fluffy. Add the remaining ingredients and stir to combine.

3. Transfer the batter to the prepared baking pan.
4. Select Bake. Set temperature to 320°F (160°C) and set time to 30 minutes. Press Start to begin preheating.
5. Once the oven has preheated, place the pan into the oven. Rotate the pan halfway through the cooking time.
6. When cooking is complete, the center of the cake should be springy.
7. Allow the cake to cool in the pan for 10 minutes before removing and serving.

Pumpkin Pudding with Vanilla Wafers

Prep time: 10 minutes | Cook time: 15 minutes | Serves 4

- 1 cup canned no-salt-added pumpkin purée (not pumpkin pie filling)
- ¼ cup packed brown sugar
- 3 tablespoons all-purpose flour
- 1 egg, whisked
- 2 tablespoons milk
- 1 tablespoon unsalted butter, melted
- 1 teaspoon pure vanilla extract
- 4 low-fat vanilla wafers, crumbled
- Cooking spray

1. Coat a baking pan with cooking spray. Set aside.
2. Mix the pumpkin purée, brown sugar, flour, whisked egg, milk, melted butter, and vanilla in a medium bowl and whisk to combine. Transfer the mixture to the baking pan.
3. Select Bake. Set temperature to 350°F (180°C) and set time to 15 minutes. Press Start to begin preheating.
4. Once the oven has preheated, place the pan into the oven.
5. When cooking is complete, the pudding should be set.
6. Remove the pudding from the oven to a wire rack to cool.
7. Divide the pudding into four bowls and serve with the vanilla wafers sprinkled on top.

Vanilla Ricotta Cake with Lemon

Prep time: 5 minutes | Cook time: 25 minutes | Serves 6

- 17.5 ounces (496 g) ricotta cheese
- ounces (153 g) sugar
- 3 eggs, beaten
- 3 tablespoons flour
- 1 lemon, juiced and zested
- 2 teaspoons vanilla extract

1. In a large mixing bowl, stir together all the ingredients until the mixture reaches a creamy consistency.
2. Pour the mixture into a baking pan and place in the oven.
3. Select Bake. Set temperature to 320°F (160°C) and set time to 25 minutes. Press Start to begin preheating.
4. Once the oven has preheated, place the pan into the oven.
5. When cooking is complete, a toothpick inserted in the center should come out clean.
6. Allow to cool for 10 minutes on a wire rack before serving.

Chapter 9 Rotisserie Recipes

Whiskey-Basted Prime Rib Roast

Prep time: 10 minutes | Cook time: 2 hours | Serves 8 to 10

- 1 4-bone prime rib roast (8 to 10 pounds / 3.6 to 4.5 kg)

Rub:
- ¼ cup coarse salt
- 1 small shallot, finely chopped
- 2 cloves garlic, minced
- 2 tablespoons olive oil
- 1 tablespoon coarsely ground black pepper
- Zest of 1 large lemon
- 1 teaspoon paprika
- 1 teaspoon sugar

Baste:
- ⅓ cup whiskey
- ¼ cup water
- Juice of 1 lemon
- ⅛ teaspoon salt

1. Trim off any straggling pieces of meat or fat from the roast. If the fat cap is too thick, cut it down to between ¼ to ½ inch in thickness depending on how you like your prime rib.
2. Run a long sword skewer through the center of the roast lengthwise to create a pilot hole. Run the rotisserie spit through the hole and secure with the forks. Balance as necessary.
3. To make the rub: Combine the rub ingredients in a small bowl to form an even paste. Use additional olive oil if necessary to get it to a thick but workable consistency. Apply evenly to the roast, focusing on the outer shell of the roast.
4. To make the baste: Combine the baste ingredients in a small bowl and set aside for 15 to 30 minutes to come to room temperature.
5. Select Roast, set temperature to 400°F (205°C), Rotate, and set time to 2 hours. Select Start to begin preheating.
6. Once preheated, place the prepared roast with rotisserie spit into the oven. Set a drip tray underneath, and add 1 to 2 cups hot water to the tray. If you intend to make a gravy from the drippings, monitor the drip tray to make sure it does not run dry. Add extra water if needed.
7. During the last hour of cooking time, begin basting. Apply the baste gently so as not to wash away the seasonings on the outside of the roast. Do this 6 to 8 times, until the roast is well coated with the baste. Roast until it is near the desired doneness: 125°F (52°C) for rare, 135°F (57°C) for medium rare, 145°F (63°C) for medium, 155°F (68°C) for medium well, or 165°F (74°C) for well done. The roast will shrink during cooking, so adjust the forks when appropriate.
8. When cooking is complete, remove the roast using the rotisserie lift. Carefully remove the rotisserie forks and slide the spit out, and then set the roast on a large cutting board. Tent the roast with aluminum foil and let the meat rest for 15 to 20 minutes. Cut away the bones first by passing a knife against the bones and cutting through (save the bones for later). Cut the meat into thin slices.

Paprika Pulled Pork Butt

Prep time: 10 minutes | Cook time: 6 hours | Serves 10

- 1 pork butt, 5 to 6 pounds (2.3 to 2.7 kg)

Rub:
- 2 tablespoons paprika
- 2 tablespoons packed brown sugar
- 1 tablespoon kosher salt
- 1 tablespoon mild chili powder
- 1 teaspoon freshly ground black pepper
- 1 teaspoon celery salt
- ½ teaspoon cayenne
- ½ teaspoon garlic powder

1. Run a long sword skewer through the center of the roast lengthwise to create a pilot hole. Run the rotisserie spit through the hole and secure with the forks. Balance as necessary.
2. To make the rub: Combine the rub ingredients in a small bowl and apply evenly all over the roast. Let sit at room temperature for 15 minutes. By this time the air fryer oven should be ready.
3. Select Roast, set temperature to 350°F (180°C), Rotate, and set time to 6 hours. Select Start to begin preheating.
4. Once preheated, place the prepared roast with rotisserie spit into the oven. Set a drip tray underneath. Roast until the internal temperature reaches 185°F (85°C). The roast will shrink during cooking, so adjust the forks when appropriate.
5. When cooking is complete, remove the roast using the rotisserie lift. Carefully remove the rotisserie forks and slide the spit out, and then set the pork on a large cutting board. Tent the roast with aluminum foil and let the meat rest for 20 minutes. Remove the foil and let stand for an additional 10 minutes.
6. Using two forks, check to see how easily the meat shreds. Some parts will do this more easily than others. Be sure to use heat-resistant gloves to break the roast apart. Begin shredding each large chunk one at a time. Add pieces to a large bowl and either add the barbecue sauce directly to the shredded meat or serve on the side. Keep the bowl covered as you're working on each section. This will help keep the meat warm. Serve by itself or with your favorite sides or in sandwiches.

Porchetta with Lemony Sage Rub

Prep time: 15 minutes | Cook time: 3½ hours | Serves 6

- 1 slab pork belly, skin on, 5 to 6 pounds (2.3 to 2.7 kg)
- 1 boneless pork loin roast, about 3 pounds (1.4 kg)

Rub:
- 2 tablespoons fennel seeds
- 1 tablespoon finely chopped fresh sage
- Zest of 1 lemon
- 4 or 5 cloves garlic
- 2 teaspoons coarse salt
- 2 teaspoons freshly ground black pepper
- 1 teaspoon chopped fresh rosemary

Toshiba Air Fryer Oven Cookbook

- 1 teaspoon red pepper flakes
- 1 teaspoon freshly ground black pepper
- 1½ teaspoons coarse salt

1. Lay the pork belly, skin-side down, on a large cutting board. Place the pork loin on top and roll the pork belly together so that the ends meet. Trim any excess pork belly and loin so that it is a uniform cylinder. Do not tie yet.
2. To make the rub: Using a mortar and pestle or spice grinder, crush the fennel seeds to a medium grind. Combine with the remaining rub ingredients in a small bowl and apply all over the pork loin.
3. Roll the pork loin inside the pork belly and tie with kitchen twine every inch into a secure, round bundle. Season the outside of the pork belly with the coarse salt and pepper. Set onto a baking sheet and place in the refrigerator, uncovered, for 24 hours.
4. Run a long sword skewer through the center of the roast lengthwise to create a pilot hole. Run the rotisserie spit through the hole and secure with the forks. Balance as necessary.
5. Select Roast, set temperature to 400°F (205°C), Rotate, and set time to 3½ hours. Select Start to begin preheating.
6. Once preheated, place the prepared porchetta with rotisserie spit into the oven. Set a drip tray underneath. Watch for burning or excessive browning and adjust the heat as necessary. Once the porchetta has reached an internal temperature of 145°F (63°C), the roast is done. If the skin is not a deep brown and crispy in texture, increase the temperature to 450°F (235°C) and roast for an additional 10 minutes.
7. When cooking is complete, remove the porchetta using the rotisserie lift. Carefully remove the rotisserie forks and slide the spit out, and then set the meat on a large cutting board. Tent the roast with aluminum foil and let the meat rest for 15 minutes. Slice the meat ½ inch thick and serve.

Orange Honey Glazed Ham

Prep time: 10 minutes | Cook time: 45 minutes | Serves 12 to 14

- 1 ham, bone in and unsliced, 7 to 8 pounds (3.2 to 3.6 kg)
- 1 cup packed brown sugar

Glaze:

- 1½ cups orange juice
- ½ cup honey
- 2 tablespoons packed brown sugar
- ¼ teaspoon ground cinnamon
- ⅛ teaspoon ground nutmeg
- ⅛ teaspoon ground allspice
- ⅛ teaspoon ground cloves
- ⅛ teaspoon white pepper
- 2 tablespoons unsalted butter

1. To make the glaze: Combine the orange juice, honey, brown sugar, and spices in a saucepan and bring almost to a boil over medium-high heat. Decrease the heat to medium and simmer for 10 minutes, stirring often. The mixture should be a little runnier than real maple syrup. Remove from the heat and add the butter, stirring until melted. Let the mixture cool.
2. Run a long sword skewer through the center of the ham lengthwise to create a pilot hole. There is a bone in the middle of this ham, but generally it is just to one side. The skewer should easily go through, but feel for the bone before you start so you will know how to navigate around it. Run the rotisserie spit through the hole and secure with the forks. Balance the ham on the spit as well as possible.
3. Select Roast, set temperature to 375°F (190°C), Rotate, and set time to 45 minutes. Select Start to begin preheating.
4. Once preheated, place the prepared ham with rotisserie spit into the oven. Set a drip tray underneath. The ham should not take too long to heat up. Look for an internal temperature around 130°F (54°C). The surface should be hot.
5. Baste the ham with the glaze after 20 minutes on the air fryer oven. Repeat the process every 5 minutes and about 3 more times.
6. During the last 5 to 10 minutes of cooking time, the ham should be hot as well as sticky from the glaze. Increase the temperature to 400°F (205°C) and sprinkle the brown sugar evenly on the surface of the ham in small amounts until it is completely coated. Continue to cook until the sugar starts to bubble. Move quickly, as sugar tends to burn.
7. Once the sugar is bubbling rapidly, remove the ham using the rotisserie lift and place on a large cutting board. Remove the rotisserie forks and slide the spit out, loosely cover the ham with aluminum foil, and let it rest for 5 minutes. Carve into thin slices and serve warm.

Ham with Dijon Bourbon Baste

Prep time: 5 minutes | Cook time: 50 minutes | Serves 10 to 12

- 1 ham, unsliced, 5 to 6 pounds (2.3 to 2.7 kg)

Baste:

- ⅓ cup apple butter
- ¼ cup packed brown sugar
- 2 tablespoons bourbon
- 1½ teaspoons Dijon mustard
- ¼ teaspoon ground ginger
- ¼ teaspoon white pepper

1. Run a long sword skewer through the center of the ham lengthwise to create a pilot hole. Run the rotisserie spit through the hole and secure with the forks. Balance as necessary and secure tightly. Place the ham on the preheated air fryer oven and cook for 50 to 60 minutes. If there is room, set a drip tray underneath.
2. To make the baste: Combine all the baste ingredients in a small saucepan and simmer over medium heat for 2 minutes, stirring often. Remove from the heat and let sit for 5 to 10 minutes before using.
3. Select Roast, set temperature to 400°F (205°C), Rotate, and set time to 45 minutes. Select Start to begin preheating.
4. Once preheated, place the prepared ham with rotisserie

spit into the oven. Set a drip tray underneath. During the last 20 minutes of the cooking time, begin basting the ham with the apple butter-bourbon mixture. Make at least 4 or 5 passes with the baste to coat evenly. Focus the coating on the outside of the ham and not on the cut side. The ham should not take too long to heat up. Look for an internal temperature around 130°F (54°C). The surface should be hot.

5. When cooking is complete, remove the ham using the rotisserie lift. Carefully remove the rotisserie forks and slide the spit out, and then set the ham on a large cutting board. Tent the ham with aluminum foil and let the meat rest for 10 minutes. Carve and serve immediately.

Spareribs with Paprika Rub

Prep time: 15 minutes | Cook time: 3½ hours | Serves 4 to 6

- 2 racks spareribs
- ¼ teaspoon cayenne

Sauce:
- 1 tablespoon olive oil
- 2 cloves garlic, minced
- 1 cup ketchup
- ¾ cup water
- ⅓ cup packed brown sugar
- 1 tablespoon paprika
- 2 teaspoons mild chili powder

Rub:
- ⅓ cup packed brown sugar
- 2 tablespoons paprika
- 2 teaspoons salt
- 2 teaspoons mild chili powder
- 1 teaspoon onion powder
- ½ teaspoon garlic powder
- ¼ teaspoon cayenne

1. To make the sauce: Heat the oil in a medium-size saucepan over medium heat and sauté the garlic for 15 seconds, until aromatic. Add the remaining sauce ingredients and simmer for 5 minutes, stirring often. Remove from the heat and let cool to room temperature before using.

2. To make the rub: Combine the rub ingredients in a small bowl and set aside.

3. Place the ribs on a cutting board and pat dry with paper towels. Cut away any excess fat from the ribs. Remove the membrane from the back of the ribs by using a blunt knife to work the membrane away from the bone in one corner. Grab hold of the membrane with a paper towel for a good grip and gently peel away. With a little practice, this becomes an easy process.

4. Lay the rib racks meat-side down. Apply a small portion of the rub, just enough to season, to the bone side of the racks. Lay one rack on top of the other, bone side to bone side, to form an even shape. Tie the two racks together with kitchen twine between every other bone. The ribs should be held tightly together. Run the rotisserie spit between the racks and secure with the forks. The fork tines should run through the meat as best as possible. The ribs will move a little as the rotisserie turns. They should not flop around, however. Secure to prevent this. Apply the remaining rub evenly over the outer surface of the ribs. A general rule with rubs is that what sticks is the amount needed.

5. Select Roast, set temperature to 375°F (190°C), Rotate, and set time to 3½ hours. Select Start to begin preheating.

6. Once preheated, place the prepared ribs with rotisserie spit into the oven. Set a drip tray underneath. Roast until the ribs reach an internal temperature of 185°F (85°C). Test the temperature in several locations. Baste the ribs several times with the sauce during the last hour of cooking to build up a sticky surface.

7. When cooking is complete, remove the ribs using the rotisserie lift. Carefully remove the rotisserie forks and slide the spit out, and then set the ribs on a large cutting board. Tent the ribs with aluminum foil and let the meat rest for 5 to 10 minutes. Cut away the twine and cut the racks into individual ribs. Serve.

Smoked Paprika Lamb Leg

Prep time: 10 minutes | Cook time: 1 hour 20 minutes | Serves 6 to 8

- 1 boneless leg of lamb (partial bone-in is fine), 4 to 5 pounds (1.8 to 2.3 kg)

Rub:
- ¼ cup packed brown sugar
- 1 tablespoon coarse salt
- 2 teaspoons smoked paprika
- 1½ to 2 teaspoons spicy chili powder or cayenne
- 2 teaspoons onion powder
- 1 teaspoon garlic powder
- 1 teaspoon freshly ground black pepper
- ½ teaspoon ground cloves
- ⅛ teaspoon ground cinnamon

1. Trim off the excess fat and any loose hanging pieces from the lamb. With kitchen twine, tie the roast into a uniform and solid roast. It will take four to five ties to hold it together properly. Run a long sword skewer through the center of the roast lengthwise to create a pilot hole. Run the rotisserie spit through the hole and secure with the forks. Balance as necessary.

2. To make the rub: Combine the rub ingredients in a small bowl and apply evenly to the lamb. Make sure you get as much of the rub on the meat as possible.

3. Select Roast, set temperature to 375°F (190°C), Rotate, and set time to 80 minutes. Select Start to begin preheating.

4. Once preheated, place the prepared lamb with rotisserie spit into the oven. Set a drip tray underneath. Roast until the lamb reaches an internal temperature of 140°F (60°C) for medium or 150°F (66°C) for medium well. The lamb will shrink during cooking, so adjust the forks when appropriate.

5. When cooking is complete, remove the lamb using the rotisserie lift. Carefully remove the rotisserie forks and slide the spit out, and then set the lamb on a large cutting board. Tent the roast with aluminum foil and let the meat rest for 10 to 12 minutes. Cut off the twine and carve. Serve.

BBQ Chicken with Mustard Rub

Prep time: 15 minutes | Cook time: 1 hour 10 minutes | Serves 4 to 6

- 1 whole chicken, 3 to 4 pounds (1.4 to 1.8 kg)
- 1 medium-size onion, peeled but whole (for cavity)

Barbecue Sauce:

- ¾ cup ketchup
- ⅔ cup cherry cola
- ¼ cup apple cider vinegar
- 2 tablespoons packed brown sugar
- 1 tablespoon molasses
- ¼ teaspoon salt
- ¼ teaspoon freshly ground black pepper

Rub:

- 2 teaspoons salt
- 2 teaspoons onion powder
- 1 teaspoon mustard powder
- ½ teaspoon freshly ground black pepper
- ½ teaspoon garlic powder

1. To make the barbecue sauce: Combine all the ingredients in a medium-size saucepan over medium heat and simmer for 5 to 6 minutes, until the mixture is smooth and well blended. Stir often and watch for burning. Remove from the heat and let the sauce cool at least 10 minutes before using.
2. To make the rub: Combine all the rub ingredients in a small bowl.
3. Pat the chicken dry inside and out with paper towels. Apply the rub all over the bird, under the breast skin, and inside the body cavity.
4. Truss the chicken with kitchen twine. Run the rotisserie spit through the onion and insert it into the chicken cavity. Use a paring knife to cut a pilot hole in the onion to make this easier. Continue to run the spit through the chicken and secure with the rotisserie forks.
5. Select Roast, set temperature to 400°F (205°C), Rotate, and set time to 70 minutes. Select Start to begin preheating.
6. Once preheated, place the prepared chicken with rotisserie spit into the oven. Set a drip tray underneath. Roast until the meat in the thighs and legs reaches 175°F (79°C). The breasts should be 165°F (74°C). Baste the chicken with the barbecue sauce during the last half of the cooking time. Do so every 7 to 10 minutes, until the bird is nearly done and well coated with the sauce.
7. When cooking is complete, remove the chicken using the rotisserie lift. Carefully remove the rotisserie forks and slide the spit out, and then set the chicken on a large cutting board. Tent the chicken with aluminum foil and let it rest for 10 to 15 minutes before cutting off the twine and carving.

Sirloin Roast with Porcini-Wine Baste

Prep time: 20 minutes | Cook time: 2 hours | Serves 8

- 1 top sirloin roast, 4 to 4½ pounds (1.8 to 2.0 kg)

Wet Rub:

- ½ cup dried porcini mushrooms
- ¼ cup olive oil
- 4 teaspoons salt
- 1 tablespoon chopped fresh thyme
- 2 cloves garlic, minced
- 1 teaspoon onion powder
- 1 teaspoon chili powder
- 1 teaspoon coarsely ground black pepper

Baste:

- ½ cup dried porcini mushrooms
- 1 or 2 cups boiling water
- ½ cup red wine (Cabernet Sauvignon recommended)
- 1 tablespoon wet rub mixture
- 1 teaspoon Worcestershire sauce

1. For the wet rub: Chop the mushrooms into small pieces. Place in a clean spice or coffee grinder and grind to a fine powder. Transfer to a bowl and add the remaining rub ingredients. Remove 1 tablespoon (6 g) of the mixture and set aside.
2. If the sirloin roast is loose or uneven, tie it with kitchen twine to hold it to a consistent and even shape. Run a long sword skewer through the center of the roast lengthwise to create a pilot hole. Run the rotisserie spit through the hole and secure with the forks. Balance as necessary. Apply the wet rub evenly to the meat.
3. Select Roast, set temperature to 400°F (205°C), Rotate, and set time to 2 hours. Select Start to begin preheating.
4. Once preheated, place the prepared roast with rotisserie spit into the oven. Set a drip tray underneath, and add 1 to 2 cups hot water to the tray. Roast until it reaches the desired doneness: 125°F (52°C) for rare, 135°F (57°C) for medium rare, 145°F (63°C) for medium, 155°F (68°C) for medium well, or 165°F (74°C) for well done. Adjust the forks when appropriate.
5. While the roast cooks, make the baste: Add the dried porcini mushrooms to 1 cup boiling water, or 2 cups boiling water if you would like to use the porcini broth for the gravy. Steep the mushrooms for 30 minutes, covered. Strain the broth and reserve the porcinis (for the gravy) and broth separately. Divide the broth into two equal portions, one for the baste and one for the gravy. Combine 1 cup broth with remaining baste ingredients. Let sit for 15 to 30 minutes to come to room temperature before using. Begin basting the roast during the last half of the cooking time and repeat every 10 to 12 minutes until the roast is ready.
6. When cooking is complete, remove the roast using the rotisserie lift. Carefully remove the rotisserie forks and slide the spit out. Tent the roast with aluminum foil and let the meat rest for 20 minutes. Cut into ¼-inch slices and serve.

Balsamic Chuck Roast

Prep time: 15 minutes | Cook time: 1 hour | Serves 8

- 1 chuck roast, 4 to 4½ pounds (1.8 to 2.0 kg)
- 1¼ teaspoons salt
- ½ teaspoon freshly ground black pepper

Marinade:

- 1 tablespoon olive oil
- 1 shallot, finely chopped
- 2 or 3 cloves garlic, minced

- 1½ cups tawny port
- ¼ cup beef broth
- 1½ tablespoons balsamic vinegar
- 1 teaspoon Worcestershire sauce
- 1 teaspoon chopped fresh thyme
- ¼ teaspoon salt
- ¼ teaspoon freshly ground black pepper

1. To make the marinade: Heat the olive oil in a saucepan over medium-low heat and cook the shallot for 3 minutes until translucent. Add the garlic and cook for 30 seconds. Increase the heat to medium-high and add the port. Stir thoroughly and cook for 1 minute. Add the remaining ingredients and simmer the sauce for 5 minutes, stirring occasionally. Remove from the heat and let cool for 10 to 15 minutes. Divide the mixture into two even portions, reserving one half for the baste and one for the marinade. Store in the refrigerator until ready to cook, then bring to room temperature before using.
2. Trim away excess fat from the outer edges of the chuck roast. Place the roast in a resealable plastic bag. Add half of the port mixture to the bag, making sure that all of the meat is well covered. Seal the bag and place in the refrigerator for 6 to 8 hours.
3. Remove the roast from the bag, discarding the marinade, and place on a large cutting board or platter. With kitchen twine, tie the roast into a round and uniform shape, pulling tightly. Start in the center and work toward the ends until it is tied into a solid round roast. This will take four or five ties. Run a long sword skewer through the center of the roast lengthwise to create a pilot hole. Run the rotisserie spit through the hole and secure with the forks. Balance as necessary. Season the roast with the salt and pepper.
4. Select Roast, set temperature to 400°F (205°C), Rotate, and set time to 1 hour. Select Start to begin preheating.
5. Once preheated, place the prepared roast with rotisserie spit into the oven. Set a drip tray underneath. Roast until it reaches the desired doneness: 125°F (52°C) for rare, 135°F (57°C) for medium rare, 145°F (63°C) for medium, 155°F (68°C) for medium well, or 165°F (74°C) for well done. Baste halfway through the cooking time, and repeat the process at least 3 times until the roast is done.
6. When cooking is complete, remove the roast using the rotisserie lift. Carefully remove the rotisserie forks and slide the spit out, and then set the roast on a large cutting board. Tent the roast with aluminum foil and let the meat rest for 15 to 20 minutes. Cut off the twine. Slice into ¼-inch slices and serve.

Baby Back Ribs with Paprika Rub

Prep time: 15 minutes | Cook time: 2½ hours | Serves 4 to 6

- 2 racks baby back ribs

Sauce:
- 1 tablespoon vegetable oil
- 1 cup finely chopped sweet onion
- 2 cloves garlic, minced
- 1½ cups ketchup
- ¼ cup red wine vinegar
- ¼ cup packed brown sugar
- 2 tablespoons yellow mustard
- ⅛ teaspoon salt

Rub:
- 1 tablespoon paprika
- 2 teaspoons salt
- 2 teaspoons freshly ground black pepper
- ½ teaspoon cayenne

1. To make the sauce: Heat the oil in a medium-size saucepan over medium heat. Add the onions and sauté for 5 minutes. Add the garlic and sauté for 15 seconds. Add the remaining sauce ingredients and simmer for 4 to 5 minutes, stirring often. Remove from the heat and let cool for 15 to 30 minutes before using.
2. To make the rub: Combine the rub ingredients in a small bowl and set aside.
3. Place the ribs on a cutting board and pat dry with paper towels. Cut away any excess fat from the ribs. Remove the membrane from the back of the ribs by using a blunt knife to work the membrane away from the bone in one corner. Grab hold of the membrane with a paper towel for a good grip and gently peel away. With a little practice, this becomes an easy process. Apply the rub all over the ribs' surface, focusing more on the meat side than the bone side.
4. Place one rack of ribs bone-side up on a large cutting board. Place the other rack of ribs bone-side down on top. Position to match up the racks of ribs as evenly as possible. With kitchen twine, tie the racks together between ever other bone, end to end. The whole bundle should be secure and tight. Run the rotisserie spit between the racks and secure tightly with the rotisserie forks. There will be a little movement in the middle, which is fine. As the ribs cook it may be necessary to tighten the forks to keep them secure. Make sure the forks pass through the meat of each rack on each end.
5. Select Roast, set temperature to 375°F (190°C), Rotate, and set time to 2½ hours. Select Start to begin preheating.
6. Once preheated, place the prepared ribs with rotisserie spit into the oven. Set a drip tray underneath. Roast until the internal temperature reaches 185°F (85°C). Test the temperature in several locations. Baste the ribs evenly with barbecue sauce during the last 45 minutes of cooking time.
7. When cooking is complete, remove the ribs using the rotisserie lift. Carefully remove the rotisserie forks and slide the spit out, and then set the ribs on a large cutting board. Tent the ribs with aluminum foil and let the meat rest for 5 to 10 minutes.
8. Cut away the twine and cut the racks into individual ribs. Serve.

Teriyaki Chicken

Prep time: 5 minutes | Cook time: 1 hour 10 minutes | Serves 4

- 1 (4-pound / 1.8-kg) chicken
- 1 tablespoon kosher salt

Teriyaki Sauce:

- ¼ cup soy sauce
- ¼ cup mirin
- ¼ cup honey (or sugar)
- ¼ inch slice of ginger, smashed

1. Season the chicken with the salt, inside and out. Gently work your fingers under the skin on the breast, then rub some of the salt directly onto the breast meat. Fold the wingtips under the wings and truss the chicken. Skewer the chicken on the rotisserie spit, securing it with the rotisserie forks. Let the chicken rest at room temperature.
2. Select Roast, set temperature to 450°F (235°C), Rotate, and set time to 1 hour. Select Start to begin preheating.
3. While the air fryer oven is preheating, combine the soy sauce, mirin, honey, and ginger in a saucepan. Bring to a boil over medium-high heat, stirring often, then decrease the heat to low and simmer for 10 minutes, until the liquid is reduced by half.
4. Once preheated, place the prepared chicken with rotisserie spit into the oven. Set a drip tray underneath. Roast until the chicken reaches 160°F (70°C) in the thickest part of the breast. During the last 15 minutes of cooking, brush the chicken with the teriyaki sauce every five minutes.
5. When cooking is complete, remove the chicken using the rotisserie lift. Remove the chicken from the rotisserie spit and transfer to a platter. Be careful - the spit and forks are blazing hot. Remove the trussing twine, then brush the chicken one last time with the teriyaki sauce. Let the chicken rest for 15 minutes, then carve and serve, passing any remaining teriyaki sauce at the table.

Chicken Roast with Mustard Paste

Prep time: 5 minutes | Cook time: 1 hour | Serves 4

- 1 (4-pound / 1.8-kg) chicken
- 1 tablespoon Herbes de Provence

Mustard Paste:

- ¼ cup Dijon mustard
- 1 tablespoon kosher salt
- 1 teaspoon freshly ground black pepper

1. Mix the mustard paste ingredients in a small bowl. Rub the chicken with the mustard paste, inside and out. Gently work your fingers under the skin on the breast, then rub some of the paste directly onto the breast meat. Refrigerate for at least two hours, preferably overnight.
2. One hour before cooking, remove the chicken from the refrigerator. Fold the wingtips under the wings and truss the chicken. Skewer the chicken on the rotisserie spit, securing it with the rotisserie forks. Let the chicken rest at room temperature.
3. Select Roast, set temperature to 450°F (235°C), Rotate, and set time to 1 hour. Select Start to begin preheating.
4. Once preheated, place the prepared chicken with rotisserie spit into the oven. Set a drip tray underneath. Roast until the chicken reaches 160°F (70°C) in the thickest part of the breast.
5. When cooking is complete, remove the chicken using the rotisserie lift. Remove the chicken from the rotisserie spit and remove the twine trussing the chicken. Be careful - the spit and forks are blazing hot. Let the chicken rest for 15 minutes, then carve and serve.

Turkey with Thyme-Sage Brine

Prep time: 5 minutes | Cook time: 2½ hours | Serves 12 to 14

- 1 (12- to 14-pound / 5.4- to 6.3-kg) turkey

Dry Brine:

- ¼ cup kosher salt
- 1 tablespoon minced fresh sage
- 1 tablespoon minced fresh thyme
- 1 teaspoon fresh ground black pepper
- Fist sized chunk of smoking wood (or 1 cup wood chips)

1. Mix the dry brine ingredients in a small bowl. Sprinkle the turkey with the dry brine, inside and out. Gently work your fingers under the skin on the breast, then rub some of the dry brine directly onto the breast meat. Refrigerate at least overnight, preferably two to three days. If dry brining more than a day in advance, cover the turkey with plastic wrap until the night before cooking, then remove the plastic wrap to let the skin dry out overnight.
2. Two hours before cooking, remove the turkey from the refrigerator. Fold the wingtips underneath the wings, then truss the turkey. Skewer the turkey on the rotisserie spit, securing it with the rotisserie forks. Let the turkey rest at room temperature. Submerge the smoking wood in water and let it soak until the air fryer oven is ready.
3. Select Roast, set temperature to 375°F (190°C), Rotate, and set time to 2½ hours. Select Start to begin preheating.
4. Once preheated, place the prepared turkey with rotisserie spit into the oven. Set a drip tray underneath. Roast until the turkey reaches 155°F (68°C) in the thickest part of the breast.
5. When cooking is complete, remove the turkey using the rotisserie lift. Remove the turkey from the rotisserie spit and remove the twine trussing the turkey. Be very careful - the spit and forks are blazing hot. Let the turkey rest for 15 to 30 minutes, then carve and serve.

Pork Loin Roast with Brown Sugar Brine

Prep time: 10 minutes | Cook time: 45 minutes | Serves 4

- 1 (4-pound / 1.8-kg) bone-in pork loin roast

Brine:

- 3 quarts water
- ½ cup table salt (or 1 cup kosher salt)
- ¼ cup brown sugar

Spice Rub:

- 4 cloves garlic, minced or pressed through a garlic press
- 1 teaspoon minced rosemary
- 1 teaspoon fresh ground black pepper
- ½ teaspoon hot red pepper flakes

1. Combine the brine ingredients in a large container and stir until the salt and sugar dissolve. Submerge the pork in the brine. Store in the refrigerator for four to eight hours.
2. One hour before cooking, remove the pork from the brine and pat dry with paper towels. Mix the rub ingredients in a small bowl, then rub over the pork shoulder, working the rub into any natural seams in the meat. Truss the pork roast, skewer it on the rotisserie spit, and secure it with the rotisserie forks. Let the pork rest at room temperature.
3. Select Roast, set temperature to 450°F (235°C), Rotate, and set time to 45 minutes. Select Start to begin preheating.
4. Once preheated, place the prepared pork roast with rotisserie spit into the oven. Set a drip tray underneath. Roast until it reaches 135°F (57°C) in its thickest part.
5. When cooking is complete, remove the pork using the rotisserie lift. Remove the pork from the rotisserie spit and remove the twine trussing the roast. Be careful - the spit and forks are blazing hot. Let the pork rest for 15 minutes, then slice and serve.

Dried Fruit Stuffed Pork Loin

Prep time: 10 minutes | Cook time: 50 minutes | Serves 4

- 2 (2-pound / 907-g) boneless pork loin roasts

Apple Cider Brine:
- 2 quarts apple cider
- 1 quart water
- ½ cup table salt

Dried Fruit Stuffing:
- 2 cups mixed dried fruit, chopped (apples, apricots, cranberries and raisins)
- 1 teaspoon fresh ground black pepper
- ½ teaspoon dried ginger

1. Combine the brine ingredients in a large container and stir until the salt and sugar dissolve. Roll cut the pork roasts to open them up like a book. Set a roast with the fat cap facing down. Make a cut the length of the roast, one third of the way from the bottom, which goes almost all the way to the other side of the roast but not through. Open the roast up like a book along that cut, then make another cut halfway up the opened part of the roast, almost all the way to the other side, and open up the roast again. Submerge the pork roasts in the brine. Store in the refrigerator for one to four hours.
2. One hour before cooking, remove the pork from the brine and pat dry with paper towels. Open up the pork with the cut side facing up, and sprinkle evenly with the chopped fruit, ginger, and pepper. Carefully roll the pork back into a cylinder, then truss each roast at the edges to hold the cylinder shape. Truss the roasts together with the fat caps facing out, then skewer on the rotisserie spit, running the spit between the roasts and securing them with the rotisserie forks. Let the pork rest at room temperature.
3. Select Roast, set temperature to 450°F (235°C), Rotate, and set time to 50 minutes. Select Start to begin preheating.
4. Once preheated, place the prepared pork with rotisserie spit into the oven. Set a drip tray underneath. Roast until it reaches 135°F (57°C) in its thickest part.
5. When cooking is complete, remove the pork using the rotisserie lift. Remove the pork from the rotisserie spit and remove the twine trussing the roast. Be careful - the spit and forks are blazing hot. Let the pork rest for 15 minutes, then slice into ½ inch thick rounds and serve.

Feta Stuffed Lamb Leg

Prep time: 5 minutes | Cook time: 45 minutes | Serves 3

- 1 (2½-pound / 1.1-kg) boneless leg of lamb roast
- 2 teaspoons kosher salt

Feta Stuffing:
- 2 ounces crumbled feta cheese
- 1 teaspoon minced fresh rosemary
- 1 teaspoon minced fresh thyme
- Zest of ½ lemon

1. Season the leg of lamb with the salt, then refrigerate for at least two hours, preferably overnight.
2. One hour before cooking, remove the lamb from the refrigerator. Just before heating the air fryer oven, mix the stuffing ingredients. Open up the lamb like a book, then spread the stuffing over the cut side of the lamb. Fold the roast back into its original shape. Truss the lamb, then skewer it on the rotisserie spit, securing it with the rotisserie forks. (You're going to lose a little of the stuffing when you tie down the trussing twine; that's OK.) Let the lamb rest at room temperature until the air fryer oven is ready.
3. Select Roast, set temperature to 450°F (235°C), Rotate, and set time to 45 minutes. Select Start to begin preheating.
4. Once preheated, place the prepared lamb with rotisserie spit into the oven. Set a drip tray underneath. Roast until it reaches 130°F (54°C) in its thickest part for medium. (Cook to 115°F (46°C) for rare, 120°F (49°C) for medium-rare.)
5. When cooking is complete, remove the lamb using the rotisserie lift. Remove the lamb from the rotisserie spit and remove the twine trussing the roast. Be careful - the spit and forks are blazing hot. Let the lamb rest for 15 minutes, then carve and serve.

Mustard Lamb Shoulder

Prep time: 5 minutes | Cook time: 2 hours | Serves 4

- 1 (4-pound / 1.8-kg) boneless lamb shoulder roast

Mustard Herb Paste:
- ¼ cup whole grain mustard
- 1 tablespoon kosher salt
- 1 tablespoon minced fresh thyme
- 1 teaspoon minced fresh oregano
- 1 teaspoon minced fresh rosemary
- 1 teaspoon fresh ground black pepper

1. Mix the paste ingredients in a small bowl. Open up the lamb like a book, then rub all over with the paste, working it into

any natural seams in the meat. Refrigerate for at least two hours, preferably overnight.

2. One hour before cooking, remove the lamb from the refrigerator. Fold the lamb into its original shape, truss the lamb, and skewer it on the rotisserie spit, securing it with the rotisserie forks. Let the lamb rest at room temperature until the air fryer oven is ready.

3. Select Roast, set temperature to 375°F (190°C), Rotate, and set time to 2 hours. Select Start to begin preheating.

4. Once preheated, place the prepared lamb with rotisserie spit into the oven. Set a drip tray underneath. Roast the lamb until it reaches 190°F (88°C) in its thickest part.

5. When cooking is complete, remove the lamb shoulder using the rotisserie lift. Remove the lamb shoulder from the rotisserie spit and remove the twine trussing the roast. Be careful - the spit and forks are blazing hot. Let the lamb rest for 15 minutes, then carve and serve.

Chapter 10 Sauces, Dips, and Dressings

Cauliflower Alfredo Sauce

Prep time: 2 minutes | Cook time: 0 minutes | Makes 4 cups

- 2 tablespoons olive oil
- 6 garlic cloves, minced
- 3 cups unsweetened almond milk
- 1 (1-pound / 454-g) head cauliflower, cut into florets
- 1 teaspoon salt
- ¼ teaspoon freshly ground black pepper
- Juice of 1 lemon
- 4 tablespoons nutritional yeast

1. In a medium saucepan, heat the olive oil over medium-high heat. Add the garlic and sauté for 1 minute or until fragrant. Add the almond milk, stir, and bring to a boil.
2. Gently add the cauliflower. Stir in the salt and pepper and return to a boil. Continue cooking over medium-high heat for 5 minutes or until the cauliflower is soft. Stir frequently and reduce heat if needed to prevent the liquid from boiling over.
3. Carefully transfer the cauliflower and cooking liquid to a food processor, using a slotted spoon to scoop out the larger pieces of cauliflower before pouring in the liquid. Add the lemon and nutritional yeast and blend for 1 to 2 minutes until smooth.
4. Serve immediately.

Red Buffalo Sauce

Prep time: 5 minutes | Cook time: 20 minutes | Makes 2 cups

- ¼ cup olive oil
- 4 garlic cloves, roughly chopped
- 1 (5-ounce / 142-g) small red onion, roughly chopped
- 6 red chiles, roughly chopped (about 2 ounces / 56 g in total)
- 1 cup water
- ½ cup apple cider vinegar
- ½ teaspoon salt
- ½ teaspoon freshly ground black pepper

1. In a large nonstick sauté pan, heat ¼ cup olive oil over medium-high heat. Once it's hot, add the garlic, onion, and chiles. Cook for 5 minutes, stirring occasionally, until onions are golden brown.
2. Add the water and bring to a boil. Cook for about 10 minutes or until the water has nearly evaporated.
3. Transfer the cooked onion and chile mixture to a food processor or blender and blend briefly to combine. Add the apple cider vinegar, salt, and pepper. Blend again for 30 seconds.
4. Using a mesh sieve, strain the sauce into a bowl. Use a spoon or spatula to scrape and press all the liquid from the pulp.

Avocado Dressing

Prep time: 5 minutes | Cook time: 0 minutes | Makes 12 tablespoons

- 1 large avocado, pitted and peeled
- ½ cup water
- 2 tablespoons tahini
- 2 tablespoons freshly squeezed lemon juice
- 1 teaspoon dried basil
- 1 teaspoon white wine vinegar
- 1 garlic clove
- ¼ teaspoon pink Himalayan salt
- ¼ teaspoon freshly ground black pepper

1. Combine all the ingredients in a food processor and blend until smooth.

Dijon and Balsamic Vinaigrette

Prep time: 5 minutes | Cook time: 0 minutes | Makes 12 tablespoons

- 6 tablespoons water
- 4 tablespoons Dijon mustard
- 4 tablespoons balsamic vinegar
- 1 teaspoon maple syrup
- ½ teaspoon pink Himalayan salt
- ¼ teaspoon freshly ground black pepper

1. In a bowl, whisk together all the ingredients.

Hemp Dressing

Prep time: 5 minutes | Cook time: 0 minutes | Makes 12 tablespoons

- ½ cup white wine vinegar
- ¼ cup tahini
- ¼ cup water
- 1 tablespoon hemp seeds
- ½ tablespoon freshly squeezed lemon juice
- 1 teaspoon garlic powder
- 1 teaspoon dried oregano
- 1 teaspoon dried basil
- 1 teaspoon red pepper flakes
- ½ teaspoon onion powder
- ½ teaspoon pink Himalayan salt
- ½ teaspoon freshly ground black pepper

1. In a bowl, combine all the ingredients and whisk until mixed well.

Lemony Tahini

Prep time: 5 minutes | Cook time: 0 minutes | Serves 4

- ¾ cup water
- ½ cup tahini
- 3 garlic cloves, minced
- Juice of 3 lemons
- ½ teaspoon pink Himalayan salt

1. In a bowl, whisk together all the ingredients until mixed well.

Cashew Mayo

Prep time: 5 minutes | Cook time: 0 minutes | Makes 18 tablespoons

- 1 cup cashews, soaked in hot water for at least 1 hour
- ¼ cup plus 3 tablespoons milk
- 1 tablespoon apple cider vinegar
- 1 tablespoon freshly squeezed lemon juice
- 1 tablespoon Dijon mustard
- 1 tablespoon aquafaba
- ⅛ teaspoon pink Himalayan salt

1. In a food processor, combine all the ingredients and blend until creamy and smooth.

Mushroom Apple Gravy

Prep time: 5 minutes | Cook time: 10 minutes | Serves 4

- 2 cups vegetable broth
- ½ cup finely chopped mushrooms
- 2 tablespoons whole wheat flour
- 1 tablespoon unsweetened applesauce
- 1 teaspoon onion powder
- ½ teaspoon dried thyme
- ¼ teaspoon dried rosemary
- ⅛ teaspoon pink Himalayan salt
- Freshly ground black pepper, to taste

1. In a nonstick saucepan over medium-high heat, combine all the ingredients and mix well. Bring to a boil, stirring frequently, reduce the heat to low, and simmer, stirring constantly, until it thickens.

Creamy Ranch Dressing

Prep time: 5 minutes | Cook time: 0 minutes | Serves 8

- 1 cup plain Greek yogurt
- ¼ cup chopped fresh dill
- 2 tablespoons chopped fresh chives
- Zest of 1 lemon
- 1 garlic clove, minced
- ½ teaspoon sea salt
- ⅛ teaspoon freshly cracked black pepper

1. Mix together the yogurt, dill, chives, lemon zest, garlic, sea salt, and pepper in a small bowl and whisk to combine.
2. Serve chilled.

Creamy Coconut Lime Dressing

Prep time: 5 minutes | Cook time: 0 minutes | Makes about 1 cup

- 8 ounces (227 g) plain coconut yogurt
- 2 tablespoons chopped fresh parsley
- 2 tablespoons freshly squeezed lemon juice
- 1 tablespoon snipped fresh chives
- ½ teaspoon salt
- Pinch freshly ground black pepper

1. Stir together the coconut yogurt, parsley, lemon juice, chives, salt, and pepper in a medium bowl until completely mixed.
2. Transfer to an airtight container and refrigerate until ready to use.
3. This dressing perfectly pairs with spring mix greens, grilled chicken or even your favorite salad.

Garlic Lime Tahini Dressing

Prep time: 5 minutes | Cook time: 0 minutes | Makes about ¾ cup

- ⅓ cup tahini
- 3 tablespoons filtered water
- 2 tablespoons freshly squeezed lime juice
- 1 tablespoon apple cider vinegar
- 1 teaspoon lime zest
- 1½ teaspoons raw honey
- ¼ teaspoon garlic powder
- ¼ teaspoon salt

1. Whisk together the tahini, water, vinegar, lime juice, lime zest, honey, salt, and garlic powder in a small bowl until well emulsified.
2. Serve immediately, or refrigerate in an airtight container for to 1 week.

Fresh Mixed Berry Vinaigrette

Prep time: 15 minutes | Cook time: 0 minutes | Makes about 1½ cups

- 1 cup mixed berries, thawed if frozen
- ½ cup balsamic vinegar
- ⅓ cup extra-virgin olive oil
- 2 tablespoons freshly squeezed lemon or lime juice
- 1 tablespoon lemon or lime zest
- 1 tablespoon Dijon mustard
- 1 tablespoon raw honey or maple syrup
- 1 teaspoon salt
- ½ teaspoon freshly ground black pepper

1. Place all the ingredients in a blender and purée until thoroughly mixed and smooth.
2. You can serve it over a bed of greens, grilled meat, or fresh fruit salad.

Lemon Dijon Vinaigrette

Prep time: 5 minutes | Cook time: 0 minutes | Makes about 6 tablespoons

- ¼ cup extra-virgin olive oil
- 1 garlic clove, minced
- 2 tablespoons freshly squeezed lemon juice
- 1 teaspoon Dijon mustard
- ½ teaspoon raw honey
- ¼ teaspoon salt
- ¼ teaspoon dried basil

1. Place all the ingredients in a mason jar. Cover and shake vigorously until thoroughly mixed and well emulsified.
2. Serve chilled.

Chimichurri

Prep time: 15 minutes | Cook time: 0 minutes | Makes 2 cups

- 1 cup minced fresh parsley
- ½ cup minced fresh cilantro
- ¼ cup minced fresh mint leaves
- ¼ cup minced garlic (about 6 cloves)
- 2 tablespoons minced fresh oregano leaves
- 1 teaspoon fine Himalayan salt
- 1 cup olive oil or avocado oil
- ½ cup red wine vinegar
- Juice of 1 lemon

1. Thoroughly mix the parsley, cilantro, mint leaves, garlic, oregano leaves, and salt in a medium bowl. Add the olive oil, vinegar, and lemon juice and whisk to combine.
2. Store in an airtight container in the refrigerator and shake before using.
3. You can serve the chimichurri over vegetables, poultry, meats, and fish. It also can be used as a marinade, dipping sauce, or condiment.

Kale and Almond Pesto

Prep time: 15 minutes | Cook time: 0 minutes | Makes about 1 cup

- 2 cups chopped kale leaves, rinsed well and stemmed
- ½ cup toasted almonds
- 2 garlic cloves
- 3 tablespoons extra-virgin olive oil
- 3 tablespoons freshly squeezed lemon juice
- 2 teaspoons lemon zest
- 1 teaspoon salt
- ½ teaspoon freshly ground black pepper
- ¼ teaspoon red pepper flakes

1. Place all the ingredients in a food processor and pulse until smoothly puréed.
2. It tastes great with the eggs, salads, soup, pasta, cracker, and sandwiches.

Marinara Sauce

Prep time: 15 minutes | Cook time: 30 minutes | Makes about 3 cups

- ¼ cup extra-virgin olive oil
- 3 garlic cloves, minced
- 1 small onion, chopped (about ½ cup)
- 2 tablespoons minced or puréed sun-dried tomatoes (optional)
- 1 (28-ounce / 794-g) can crushed tomatoes
- ½ teaspoon dried basil
- ½ teaspoon dried oregano
- ¼ teaspoon red pepper flakes
- 1 teaspoon kosher salt or ½ teaspoon fine salt, plus more as needed

1. Heat the oil in a medium saucepan over medium heat.
2. Add the garlic and onion and sauté for 2 to 3 minutes, or until the onion is softened. Add the sun-dried tomatoes (if desired) and cook for 1 minute until fragrant. Stir in the crushed tomatoes, scraping any brown bits from the bottom of the pot. Fold in the basil, oregano, red pepper flakes, and salt. Stir well.
3. Bring to a simmer. Cook covered for about 30 minutes, stirring occasionally.
4. Turn off the heat and allow the sauce to cool for about 10 minutes.
5. Taste and adjust the seasoning, adding more salt if needed.
6. Use immediately.

Shawarma Spice Blend

Prep time: 5 minutes | Cook time: 0 minutes | Makes about 1 tablespoon

- 1 teaspoon smoked paprika
- 1 teaspoon cumin
- ¼ teaspoon turmeric
- ¼ teaspoon cinnamon
- ¼ teaspoon allspice
- ¼ teaspoon red pepper flakes
- ¼ teaspoon kosher salt or ⅛ teaspoon fine salt
- ¼ teaspoon freshly ground black pepper

1. Stir together all the ingredients in a small bowl.
2. Use immediately or place in an airtight container in the pantry.

Spicy Southwest Seasoning

Prep time: 5 minutes | Cook time: 0 minutes | Makes about ¾ cups

- 1 tablespoon granulated onion
- 1 tablespoon granulated garlic
- 2 tablespoons dried oregano
- 2 tablespoons freshly ground black pepper
- 3 tablespoons ancho chile powder
- 3 tablespoons paprika
- 2 teaspoons cayenne
- 2 teaspoons cumin

1. Stir together all the ingredients in a small bowl.
2. Use immediately or place in an airtight container in the pantry.

Baked White Rice

Prep time: 3 minutes | Cook time: 35 minutes | Makes about 4 cups

- 1 cup long-grain white rice, rinsed and drained
- 2 cups water
- 1 tablespoon unsalted butter, melted, or 1 tablespoon extra-virgin olive oil
- 1 teaspoon kosher salt or ½ teaspoon fine salt

1. Add the butter and rice to the baking pan and stir to coat. Pour in the water and sprinkle with the salt. Stir until the salt is dissolved.
2. Place the pan on the bake position. Select Bake, set the temperature to 325°F (163°C), and set the time for 35 min-

utes.

3. After 20 minutes, remove the pan from the air fryer grill. Stir the rice. Transfer the pan back to the air fryer grill and continue cooking for 10 to 15 minutes, or until the rice is mostly cooked through and the water is absorbed.

4. When done, remove the pan from the air fryer grill and cover with aluminum foil. Let stand for 10 minutes. Using a fork, gently fluff the rice.

5. Serve immediately.

Red Enchilada Sauce

Prep time: 15 minutes | Cook time: 0 minutes | Makes 2 cups

- 3 large ancho chiles, stems and seeds removed, torn into pieces
- 1½ cups very hot water
- 2 garlic cloves, peeled and lightly smashed
- 2 tablespoons wine vinegar
- 2 teaspoons kosher salt or 1 teaspoon fine salt
- 1½ teaspoons sugar
- ½ teaspoon dried oregano
- ½ teaspoon ground cumin

1. Mix together the chile pieces and hot water in a bowl and let stand for 10 to 15 minutes.

2. Pour the chiles and water into a blender jar. Fold in the garlic, vinegar, salt, sugar, oregano, and cumin, and salt and blend until smooth.

3. Use immediately.

Chapter 11 Dehydrate

Dehydrated Pineapple Slices

Prep time: 10 minutes | Cook time: 12 hours | Serves 6

- 1 pineapple, peeled, cored and sliced ¼ inch thick
- 1 tablespoon coconut palm sugar
- 2 teaspoons ground cinnamon
- ½ teaspoon ground ginger
- ½ teaspoon Himalayan pink salt

1. Toss the pineapple slices with the sugar, cinnamon, ginger and salt.
2. Place the pineapple slices in a single layer on three air flow racks. Place the racks on the bottom, middle, and top shelves of the air fryer oven.
3. Press the Power Button. Cook at 120°F (49°C) for 12 hours.

Pork Jerky

Prep time: 10 minutes | Cook time: 3 hours | Makes 35 jerky strips

- 2 pounds (907 g) ground pork
- 1 tablespoon sesame oil
- 1 tablespoon Sriracha
- 1 tablespoon soy sauce
- 1 tablespoon rice vinegar
- ½ teaspoon salt
- ½ teaspoon black pepper
- ½ teaspoon onion powder
- ½ teaspoon pink curing salt

1. Combine ground pork, sesame oil, Sriracha, soy sauce, rice vinegar, salt, black pepper, onion powder, and pink curing salt in a large bowl; mix until evenly combined. Cover and refrigerate for 8 hours.
2. Using a jerky gun, form as many sticks as you can fit on all three air flow racks. They will shrink almost immediately so you can put them close together and utilize the full length of the racks.
3. Slide the racks into the air fryer oven. Press the Power Button. Cook at 160°F (70°C) for 1 hour.
4. Remove racks from the air fryer oven and blot excess moisture with paper towels. Flip each stick and cook for 1 more hour.
5. Repeat step 4 for a total cook time of 3 hours. Transfer jerky sticks to a paper towel-lined baking sheet. Cover with another layer of paper towels and let sit out 8 hours for final drying. Repeat with any remaining jerky mix.
6. Transfer jerky to an airtight container and refrigerate for up to 30 days.

Strawberry Roll Ups

Prep time: 10 minutes | Cook time: 9 hours | Serves 2

- 2 cups fresh strawberries
- 3 tablespoons Splenda
- ½ lemon, juiced

1. Blend your strawberries, sugar and lemon juice until smooth.
2. Line the air flow racks with parchment paper.
3. Spread the fruit mixture evenly across the racks.
4. Slide the racks into the air fryer oven. Press the Power Button. Cook at 140°F (60°C) for 9 hours, or until it is no longer sticky.
5. Cut into slices and roll.
6. Store in an air tight container at room temperature for up to a month or in the freezer for up to a year.

Dehydrated Strawberries

Prep time: 10 minutes | Cook time: 2 hours | Serves 4

- 1 pound (454 g) fresh strawberries

1. Line three air flow racks with parchment paper.
2. Wash strawberries and cut off stem ends. Cut strawberries into slices, about ⅛ inch thick.
3. Place sliced strawberries on the air flow racks. Space them so the pieces are not touching.
4. Slide the racks into the air fryer oven. Press the Power Button. Cook at 170°F (77°C) for 30 minutes. Use tongs to turn the berries. Cook for another 30 minutes. Repeat this until strawberry slices are leathery.
5. Allow the slices to cool completely. Transfer dried strawberry slices to an airtight container. They will keep up to 5 days.

Peach Fruit Leather

Prep time: 15 minutes | Cook time: 6 hours 15 minutes | Serves 4

- 4 peaches, pitted and each peach cut into 6 pieces

1. Line three air flow racks with parchment paper. Place peach slices on parchment.
2. Slide the racks into the air fryer oven. Press the Power Button. Cook at 400°F (205°C) for 15 minutes.
3. Transfer the cooked peaches to a blender or food processor and blend until smooth.
4. Line a baking sheet with parchment paper and pour peach purée onto paper, spreading as necessary with a spatula into an even layer.
5. Slide the sheet into the air fryer oven. Press the Power Button. Cook at 130°F (54°C) for 6 hours or until leather is desired consistency.

Smoky Venison Jerky

Prep time: 30 minutes | Cook time: 4 hours | Makes 1 to 2 pounds

- 3 to 5 pounds (1.4 to 2.3 kg) deer roast

- Hi-Mountain cure and jerky mix or another brand
- 3 to 5 teaspoons liquid smoke

1. Start by slicing your roast into thin strips, and removing any silver skin on each piece of the meat.
2. Lay it all out flat, and then mix up your seasoning per the box. Sprinkle on both sides of the meat, massaging it in.
3. Then transfer the meat into a bag and add in the liquid smoke. Massage bag.
4. Store in the fridge for 24 hours to let it marinade and cure.
5. Lay the jerky out on the air flow racks, don't let the pieces touch.
6. Slide the racks into the air fryer oven. Press the Power Button. Cook at 160°F (70°C) for 3 to 4 hours.
7. Make sure to flip and randomly check, and remove the meat when it is cooked to your texture liking.

Dried Mushrooms

Prep time: 30 minutes | Cook time: 4 hours | Makes 2½ quarts

- 4 to 5 pounds (1.8 to 2.3 kg) fresh mushrooms, washed, rinsed and drained well.

1. Rinse whole mushrooms well under cold running water. Gently scrub any visible dirt away with out damaging the mushroom. Pat dry with paper towels if needed.
2. Break the stem off of each mushroom and slice into ¼ to ½ inch thick slices with a sharp knife.
3. Place the sliced mushrooms on the parchment-lined air flow racks.
4. Slide the racks into the air fryer oven. Press the Power Button. Cook at 170°F (77°C) for 4 hours.
5. Check the mushrooms after 1 hour and flip them over for even drying. Check the mushroom slices every hour.
6. As the mushroom slices dry, remove them from the air fryer oven and allow to cool on the racks or a paper towel.
7. Store dried mushroom slices in an airtight glass container.

Dehydrated Zucchini Chips

Prep time: 10 minutes | Cook time: 3 hours | Serves 4

- 4 to 5 medium zucchini, thinly sliced
- Garlic salt and black pepper, to taste
- 2 tablespoons olive oil

1. Toss the zucchini with the olive oil, garlic salt and pepper.
2. Lay in a single layer on the air flow racks. Slide the racks into the air fryer oven. Press the Power Button. Cook at 170°F (77°C) for 3 hours, until dry and crisp.
3. Store in a plastic container for up to two weeks.

Cinnamon Pear Chips

Prep time: 20 minutes | Cook time: 2 hours | Serves 2

- 2 pears
- 3 tablespoons cinnamon and sugar mixture

1. Line a baking pan with parchment paper.
2. Slice the pears very thin and lay them on the pan in a single layer.
3. Sprinkle them with the cinnamon and sugar mixture.
4. Slide the pan into the air fryer oven. Press the Power Button. Cook at 170°F (77°C) for 2 hours, turning pears over halfway through.
5. Transfer to wire rack to cool.

Dried Hot Peppers

Prep time: 10 minutes | Cook time: 10 hours | Serves 2

- 10 hot peppers

1. Place the peppers on the air flow racks.
2. Slide the racks into the air fryer oven. Press the Power Button. Cook at 160°F (70°C) for 8 to 10 hours.
3. They should be very dry.

Lemon-Pepper Salmon Jerky

Prep time: 20 minutes | Cook time: 3 hours | Serves 10

- 1¾ pounds (794 g) filet wild Alaskan salmon, skin on, bones removed
- ½ cup low sodium soy sauce
- 1 tablespoon lemon juice
- 1 tablespoon brown sugar
- 2 teaspoons mixed whole peppercorns
- 1 teaspoon lemon zest
- ½ teaspoon liquid smoke
- ½ teaspoon celery seeds
- ½ teaspoon onion powder
- ½ teaspoon garlic powder
- ¼ teaspoon kosher salt

1. Freeze salmon for 1 hour.
2. In the meantime, in a large bowl, combine the soy sauce, lemon juice, sugar, peppercorns, lemon zest, liquid smoke, celery seeds, onion and garlic powders, and salt.
3. Remove the salmon from the freezer and cut it into thin strips (about ½ inch), then place in the marinade. Cover and marinate for 1 to 3 hours in the fridge.
4. Remove strips and place on a plate, patting dry with a paper towel.
5. Place the salmon strips on three air flow racks in a single layer. Slide the racks into the air fryer oven. Press the Power Button. Cook at 170°F (77°C) for 3 hours, flipping over halfway through. Salmon is done when dried all the way through, but slightly chewy.
6. Store in a cool dry place in a sealed container.

Kiwi Chips

Prep time: 15 minutes | Cook time: 6 to 12 hours | Makes 10 to 12 slices

Dehydrate

- 2 kiwis

1. Peel the kiwis, using a paring knife to slice the skin off or a vegetable peeler.
2. Slice the peeled kiwis into ¼ inch slices.
3. Place the kiwi slices on the air flow racks. Slide the racks into the air fryer oven. Press the Power Button. Cook at 135°F (57°C) for 6 to 12 hours.
4. These should be slightly chewy when done.

Dehydrated Onions

Prep time: 15 minutes | Cook time: 9 hours | Makes 6 tablespoons dried minced onions and 1 tablespoon onion powder

- 1 medium onion

To dry the onions:

1. Prepare your onions by removing the skins, trimming the ends, and slicing into even sized pieces.
2. Separate the onion segments and spread them out evenly on the air flow racks in a single layer.
3. Slide the racks into the air fryer oven. Press the Power Button. Cook at 125°F (52°C) for 3 to 9 hours.
4. The timing will depend on the size of your onion pieces and moisture content. The dehydrated onions should be crisp and snap when your break them.
5. Let the dried onion pieces cool, crush into onion flakes, and package into airtight glass containers or process further into dried onion flakes and onion powder.

Candied Bacon

Prep time: 10 minutes | Cook time: 4 hours | Makes 6 slices

- 6 slices bacon
- 3 tablespoons light brown sugar
- 2 tablespoons rice vinegar
- 2 tablespoons chili paste
- 1 tablespoon soy sauce

1. Mix brown sugar, rice vinegar, chili paste, and soy sauce in a bowl.
2. Add bacon slices and mix until the slices are evenly coated.
3. Marinate for up to 3 hours or until ready to dehydrate.
4. Discard the marinade, then place the bacon onto the air flow racks.
5. Slide the racks into the air fryer oven. Press the Power Button. Cook at 170°F (77°C) for 4 hours.
6. Remove from the air fryer oven when done and let the bacon cool down for 5 minutes, then serve.

Cinnamon Orange Slices

Prep time: 10 minutes | Cook time: 6 hours | Serves 3

- 2 large oranges, cut into ⅛-inch-thick slices
- ½ teaspoon ground star anise
- ½ teaspoon ground cinnamon
- 1 tablespoon chocolate hazelnut spread (optional)

1. Sprinkle spices on the orange slices.
2. Place orange slices on the air flow racks. Slide the racks into the air fryer oven. Press the Power Button. Cook at 140°F (60°C) for 6 hours.
3. Remove when done, and if desired serve with chocolate hazelnut spread.

Chapter 12 Pizza

Simple Pizza Dough

Prep time: 15 minutes | Cook time: 0 minutes | Makes 2 (12- to 14-inch) pizzas

- 1 package active dry yeast
- 1½ cups warm water (about 110o F)
- 2 tablespoons extra-virgin olive oil
- 4 cups all-purpose flour, plus more for dusting
- 1½ teaspoons salt

1. In a medium bowl, add the yeast to the warm water and let bloom for about 10 minutes. Add the olive oil.
2. In a food processor or standing mixer fitted with a paddle attachment, pulse to blend the flour and salt. With the machine running, add the yeast mixture in a slow, steady stream, mixing just until the dough comes together. Turn the dough out onto a well-floured board, and with lightly floured hands, knead the dough using the heels of your hands, pushing the dough and then folding it over. Shape it into a ball, then cut it into 2 or 4 equal pieces.
3. Place the balls of dough on a lightly floured baking sheet and cover with a clean dishtowel. Let them rise in a warm, draft-free spot until they are doubled in size, about 45 minutes.
4. Proceed with the desired recipe.

Pro Dough

Prep time: 40 minutes | Cook time: 0 minutes | Makes 2 (12- to 14-inch) pizzas

- ¼ teaspoon active dry yeast
- 1½ cups warm water
- 4 cups "00" flour or all-purpose flour, plus more for dusting
- 2 teaspoons salt
- Extra-virgin olive oil, for greasing

1. In a medium bowl, add the yeast to the warm water and let it stand for 10 minutes. While the yeast is blooming, rinse the bowl of a standing mixer with hot water and dry thoroughly. It should be warm to the touch. In the warm mixing bowl, combine the flour and salt. Add the yeast mixture and mix on low speed with a dough hook for 2 minutes. Raise the speed to medium-low and continue to mix for about 10 minutes, until the dough is cohesive and smooth and has pulled away from the sides of the bowl.
2. Knead again on medium-low speed for an additional 10 minutes, or until the dough is soft and warm to the touch.
3. Transfer the dough to a large, lightly oiled bowl, rolling the dough to coat it on all sides. Cover with plastic wrap and refrigerate overnight.
4. The next day, transfer the dough to a lightly floured board and punch it down. Cut it into 2 or 4 equal pieces and shape into smooth balls. Lightly flour the balls, place them on a baking tray, and cover with a damp kitchen towel. Let the dough rise again in the refrigerator for at least 4 hours or overnight.
5. Remove the dough from the refrigerator, place on a lightly floured baking sheet, and cover with a damp kitchen towel. Let it rise for 1½ to 2 hours, until it is doubled in size.
6. Proceed with the desired recipe.

No-Knead Pan Pizza Dough

Prep time: 5 minutes | Cook time: 0 minutes | Makes 2 (13-by-18-inch) pizzas

- 3½ cups bread flour, plus more for dusting
- ¼ teaspoon active dry yeast
- 1 teaspoon kosher salt
- ¾ teaspoon sugar
- 1⅓ cups warm water
- Extra-virgin olive oil, for drizzling

1. In the bowl of a standing mixer fitted with the paddle attachment, combine the flour, yeast, salt, and sugar. With the mixer on low, add the water and mix just until combined, about 3 minutes.
2. Cover the bowl with a towel and let the mixture rise at room temperature for 8 to 18 hours, or until it is doubled in volume.
3. Turn the dough onto a well-floured board and divide in half. Lightly drizzle two large (13-by-18-inch) sheet pans with olive oil, and spread to cover with a thin, even coating.
4. Stretch one piece of dough to the length of the pan, then place it in the center of one pan. Gently pull and stretch the dough to fit the width. If it resists, refrigerate the dough for 10 minutes. When the dough fits the pan, cover the pan with a damp kitchen towel and let it rest for 30 minutes at room temperature. Repeat with the second piece of dough and the second sheet pan.
5. Proceed with the desired recipe.

Garlic Tomato Pizza Sauce

Prep time: 10 minutes | Cook time: 25 minutes | Makes 1 quart

- 2 tablespoons extra-virgin olive oil
- 1 small yellow onion, chopped (½ cup)
- 3 garlic cloves, smashed
- 1 (28-ounce / 794-g) can whole peeled San Marzano tomatoes, undrained
- 1 teaspoon fine sea salt
- ⅛ teaspoon freshly ground black pepper
- 1 to 2 tablespoons sugar

1. In a large saucepan over medium-high heat, heat the olive oil until it shimmers. Reduce the heat to medium and add the chopped onion. Cook, stirring occasionally, for 5 minutes. Add the garlic and continue to cook for 2 to 3 minutes more, until the onion is translucent and the garlic is aromatic.
2. Add the tomatoes and their juice, and bring to a simmer, stirring occasionally with a wooden spoon to break them

apart. Simmer for 10 to 15 minutes, until the sauce has thickened.

3. Using an immersion blender or food processor, pulse until the sauce is smooth. Season with the salt, pepper, and sugar.

Pepperoni Pizza with Mozzarella

Prep time: 5 minutes | Cook time: 20 minutes | Makes 2 (12-inch) pizzas

- Extra-virgin olive oil, for brushing
- Simple Pizza Dough
- 1 cup Garlic Tomato Pizza Sauce
- 1 cup grated Mozzarella cheese
- 6 ounces (170 g) pepperoni, sliced thin
- ¼ teaspoon salt

1. Brush two baking sheets with olive oil.
2. Roll out one of the dough balls and place it on the prepared baking sheet.
3. Leaving a 1-inch border, spread half of the sauce evenly over the dough. Top with half the Mozzarella and then half the pepperoni. Sprinkle with half the salt.
4. Slide the baking sheet into the air fryer oven. Press the Power Button. Cook at 400°F (205°C) for 10 minutes, until the crust is golden and the cheese has melted.
5. Remove the pizza from the air fryer oven and transfer it to a cutting board. Let it rest for 5 minutes, then slice and serve.
6. Repeat with the remaining dough ball and toppings.

Italian Sausage and Bell Pepper Pizza

Prep time: 10 minutes | Cook time: 40 minutes | Makes 2 (12-inch) pizzas

- 3 tablespoons extra-virgin olive oil, plus more for brushing
- ¾ pound (340 g) sweet Italian sausage (3 sausages)
- 1 medium yellow onion, sliced
- 1 red bell pepper, cut into ½-inch strips
- 1 green bell pepper, cut into ½-inch strips
- 2 garlic cloves, minced
- ¼ teaspoon red pepper flakes
- Simple Pizza Dough or Pro Dough
- Garlic Tomato Pizza Sauce
- 1⅓ cups grated Mozzarella cheese
- 1 teaspoon fine sea salt
- ⅛ teaspoon freshly ground black pepper
- ½ teaspoon dried oregano

1. Brush two baking sheets with olive oil.
2. In a large skillet over medium heat, heat the olive oil until it shimmers. Add the sausages and cook until they are browned on all sides and register 160°F (70°C) on an instant-read thermometer, about 8 minutes total. Transfer to a cutting board.
3. Add the onion to the hot pan (adding more oil if necessary), and sauté over medium heat until translucent, about 4 minutes. Add the red and green bell peppers. Sauté the mixture until the onions turn golden, about 4 minutes more, and then add the garlic and red pepper flakes. Cook, stirring, for about 2 additional minutes to infuse the mixture with the garlic. Using a slotted spoon, transfer the mixture to a small bowl.
4. Cut the sausages into ¼-inch-thick slices.
5. Roll out one of the dough balls to the desired size, and place it on the prepared baking sheet.
6. Leaving a 1-inch border, spread half of the sauce evenly over the dough. Sprinkle half of the grated Mozzarella over the pizza and then arrange half of the sausage slices on top. Spread half of the peppers and onions evenly over all.
7. Slide the baking sheet into the air fryer oven. Press the Power Button. Cook at 400°F (205°C) for 10 minutes, until the cheese has melted and the crust has browned.
8. Transfer the pizza to a cutting board and season with the salt, pepper, and dried oregano. Let it rest for 5 minutes, then slice and serve.
9. Repeat with the remaining dough ball and toppings.

Mushroom and Spinach Pizza

Prep time: 10 minutes | Cook time: 30 minutes | Makes 2 (12- to 14-inch) pizzas

- 4 tablespoons extra-virgin olive oil, divided, plus more for brushing
- 2 cups sliced cremini mushrooms
- ¼ teaspoon fine sea salt
- ⅛ teaspoon freshly ground black pepper
- 1 garlic clove
- Pinch red pepper flakes,
- plus more for seasoning
- 4 cups baby spinach, stems removed
- Simple Pizza Dough or Pro Dough
- 1 cup Garlic Tomato Pizza Sauce
- 1 cup grated Mozzarella cheese

1. Brush two baking sheets with olive oil.
2. In a large skillet over medium-high heat, heat 3 tablespoons of olive oil until it shimmers. Add the mushrooms and the salt, and let the mushrooms sit undisturbed for 2 minutes. Give the pan a shake and continue to cook for 3 minutes more, stirring occasionally, until the mushrooms have darkened in color but are still firm and vibrant. Season with the pepper and transfer to a medium bowl.
3. Reduce the heat to medium and add the remaining 1 tablespoon of olive oil, the garlic, and the red pepper flakes. Swirl the garlic and red pepper flakes to flavor the oil, then add the spinach. Use tongs to turn the spinach, watching it decrease in volume. Cook the spinach for 2 to 3 minutes, until it's wilted but still has structure. Remove the skillet from the heat.

Toshiba Air Fryer Oven Cookbook

4. Roll out one of the dough balls to the desired size and place it on the prepared baking sheet.
5. Leaving a 1-inch border, spoon half of the sauce evenly over the dough, then sprinkle on half of the Mozzarella. Scatter half of the spinach over the pizza, followed by half of the mushrooms. The toppings should intermingle. Season with freshly ground black pepper or more red pepper flakes as desired.
6. Slide the baking sheet into the air fryer oven. Press the Power Button. Cook at 400°F (205°C) for 10 minutes, until the crust is golden and the cheese has melted.
7. Remove the pizza from the air fryer oven and transfer it to a cutting board. Let it rest for 5 minutes, then slice and serve.
8. Repeat with the remaining dough ball and toppings.

Ham and Pineapple Pizza

Prep time: 10 minutes | Cook time: 25 minutes | Makes 2 (12- to 14-inch) pizzas

- Extra-virgin olive oil, for brushing
- 4 slices center-cut bacon
- Simple Pizza Dough or Pro Dough
- 1 cup Garlic Tomato Pizza Sauce
- 1 cup grated Mozzarella cheese
- ¼ pound (113 g) smoked ham, cut into ½-inch dice
- 1 cup diced fresh pineapple
- 2 tablespoons grated Parmesan cheese

1. Brush two baking sheets with olive oil.
2. In a medium skillet over medium heat, cook the bacon until crisp, 2 to 3 minutes per side. Transfer to a paper towel-lined plate to cool. Cut into bits.
3. Roll out one of the dough balls to the desired size and place it on the prepared baking sheet.
4. Leaving a 1-inch border, spread half of the sauce evenly onto the dough. Sprinkle on half of the Mozzarella, followed by half of the ham, chopped bacon, pineapple, and grated Parmesan cheese.
5. Slide the baking sheet into the air fryer oven. Press the Power Button. Cook at 400°F (205°C) for 10 minutes, until the crust is golden and the cheese has melted.
6. Remove the pizza from the air fryer oven and transfer it to a cutting board. Let it rest for 5 minutes, then slice and serve.
7. Repeat with the remaining dough ball and toppings.

Mozzarella Meatball Pizza

Prep time: 10 minutes | Cook time: 25 minutes | Makes 2 (12- to 14-inch) pizzas

- All-purpose flour, for coating
- ½ pound (227 g) ground pork
- ½ pound (227 g) ground veal
- 1 cup ricotta cheese
- ¼ cup grated Parmesan cheese plus 2 tablespoons, divided
- 2 tablespoons finely chopped fresh flat-leaf parsley
- ¼ teaspoon salt, plus more for sprinkling
- ⅛ teaspoon freshly ground black pepper, plus more
- 2½ cups Garlic Tomato Pizza Sauce, divided
- 2 tablespoons olive oil, plus more for brushing
- Simple Pizza Dough
- 2 cups grated Mozzarella cheese

1. Lightly flour a baking sheet.
2. In a large mixing bowl, use your hands to combine the ground pork and veal, ricotta, ¼ cup of Parmesan, and the parsley. Season with the salt and pepper, and mix again.
3. Form each meatball by rolling 1 heaping tablespoon of the meat mixture between your palms. Place the meatballs on the prepared baking sheet, lightly rolling each one in flour.
4. In a medium saucepan over medium heat, heat 1½ cups of sauce; let it come to a gentle simmer.
5. Meanwhile, in a large skillet over medium-high heat, heat the olive oil. When it shimmers, add the meatballs, cooking on all sides for about 3 minutes, until browned. As they brown, transfer the meatballs to the simmering sauce to finish cooking, about 5 minutes total.
6. Brush two baking sheets with olive oil.
7. Roll out one of the dough balls to the desired size and place it on the prepared baking sheet.
8. Leaving a 1-inch border, spread ½ cup of the remaining sauce evenly onto the dough. Top the sauce with half of the Mozzarella and half of the meatballs. Spoon a little extra sauce from the pan onto the pizza, and finish with 1 tablespoon of the remaining Parmesan cheese and a sprinkling of salt and pepper.
9. Slide the baking sheet into the air fryer oven. Press the Power Button. Cook at 400°F (205°C) for 10 minutes, until the crust is golden and the cheese has melted.
10. Remove the pizza from the air fryer oven and transfer it to a cutting board. Let it rest for 5 minutes, then slice and serve.
11. Repeat with the remaining dough ball and toppings.

Cheese Tomato Pizza with Basil

Prep time: 15 minutes | Cook time: 20 minutes | Makes 2 (12- to 14-inch) pizzas

- Extra-virgin olive oil, for brushing
- Simple Pizza Dough
- 1 cup Garlic Tomato Pizza Sauce
- ¾ cup grated Mozzarella
- ¾ cup grated fontina cheese
- 2 plum tomatoes, sliced thin
- ⅓ cup crumbled goat cheese
- ½ cup Parmesan cheese
- 8 fresh basil leaves, torn or roughly chopped
- 1 tablespoon chopped

- fresh parsley
- ¼ teaspoon salt
- ⅛ teaspoon freshly ground black pepper

1. Brush two baking sheets with olive oil.
2. Roll out one of the dough balls to the desired size, and place it on the prepared baking sheet.
3. Leaving a 1-inch border, spread half of the sauce evenly over the dough. Sprinkle on half of the Mozzarella and fontina. Arrange half of the tomato slices on top, and finish with half of the goat cheese and Parmesan.
4. Slide the baking sheet into the air fryer oven. Press the Power Button. Cook at 400°F (205°C) for 10 minutes, until the crust is golden and the cheese has melted.
5. Remove the pizza from the air fryer oven and transfer it to a cutting board. Let it rest for 5 minutes, then top with half of the basil and parsley and season with half of the salt and pepper. Slice and serve.
6. Repeat with the remaining dough ball and toppings.

Prosciutto and Bacon Pizza

Prep time: 15 minutes | Cook time: 35 minutes | Makes 2 (12- to 14-inch) pizzas

- Extra-virgin olive oil, for brushing and drizzling
- 4 slices center-cut bacon
- 4 slices prosciutto, cut into strips
- ½ pound (227 g) sweet or hot Italian sausage, casings removed
- Simple Pizza Dough or Pro Dough
- 1 cup Garlic Tomato Pizza Sauce
- 1½ cups grated Mozzarella cheese
- ¼ cup thinly sliced pepperoni
- 2 tablespoons chopped fresh flat-leaf parsley
- ½ teaspoon fine sea salt
- ¼ teaspoon freshly ground black pepper

1. Brush two baking sheets with olive oil.
2. In a medium skillet over medium heat, cook the bacon until crisp, 2 to 3 minutes per side. Transfer to a paper towel-lined plate and set aside to cool.
3. Add the prosciutto to the skillet and cook over medium heat for about 3 minutes, stirring constantly, until crisp. Transfer the prosciutto to the plate with the bacon. Chop the bacon and prosciutto into bite-size pieces.
4. If there's not enough bacon fat in the skillet to prevent sticking, add a drizzle of olive oil and return the skillet to medium heat. Add the sausage to the skillet and cook for about 5 minutes, stirring constantly and breaking it up with a wooden spoon, until no pink color remains. Use a slotted spoon to transfer the sausage to another paper towel-lined plate.
5. Roll out one of the dough balls to the desired size, and place it on the prepared baking sheet.
6. Leaving a 1-inch border, spread half of the sauce evenly onto the dough. Sprinkle on half of the Mozzarella, then half of the sausage, bacon, and prosciutto. Finish with half of the pepperoni so that the meat forms a single, even layer.
7. Slide the baking sheet into the air fryer oven. Press the Power Button. Cook at 400°F (205°C) for 10 minutes, until the crust is golden and the pepperoni is sizzling.
8. Remove the pizza from the air fryer oven and transfer it to a cutting board. Let it rest for 5 minutes, then top with half of the chopped parsley, salt, and pepper. Slice and serve.
9. Repeat with the remaining dough ball and toppings.

Arugula and Prosciutto Pizza

Prep time: 10 minutes | Cook time: 20 minutes | Makes 2 (12- to 14-inch) pizzas

- 2 tablespoons extra-virgin olive oil, plus more for brushing
- Simple Pizza Dough or Pro Dough
- 1 cup Garlic Tomato Pizza Sauce
- 8 slices prosciutto
- 6 ounces (170 g) fresh Mozzarella cheese, sliced or shredded
- 3 cups arugula
- ¼ teaspoon salt
- ⅛ teaspoon freshly ground black pepper
- 3 ounces (85 g) Parmesan cheese, shaved with a vegetable peeler

1. Brush two baking sheets with olive oil.
2. Roll out one of the dough balls to the desired size, and place it on the prepared baking sheet.
3. Leaving a 1-inch border, spread half of the sauce evenly onto the dough. Lay half of the prosciutto slices on top, then finish with half of the Mozzarella.
4. Slide the baking sheet into the air fryer oven. Press the Power Button. Cook at 400°F (205°C) for 10 minutes, until the crust is golden and the cheese has melted.
5. Remove the pizza from the air fryer oven and transfer it to a cutting board. Let it rest for 5 minutes, then top with half of the arugula, olive oil, salt, pepper, and Parmesan. Slice and serve.
6. Repeat with the remaining dough ball and toppings.

Spinach, Egg and Pancetta Pizza

Prep time: 10 minutes | Cook time: 30 minutes | Makes 2 (12- to 14-inch) pizzas

- 1 tablespoon extra-virgin olive oil, plus more for brushing
- 3 ounces (85 g) pancetta, finely diced
- 2 garlic cloves, minced
- 4 cups baby spinach, stems removed
- ¼ teaspoon salt
- Simple Pizza Dough or Pro Dough
- 1 cup Garlic Tomato Pizza Sauce
- 1 cup grated fontina cheese

- 2 large eggs
- 2 tablespoons grated Parmesan cheese
- 2 tablespoons chopped fresh flat-leaf parsley
- ⅛ teaspoon freshly ground black pepper

1. Brush two baking sheets with olive oil.
2. In a large skillet over medium heat, cook the pancetta until crisp, about 5 minutes, turning frequently. Transfer to a paper towel–lined plate.
3. Discard the rendered fat from the skillet and add the olive oil. Return the skillet to medium heat and, when the oil begins to shimmer, add the garlic. Swirl the garlic in the pan for a minute, then add the spinach. Use tongs to turn the spinach, watching it decrease in volume. Cook the spinach for 2 to 3 minutes, until it's wilted but still has structure. Season with the salt and remove the skillet from the heat. Roughly chop the spinach.
4. Roll out one of the dough balls to the desired size, and place it on the prepared baking sheet.
5. Leaving a 1-inch border, spread the sauce evenly onto the dough.
6. Top with half of the fontina followed by half of the spinach. Crack one egg, positioning the yolk in the center of the pizza. Sprinkle with half of the Parmesan.
7. Slide the baking sheet into the air fryer oven. Press the Power Button. Cook at 400°F (205°C) for 10 minutes, until the crust is golden and the egg yolk holds its shape when jiggled.
8. Remove the pizza from the air fryer oven and transfer it to a cutting board. Let it rest for 5 minutes, then season with half of the parsley and black pepper. Slice and serve.
9. Repeat with the remaining dough ball and toppings.

Chicken and Butternut Squash Pizza

Prep time: 10 minutes | Cook time: 40 minutes | Makes 2 (12- to 14-inch) pizzas

- 3 tablespoons extra-virgin olive oil, divided, plus more for brushing and drizzling
- 2 cups diced butternut squash
- 1 fresh rosemary sprig, stemmed and chopped
- Salt
- Freshly ground black pepper
- 3 cups stemmed, roughly chopped kale
- 1½ cups shredded cooked chicken
- Simple Pizza Dough
- 1½ cups grated Gruyère cheese
- 3 tablespoons grated Asiago cheese
- 2 tablespoons toasted walnuts, roughly chopped

1. Brush two baking sheets with olive oil.
2. In a medium skillet over medium-high heat, heat 1 tablespoon of olive oil. When it shimmers, add the butternut squash and rosemary. Season with salt and pepper. Cook the squash until tender and browned, about 20 minutes, stirring frequently.
3. In a large bowl, use your hands to toss the kale and shredded chicken with the remaining 2 tablespoons of olive oil, and season with salt and pepper.
4. Roll out one of the dough balls to the desired size, and place it on the prepared baking sheet.
5. Sprinkle half of the Gruyère over the dough and top with half of the kale and chicken, followed by half of the caramelized butternut squash and Asiago.
6. Slide the baking sheet into the air fryer oven. Press the Power Button. Cook at 400°F (205°C) for 10 minutes, until the crust is golden and the cheese has melted.
7. Remove the pizza from the air fryer oven and transfer it to a cutting board. Let it rest for 5 minutes, then drizzle it with a little olive oil, season with salt and pepper, and sprinkle on half of the walnuts. Slice and serve.
8. Repeat with the remaining dough ball and toppings.

Prosciutto and Fig Pizza

Prep time: 10 minutes | Cook time: 20 minutes | Makes 2 (12- to 14-inch) pizzas

- 2 tablespoons extra-virgin olive oil, plus more for brushing
- Simple Pizza Dough or Pro Dough
- ¼ cup fig jam
- ½ cup shredded Mozzarella cheese
- ½ cup crumbled goat cheese
- 8 slices prosciutto
- 8 figs, stemmed and quartered
- 4 fresh thyme sprigs, stemmed
- ¼ teaspoon fine sea salt
- ⅛ teaspoon freshly ground black pepper

1. Brush two baking sheets with olive oil.
2. Roll out one of the dough balls to the desired size, and place it on the prepared baking sheet.
3. Leaving a 1-inch border, spoon half of the fig jam evenly onto the dough. Top with half of the Mozzarella, goat cheese, and prosciutto. Arrange half of the figs on the pizza, sprinkle on half of the thyme, and season with half of the salt and pepper.
4. Slide the baking sheet into the air fryer oven. Press the Power Button. Cook at 400°F (205°C) for 10 minutes, until the crust is golden and the cheese has melted.
5. Remove the pizza from the air fryer oven and transfer it to a cutting board. Let it rest for 5 minutes, then drizzle with half of the olive oil. Slice and serve.
6. Repeat with the remaining dough ball and toppings.

Ricotta Margherita with Basil

Prep time: 10 minutes | Cook time: 20 minutes | Makes 2 (12- to

14-inch) pizzas

- 1 tablespoon extra-virgin olive oil, plus more for brushing
- Simple Pizza Dough or Pro Dough
- 1 cup Garlic Tomato Pizza Sauce
- 1 teaspoon dried oregano
- ½ cup fresh ricotta cheese
- 6 ounces (170 g) fresh Mozzarella cheese, sliced thin
- ¼ teaspoon fine sea salt
- ⅛ teaspoon freshly ground black pepper
- 8 fresh basil leaves, torn

1. Brush two baking sheets with olive oil.
2. Roll out one of the dough balls to the desired size, and place it on the prepared baking sheet.
3. Leaving a 1-inch border, spoon half of the sauce onto the dough, spreading it evenly. Sprinkle on half of the oregano.
4. Spoon half of the ricotta cheese in small dollops all over the pizza, then arrange half of the Mozzarella slices on top. Season with half of the salt and pepper, and scatter on half of the torn basil leaves.
5. Slide the baking sheet into the air fryer oven. Press the Power Button. Cook at 400°F (205°C) for 10 minutes, until the crust is golden and the cheese has melted.
6. Remove the pizza from the air fryer oven and transfer it to a cutting board. Let it rest for 5 minutes. Slice and serve.
7. Repeat with the remaining dough ball and toppings.

Zucchini and Summer Squash Pizza

Prep time: 15 minutes | Cook time: 50 minutes | Makes 1 pan pizza

- 2 red bell peppers, cut into strips
- 1 zucchini, trimmed and cut into ¼-inch rounds
- 1 yellow summer squash, trimmed and cut into ¼-inch rounds
- 1 medium red onion, sliced
- 10 ounces (284 g) fingerling or red bliss potatoes, scrubbed and cut into ¼-inch slices
- 3 tablespoons extra-virgin olive oil
- 5 fresh thyme sprigs, stemmed
- ½ teaspoon fine sea salt
- ¼ teaspoon freshly ground black pepper
- 1 cup Garlic Tomato Pizza Sauce
- No-Knead Pan Pizza Dough
- 1¼ cups grated fontina cheese
- 1½ cups arugula

1. On a foil-lined baking sheet, spread the bell peppers, zucchini, summer squash, onion, and potatoes. Drizzle with the olive oil, sprinkle on the thyme, and season with the salt and pepper. Toss well, then transfer the baking sheet to the air fryer oven and Press the Power Button. Cook at 400°F (205°C) for about 30 minutes, stirring twice during cooking. The potatoes should be fork tender.
2. Remove the vegetables from the air fryer oven and set aside. At this point, they can be used immediately or cooled to room temperature and refrigerated overnight in an airtight container.
3. Roll out the dough ball to the desired size, and place it on a greased baking pan.
4. Leaving a 1-inch border, spoon the sauce onto the dough, spreading it evenly. Scatter the fontina cheese over the dough, followed by the cooked vegetables.
5. Slide the baking sheet into the air fryer oven. Press the Power Button. Cook at 400°F (205°C) for 10 minutes, until the cheese has melted and the crust is golden. Remove it from the air fryer oven and let it cool for 5 minutes, then top it with the fresh arugula. Slice and serve.

Pear Pizza with Basil

Prep time: 15 minutes | Cook time: 25 minutes | Makes 1 (12- to 14-inch) pizza

- ½ recipe Simple Pizza Dough
- 4 Bosc pears
- ½ lemon
- Zest of 1 orange
- 1 tablespoon chopped fresh basil leaves
- 1 teaspoon chopped fresh rosemary leaves
- 2 tablespoons sugar
- ⅛ teaspoon freshly ground black pepper
- 2 tablespoons extra-virgin olive oil

1. On a baking sheet, roll out the pizza dough to form a 12- to 14-inch disc.
2. Peel, halve, and cut away the core of the pears. Slice each pear half into thin wedges. Squeeze lemon juice over the pears.
3. Arrange the pears, starting at the outer edge of the crust (leaving no border), in a spiral toward the center. Sprinkle the orange zest, basil, rosemary, sugar, and pepper over the pears. Drizzle with the olive oil.
4. Slide the baking sheet into the air fryer oven. Press the Power Button. Cook at 400°F (205°C) for 25 minutes, until the pizza appears golden and crisp.
5. Remove the pizza from the air fryer oven and let sit for 5 minutes. Slice and serve warm or at room temperature.

Black Bean Pizza with Chipotle

Prep time: 15 minutes | Cook time: 30 minutes | Makes 2 (12- to 14-inch) pizzas

- 2 tablespoons extra-virgin olive oil, plus more for brushing
- ¼ teaspoon dried oregano
- 1 medium yellow onion, diced
- ½ teaspoon salt, plus more for seasoning
- 2 garlic cloves
- ⅛ teaspoon freshly ground black pepper, plus more for seasoning
- ¼ cup low-sodium vegetable broth

- 2 cups canned black beans, rinsed
- 2 chipotle chilies in adobo, chopped, plus 1 tablespoon of the adobo sauce
- Simple Pizza Dough
- 1 cup grated vegan Mozzarella cheese
- 1 red bell pepper, diced
- 1 cup diced avocado
- ½ cup fresh cilantro leaves

1. Brush two baking sheets with olive oil.
2. In a large skillet over medium-high heat, heat the olive oil and oregano. When it shimmers, add the diced onion and salt and cook, stirring occasionally, until the onions are soft and translucent, about 5 minutes. Add the garlic and cook 1 minute more, stirring to combine. Season with salt and add the pepper. Transfer to a small bowl.
3. Add the vegetable broth to the sauté pan, then add the black beans, chipotle chilies, and reserved adobo sauce. Bring to a simmer and begin to mash the beans using a potato masher or immersion blender until they form a rough paste (add more vegetable broth if necessary). Season with salt and pepper. Remove from the heat and set aside.
4. Roll out one of the dough balls to the desired size, and place it on the prepared baking sheet.
5. Leaving a 1-inch border, spoon half of the black beans onto the crust, spreading them evenly. Top with half of the Mozzarella and red pepper.
6. Slide the baking sheet into the air fryer oven. Press the Power Button. Cook at 400°F (205°C) for 10 minutes, until the crust is golden and the cheese has melted.
7. Remove the pizza from the air fryer oven, transfer it to a cutting board, and let it sit for 5 minutes. Top the pizza with half of the avocado, cilantro, and freshly ground black pepper. Slice and serve.
8. Repeat with the remaining dough ball and toppings.

Spring Pea Pizza with Ramps

Prep time: 10 minutes | Cook time: 25 minutes | Makes 2 (12- to 14-inch) pizzas

- 2 tablespoons extra-virgin olive oil, plus more for brushing
- ½ cup shelled fresh English peas (or frozen and thawed peas)
- 10 ramps
- ¼ teaspoon fine sea salt
- Simple Pizza Dough or Pro Dough
- ¾ cup ricotta cheese
- 2 tablespoons chopped fresh mint

1. Brush two baking sheets with olive oil.
2. If using fresh peas, bring a large pot of salted water to a boil. Fill a large bowl with ice water. Blanch the peas for 1 minute then, using a slotted spoon, transfer them to the ice water. Drain and set aside.
3. Spread the ramps on a baking sheet, drizzle with the olive oil, and sprinkle with the salt. Press the Power Button. Cook at 400°F (205°C) for 5 minutes to wilt. Transfer to a cutting board and cut into thirds.
4. Roll out one of the dough balls to the desired size, and place it on the prepared baking sheet.
5. Spoon half of the ricotta in dollops all over the dough. Scatter on half of the peas, ramps, and mint.
6. Slide the baking sheet into the air fryer oven. Press the Power Button. Cook at 400°F (205°C) for 10 minutes, until the crust is golden.
7. Remove the pizza from the air fryer oven, transfer it to a cutting board, and let it sit for 5 minutes. Slice and serve.
8. Repeat with the remaining dough ball and toppings.

Zucchini Pizza with Pistachios

Prep time: 15 minutes | Cook time: 30 minutes | Makes 2 (12- to 14-inch) pizzas

- 2 tablespoons extra-virgin olive oil, plus more for brushing
- 1 medium green zucchini, halved lengthwise and cut thinly into half-moons
- 1 medium yellow summer squash, halved lengthwise and cut thinly into half-moons
- ¼ teaspoon salt
- Simple Pizza Dough
- 1 medium red onion, sliced thin
- 1 teaspoon fresh thyme leaves
- ¼ teaspoon red pepper flakes
- 1 teaspoon freshly squeezed lemon juice
- ¼ cup shelled pistachios, toasted

1. Brush two baking sheets with olive oil.
2. In a large strainer set over a large bowl, toss the zucchini and summer squash well with the salt, and let it sit for about 5 minutes. Use a kitchen towel to press and squeeze the liquid from the squash mixture, removing as much moisture as possible.
3. Roll out one of the dough balls to the desired size, and place it on the prepared baking sheet.
4. In a large mixing bowl, toss together the drained squash mixture, onion, thyme, red pepper flakes, olive oil, and lemon juice. Arrange half of the vegetables on the dough.
5. Slide the baking sheet into the air fryer oven. Press the Power Button. Cook at 400°F (205°C) for 10 minutes, until the crust is golden and the cheese has melted.
6. Remove the pizza from the air fryer oven and transfer it to a cutting board. Let it rest for 5 minutes, then garnish with half of the toasted pistachios. Slice and serve.
7. Repeat with the remaining dough ball and toppings.

Escarole and Radicchio Pizza with Walnuts

Prep time: 10 minutes | Cook time: 25 minutes | Makes 1 pan pizza

- 1 head escarole, cored, center ribs removed, leaves chopped
- ½ head radicchio, sliced
- 1 small red onion, sliced thin
- 1 tablespoon extra-virgin olive oil
- ¼ teaspoon fine sea salt
- Pinch red pepper flakes
- No-Knead Pan Pizza Dough
- 6 slices provolone cheese
- ½ cup grated pecorino Romano cheese
- ¼ cup walnuts, toasted

1. Toss the escarole, radicchio, and red onion slices in a bowl with the olive oil. Season with the salt and red pepper flakes. Cover the dough with the slices of provolone. Top the pizza with the escarole mixture, spreading it into a thin, even layer. Sprinkle with the pecorino.
2. Slide the baking sheet into the air fryer oven. Press the Power Button. Cook at 400°F (205°C) for 25 minutes, until the crust is golden.
3. Remove the pizza from the air fryer oven and use a spatula to transfer it to a cutting board. Let it sit for 5 minutes. Top the pizza with a drizzle of olive oil and the toasted walnuts. Slice and serve.

Mozzarella Brussels Sprout Pizza

Prep time: 10 minutes | Cook time: 30 minutes | Makes 2 (12- to 14-inch) pizzas

- 2 tablespoons extra-virgin olive oil, plus more for brushing and drizzling
- 1 red onion, sliced
- ½ teaspoon fine sea salt, divided
- ⅛ teaspoon freshly ground black pepper
- Simple Pizza Dough or Pro Dough
- 6 ounces (170 g) fresh Mozzarella cheese, shredded
- 12 Brussels sprouts, shredded or finely sliced
- 8 sage leaves, rolled and sliced thin
- ¼ cup grated Parmesan cheese
- 2 pinches red pepper flakes

1. Brush two baking sheets with olive oil.
2. Spread the onion on a sheet tray, drizzle with the olive oil, and toss to coat. Season with ¼ teaspoon of salt, and the pepper. Transfer the baking sheet to the air fryer oven and Press the Power Button. Cook at 400°F (205°C) for 12 minutes, or until the onions are caramelized. Remove from the air fryer oven and set aside.
3. Roll out one of the dough balls to the desired size, and place it on the prepared baking sheet.
4. Top the dough with half of the Mozzarella, Brussels sprouts, and cooked red onion. Sprinkle on the remaining ¼ teaspoon of salt, half of the sage, and half of the Parmesan, followed by a drizzle of olive oil and a pinch of red pepper flakes.
5. Slide the baking sheet into the air fryer oven. Press the Power Button. Cook at 400°F (205°C) for 10 minutes, until the crust is golden and the cheese has melted.
6. Remove the pizza from the air fryer oven and transfer it to a cutting board. Let it rest for 5 minutes. Slice and serve.
7. Repeat with the remaining dough ball and toppings.

Butternut Squash and Arugula Pizza

Prep time: 10 minutes | Cook time: 1 hour | Makes 2 (12- to 14-inch) pizzas

- 1 small (1-pound / 454-g) butternut squash, peeled, seeded, and cut into small dice
- 3 tablespoons extra-virgin olive oil, plus more for brushing
- ¼ teaspoon salt, plus more for finishing
- ⅛ teaspoon freshly ground black pepper, plus more for finishing
- 3 fresh thyme sprigs, stemmed
- 4 slices center-cut bacon
- Simple Pizza Dough
- ½ cup grated fontina cheese
- ¼ cup crumbled blue cheese
- 4 cups arugula

1. Spread the butternut squash on a foil-lined baking pan and drizzle with the olive oil. Season with the salt, pepper, and thyme, and toss well. Press the Power Button. Cook at 400°F (205°C) for about 35 minutes, until the squash is fork tender and golden, stirring and rotating the pan halfway through. Remove from the air fryer oven and cool briefly.
2. Meanwhile, in a sauté pan over medium heat, brown the bacon until crisp, 2 to 3 minutes per side. Transfer to a paper towel–lined plate and, when cool, roughly chop.
3. Brush two baking sheets with olive oil.
4. Roll out one of the dough balls to the desired size, and place it on the prepared baking sheet.
5. Spread half of the fontina and blue cheeses evenly over the dough. Top with half of the cooked butternut squash and half of the bacon.
6. Slide the baking sheet into the air fryer oven. Press the Power Button. Cook at 400°F (205°C) for 10 minutes, until the crust is golden and the cheese is bubbly.
7. Remove the pizza from the air fryer oven and transfer it to a cutting board. Let it rest for 5 minutes, then top with half of the arugula. Slice and serve.
8. Repeat with the remaining dough ball and toppings.

Double-Cheese Clam Pizza

Prep time: 15 minutes | Cook time: 15 minutes | Serves 4

- ¼ cup extra-virgin olive oil, plus a little extra for forming the crust
- 2 large garlic cloves, chopped
- ¼ teaspoon red pepper flakes
- 1 pound (454 g) store-bought pizza dough
- ½ cup shredded

- Mozzarella cheese (4 ounces / 113 g)
- 2 (6.5-ounce / 184-g) cans chopped clams, drained
- ¼ cup grated Parmesan cheese
- ½ cup coarsely chopped fresh parsley
- 2 teaspoons chopped fresh oregano (optional)

1. In a small bowl, whisk together the olive oil with the garlic and red pepper flakes. Let it sit while you work on the dough.
2. Punch down the pizza dough to release as much air as possible. Place the dough in the baking pan and press it out toward the edges. The dough will likely spring back and shrink. Be patient and keep working at it, leaving it to relax for a few minutes from time to time. As it stretches, I find it helpful to coat my fingers with some olive oil and then poke the dough lightly with my fingertips to keep it from shrinking as much. Don't worry if you can't get it all the way to the edges of the pan.
3. Brush half of the garlic oil over the dough. Evenly distribute the Mozzarella cheese over the dough.
4. Slide the baking pan into the air fryer oven. Press the Power Button. Cook at 400°F (205°C) for 15 minutes.
5. After about 8 minutes, remove the pan from the air fryer oven. Scatter the clams over the pizza and sprinkle the Parmesan cheese on top. Return the pan to the air fryer oven and continue cooking for another 7 minutes.
6. When cooking is complete, the cheese on top is lightly browned and bubbling and the crust is deep golden brown. Remove the pan from the air fryer oven. Place the pizza on a wire rack to cool for a few minutes (a rack will keep the crust from getting soggy as it cools). Sprinkle the parsley and oregano (if using) over the pizza and drizzle with the remaining garlic oil. Slice and serve.

Egg and Arugula Pizza

Prep time: 10 minutes | Cook time: 10 minutes | Serves 2

- 2 tablespoons all-purpose flour, plus more as needed
- ½ store-bought pizza dough (about 8 ounces / 227 g)
- 1 tablespoon canola oil, divided
- 1 cup fresh ricotta cheese
- 4 large eggs
- Sea salt, to taste
- Freshly ground black pepper, to taste
- 4 cups arugula, torn
- 1 tablespoon extra-virgin olive oil
- 1 teaspoon freshly squeezed lemon juice
- 2 tablespoons grated Parmesan cheese

1. Dust a clean work surface with flour. Place the dough on the floured surface and roll it into a 9-inch round of even thickness. Dust your rolling pin and work surface with additional flour, as needed, to ensure the dough does not stick.
2. Brush the surface of the rolled-out dough evenly with ½ tablespoon of canola oil. Flip the dough over and brush with the remaining ½ tablespoon oil. Poke the dough with a fork 5 or 6 times across its surface to prevent air pockets from forming during cooking.
3. Place the dough on a greased baking sheet. Slide the baking sheet into the air fryer oven. Press the Power Button. Cook at 400°F (205°C) for 10 minutes.
4. After 5 minutes, flip the dough, then spoon teaspoons of ricotta cheese across the surface of the dough, leaving a 1-inch border around the edges.
5. Crack one egg into a ramekin or small bowl. This way you can easily remove any shell that may break into the egg and keep the yolk intact. Imagine the dough is split into four quadrants. Pour one egg into each. Repeat with the remaining 3 eggs. Season the pizza with salt and pepper.
6. Continue cooking for the remaining 5 minutes until the egg whites are firm.
7. Meanwhile, in a medium bowl, toss together the arugula, oil, and lemon juice, and season with salt and pepper.
8. Transfer the pizza to a cutting board and let it cool. Top it with the arugula mixture, drizzle with olive oil, if desired, and sprinkle with Parmesan cheese. Cut into pieces and serve.

Zucchini and Onion Pizza

Prep time: 10 minutes | Cook time: 10 minutes | Serves 2

- 2 tablespoons all-purpose flour, plus more as needed
- ½ store-bought pizza dough (about 8 ounces / 227 g)
- 1 tablespoon canola oil, divided
- ½ cup pizza sauce
- 1 cup shredded Mozzarella cheese
- ½ zucchini, thinly sliced
- ½ red onion, sliced
- ½ red bell pepper, seeded and thinly sliced

1. Dust a clean work surface with the flour.
2. Place the dough on the floured surface and roll it into a 9-inch round of even thickness. Dust your rolling pin and work surface with additional flour, as needed, to ensure the dough does not stick.
3. Evenly brush the surface of the rolled-out dough with ½ tablespoon of oil. Flip the dough over and brush the other side with the remaining ½ tablespoon of oil. Poke the dough with a fork 5 or 6 times across its surface to prevent air pockets from forming while it cooks.
4. Place the dough on a greased baking sheet. Slide the baking sheet into the air fryer oven. Press the Power Button. Cook at 400°F (205°C) for 10 minutes.
5. After 5 minutes, flip the dough, then spread the pizza sauce evenly over it. Sprinkle with the cheese, and top with the zucchini, onion, and pepper.
6. Continue cooking for the remaining 5 minutes until the cheese is melted and the veggie slices begin to crisp.

7. When cooking is complete, let cool slightly before slicing.

Pizza Margherita

Prep time: 15 minutes | Cook time: 15 minutes | Serves 4

- 1 pound (454 g) store-bought pizza dough
- 2 tablespoons extra-virgin olive oil, divided
- ½ cup Marinara Sauce or store-bought variety
- 6 ounces (170 g) shredded Mozzarella cheese
- ½ cup coarsely shredded Parmesan cheese (about 1½ ounces / 43 g)
- 2 large tomatoes, seeded and chopped (about 1½ cups)
- ¼ teaspoon kosher salt or ⅛ teaspoon fine salt
- ¼ cup chopped fresh basil
- 2 teaspoons wine vinegar

1. Punch down the pizza dough to release as much air as possible. Place the dough in the baking pan and press it out toward the edges. The dough will likely spring back and shrink. Be patient and keep working at it, leaving it alone to relax for a few minutes from time to time. As it stretches, I find it helpful to coat my fingers with 1 tablespoon of olive oil and then poke the dough lightly with my fingertips to keep it from shrinking as much. Don't worry if you can't get it all the way to the pan's edges.

2. Spread the marinara sauce over the dough. You'll be able to see the dough through the sauce in places; you don't want a thick coating. Evenly top the sauce with the Mozzarella cheese.

3. Slide the baking pan into the air fryer oven. Press the Power Button. Cook at 400°F (205°C) for 15 minutes.

4. After about 8 minutes, remove the pan from the air fryer oven. Sprinkle the Parmesan cheese over the pizza. Return the pan to the air fryer oven. Continue cooking for 7 minutes.

5. While the pizza cooks, place the tomatoes in a colander or fine-mesh strainer and sprinkle with the salt. Let them drain for a few minutes, then place in a small bowl. Mix in the remaining 1 tablespoon of olive oil, basil, and vinegar.

6. When cooking is complete, the cheese on top will be lightly browned and bubbling and the crust a deep golden brown. Remove the pizza from the baking pan, if you haven't already, and place it on a wire rack to cool for a few minutes (a rack will keep the crust from getting soggy as it cools). Distribute the tomato mixture evenly over the pizza, then transfer to a cutting board to slice and serve.

Appendix 1 Measurement Conversion Chart

VOLUME EQUIVALENTS(DRY)

US STANDARD	METRIC (APPROXIMATE)
1/8 teaspoon	0.5 mL
1/4 teaspoon	1 mL
1/2 teaspoon	2 mL
3/4 teaspoon	4 mL
1 teaspoon	5 mL
1 tablespoon	15 mL
1/4 cup	59 mL
1/2 cup	118 mL
3/4 cup	177 mL
1 cup	235 mL
2 cups	475 mL
3 cups	700 mL
4 cups	1 L

VOLUME EQUIVALENTS(LIQUID)

US STANDARD	US STANDARD (OUNCES)	METRIC (APPROXIMATE)
2 tablespoons	1 fl.oz.	30 mL
1/4 cup	2 fl.oz.	60 mL
1/2 cup	4 fl.oz.	120 mL
1 cup	8 fl.oz.	240 mL
1 1/2 cup	12 fl.oz.	355 mL
2 cups or 1 pint	16 fl.oz.	475 mL
4 cups or 1 quart	32 fl.oz.	1 L
1 gallon	128 fl.oz.	4 L

TEMPERATURES EQUIVALENTS

FAHRENHEIT(F)	CELSIUS(C) (APPROXIMATE)
225 °F	107 °C
250 °F	120 °C
275 °F	135 °C
300 °F	150 °C
325 °F	160 °C
350 °F	180 °C
375 °F	190 °C
400 °F	205 °C
425 °F	220 °C
450 °F	235 °C
475 °F	245 °C
500 °F	260 °C

WEIGHT EQUIVALENTS

US STANDARD	METRIC (APPROXIMATE)
1 ounce	28 g
2 ounces	57 g
5 ounces	142 g
10 ounces	284 g
15 ounces	425 g
16 ounces (1 pound)	455 g
1.5 pounds	680 g
2 pounds	907 g

Appendix 2 Air Fryer Cooking Chart

Beef

Item	Temp (°F)	Time (mins)	Item	Temp (°F)	Time (mins)
Beef Eye Round Roast (4 lbs.)	400 °F	45 to 55	Meatballs (1-inch)	370 °F	7
Burger Patty (4 oz.)	370 °F	16 to 20	Meatballs (3-inch)	380 °F	10
Filet Mignon (8 oz.)	400 °F	18	Ribeye, bone-in (1-inch, 8 oz)	400 °F	10 to 15
Flank Steak (1.5 lbs.)	400 °F	12	Sirloin steaks (1-inch, 12 oz)	400 °F	9 to 14
Flank Steak (2 lbs.)	400 °F	20 to 28			

Chicken

Item	Temp (°F)	Time (mins)	Item	Temp (°F)	Time (mins)
Breasts, bone in (1 ¼ lb.)	370 °F	25	Legs, bone-in (1 ¾ lb.)	380 °F	30
Breasts, boneless (4 oz)	380 °F	12	Thighs, boneless (1 ½ lb.)	380 °F	18 to 20
Drumsticks (2 ½ lb.)	370 °F	20	Wings (2 lb.)	400 °F	12
Game Hen (halved 2 lb.)	390 °F	20	Whole Chicken	360 °F	75
Thighs, bone-in (2 lb.)	380 °F	22	Tenders	360 °F	8 to 10

Pork & Lamb

Item	Temp (°F)	Time (mins)	Item	Temp (°F)	Time (mins)
Bacon (regular)	400 °F	5 to 7	Pork Tenderloin	370 °F	15
Bacon (thick cut)	400 °F	6 to 10	Sausages	380 °F	15
Pork Loin (2 lb.)	360 °F	55	Lamb Loin Chops (1-inch thick)	400 °F	8 to 12
Pork Chops, bone in (1-inch, 6.5 oz)	400 °F	12	Rack of Lamb (1.5 – 2 lb.)	380 °F	22

Fish & Seafood

Item	Temp (°F)	Time (mins)	Item	Temp (°F)	Time (mins)
Calamari (8 oz)	400 °F	4	Tuna Steak	400 °F	7 to 10
Fish Fillet (1-inch, 8 oz)	400 °F	10	Scallops	400 °F	5 to 7
Salmon, fillet (6 oz)	380 °F	12	Shrimp	400 °F	5
Swordfish steak	400 °F	10			

Vegetables

INGREDIENT	AMOUNT	PREPARATION	OIL	TEMP	COOK TIME
Asparagus	2 bunches	Cut in half, trim stems	2 Tbsp	420°F	12-15 mins
Beets	1½ lbs	Peel, cut in ½-inch cubes	1 Tbsp	390°F	28-30 mins
Bell peppers (for roasting)	4 peppers	Cut in quarters, remove seeds	1 Tbsp	400°F	15-20 mins
Broccoli	1 large head	Cut in 1-2-inch florets	1 Tbsp	400°F	15-20 mins
Brussels sprouts	1 lb	Cut in half, remove stems	1 Tbsp	425°F	15-20 mins
Carrots	1 lb	Peel, cut in ¼-inch rounds	1 Tbsp	425°F	10-15 mins
Cauliflower	1 head	Cut in 1-2-inch florets	2 Tbsp	400°F	20-22 mins
Corn on the cob	7 ears	Whole ears, remove husks	1 Tbps	400°F	14-17 mins
Green beans	1 bag (12 oz)	Trim	1 Tbps	420°F	18-20 mins
Kale (for chips)	4 oz	Tear into pieces, remove stems	None	325°F	5-8 mins
Mushrooms	16 oz	Rinse, slice thinly	1 Tbps	390°F	25-30 mins
Potatoes, russet	1½ lbs	Cut in 1-inch wedges	1 Tbps	390°F	25-30 mins
Potatoes, russet	1 lb	Hand-cut fries, soak 30 mins in cold water, then pat dry	½-3 Tbps	400°F	25-28 mins
Potatoes, sweet	1 lb	Hand-cut fries, soak 30 mins in cold water, then pat dry	1 Tbps	400°F	25-28 mins
Zucchini	1 lb	Cut in eighths lengthwise, then cut in half	1 Tbps	400°F	15-20 mins

Appendix 3 Index

A-B

Air Fried Cream Cheese Wontons	31
Arugula and Prosciutto Pizza	74
Asparagus Casserole with Grits	24
Avocado Chips with Lime	45
Avocado Dressing	64
Baby Back Ribs with Paprika Rub	60
Bacon Knots with Maple Sugar	1
Baked Cornmeal Pancake	3
Baked Eggs with Spinach and Basil	35
Baked Salmon in Wine	19
Baked White Rice	66
Balsamic Chuck Roast	59
Balsamic Prosciutto-Wrapped Pears	42
Barbecue Chicken with Coleslaw	8
BBQ Chicken with Mustard Rub	58
Beef and Bean Casserole	26
Beef Hash with Eggs	5
Bell Pepper Rings with Eggs	4
Black Bean and Salsa Tacos	34
Black Bean Pizza with Chipotle	76
Blueberry and Peach Tart	49
Blueberry Cake with Lemon	5
Breaded Chicken Fingers	7
Breaded Chicken Livers	7
Breaded Chicken Tenders with Thyme	8
Breaded Fish Fillets with Mustard	17
Breaded Zucchini Tots	42
Breakfast Sausage Quiche	5
Brie Pear Sandwiches	45
Bulgogi Burgers	32
Buttermilk Biscuits	2
Buttermilk Chicken Drumsticks	11
Buttermilk-Marinated Chicken Wings	45
Butternut Squash and Arugula Pizza	78
Butternut Squash and Parsnip with Thyme	37
Butternut Squash with Goat Cheese	37
Butter Shortbread with Lemon	49
Buttery Chicken with Corn	13

C

Cabbage and Pork Gyoza	31
Cajun Catfish Cakes with Parmesan	20
Cajun Tilapia Tacos	16
Candied Bacon	70
Cashew Mayo	64
Cauliflower Alfredo Sauce	64
Cauliflower and Okra Casserole	25
Cauliflower Casserole with Pecan Butter	23
Cayenne Cod Fillets with Garlic	17
Cheddar and Egg Frittata with Parsley	27
Cheddar Baked Potatoes with Chives	39
Cheddar Broccoli and Carrot Quiche	27
Cheddar Broccoli Casserole	24
Cheddar Chicken and Broccoli Divan	27
Cheddar Chicken Sausage Casserole	23
Cheddar Ham Toast	1
Cheddar Mushrooms with Pimientos	40
Cheddar Pastrami Casserole	25
Cheddar Sausage Balls	41
Cheese and Bacon Muffin Sandwiches	4
Cheese Tomato Pizza with Basil	73
Cheesy Broccoli with Rosemary	35
Cheesy Chicken Sandwich	30
Cheesy Potato Taquitos	30
Chicken and Butternut Squash Pizza	75
Chicken and Ham Rochambeau	7
Chicken and Yogurt Taquitos	30
Chicken Drumsticks with Cajun Seasoning	9
Chicken Gnocchi with Spinach	13
Chicken-Lettuce Wraps	29
Chicken Roast with Mustard Paste	61
Chicken Tacos with Lettuce	11
Chicken Thighs with Cabbage Slaw	12
Chicken Thighs with Cherry Tomatoes	11
Chickpea and Spinach Casserole	26
Chili Chicken Fries	15
Chili Chicken Skin with Dill	9
Chimichurri	65
Chocolate Blueberry Cupcakes	52
Chocolate Coconut Cake	49
Chocolate Vanilla Cheesecake	50
Cinnamon Apple Chips	44
Cinnamon Apple Fritters	52
Cinnamon Apple Turnovers	5

Cinnamon Apple with Apricots	54
Cinnamon Monkey Bread	2
Cinnamon Orange Slices	70
Cinnamon Pear Chips	69
Coconut Curried Fish with Chilies	20
Coconut Orange Cake	53
Coffee Chocolate Cake with Cinnamon	49
Corn Casserole with Bell Pepper	23
Corn Frittata with Avocado Dressing	4
Creamy Coconut Lime Dressing	65
Creamy Ranch Dressing	65
Crispy Crab and Cream Cheese Wontons	31

D-G

Dehydrated Onions	70
Dehydrated Pineapple Slices	68
Dehydrated Strawberries	68
Dehydrated Zucchini Chips	69
Deviled Eggs with Mayo	43
Dijon and Balsamic Vinaigrette	64
Double-Cheese Clam Pizza	78
Dried Fruit Stuffed Pork Loin	62
Dried Hot Peppers	69
Dried Mushrooms	69
Egg and Arugula Pizza	79
Egg and Bacon Bread Cups	3
Eggplant and Bell Peppers with Basil	34
Eggplant Hoagies	33
English Muffins with Spinach and Pear	4
Escarole and Radicchio Pizza with Walnuts	77
Feta Stuffed Lamb Leg	62
Flounder Fillets with Lemon Pepper	21
Fresh Mixed Berry Vinaigrette	65
Fried Cod Fillets in Beer	20
Fried Pickle Spears with Chili	44
Garlic Carrots with Sesame Seeds	36
Garlic Lime Tahini Dressing	65
Garlic Tomato Pizza Sauce	71
Ginger Chicken Bites in Sherry	9
Ginger-Pepper Broccoli	38
Ginger Shrimp with Sesame Seeds	42
Ginger Swordfish Steaks with Jalapeño	19
Gochujang Chicken Wings	9
Green Chiles and Cheese Nachos	40
Grits with Cheddar Cheese	3

H-L

Ham and Pineapple Pizza	73
Ham with Dijon Bourbon Baste	57
Hash Brown Cups with Cheddar Cheese	2
Hemp Dressing	64
Hoisin Tuna with Lemongrass	16
Honey Apple-Peach Crumble	54
Honey Cashew Granola with Cranberries	6
Honey Eggplant with Yogurt Sauce	36
Honey-Ginger Chicken Breasts	10
Honey-Glazed Peach and Plum Kebabs	54
Honey-Lemon Snapper with Grapes	19
Honey Roasted Grapes with Basil	39
Honey Snack Mix	43
Honey Walnut and Pistachios Baklava	48
Horseradish Green Tomatoes	46
Hush Puppies with Jalapeño	44
Italian Rice Balls with Olives	46
Italian Sausage and Bell Pepper Pizza	72
Jalapeño Poppers with Cheddar	40
Kale and Almond Pesto	66
Kale with Tahini-Lemon Dressing	35
Kiwi Chips	69
Lamb and Feta Hamburgers	33
Lemon Caramelized Pear Tart	48
Lemon Dijon Vinaigrette	65
Lemon-Pepper Salmon Jerky	69
Lemon Ricotta with Capers	43
Lemony Tahini	64
Lettuce Fajita Meatball Wraps	29

M-P

Maple French Toast Casserole	6
Maple Granola	1
Marinara Sauce	66
Mixed Berry Bake with Almond Topping	51
Monk Fruit and Hazelnut Cake	48
Mozzarella Brussels Sprout Pizza	78
Mozzarella Chicken Breasts with Basil	12
Mozzarella Meatball Pizza	73
Muffuletta Sliders with Olive Mix	47
Mushroom and Beef Casserole	23
Mushroom and Spinach Pizza	72

Mushroom Apple Gravy	65	Red Buffalo Sauce	64
Mustard Chicken Thighs in Waffles	8	Red Enchilada Sauce	67
Mustard Lamb Shoulder	62	Ricotta Margherita with Basil	75
No-Knead Pan Pizza Dough	71	Roasted Mushrooms with Garlic	40
Nugget and Veggie Taco Wraps	29	Roasted Veggie and Tofu	34
Orange Honey Glazed Ham	57	Rosemary Chicken Breasts with Tomatoes	10
Orange Shrimp with Cayenne	21	Salmon Spring Rolls with Parsley	16
Paprika Hens in Wine	14	Salmon with Cherry Tomatoes	18
Paprika Hens with Creole Seasoning	14	Salmon with Roasted Asparagus	18
Paprika Polenta Fries with Chili-Lime Mayo	42	Sausage and Onion Rolls with Mustard	39
Paprika Potato Chips	44	Sesame Mushrooms with Thyme	36
Paprika Pulled Pork Butt	56	Shawarma Spice Blend	66
Paprika Tiger Shrimp	22	Shrimp and Veggie Spring Rolls	21
Parmesan Brussels Sprouts	38	Simple Pizza Dough	71
Parmesan Cabbage Wedges	36	Sirloin Roast with Porcini-Wine Baste	59
Parmesan Cauliflower with Turmeric	39	Smoked Paprika Lamb Leg	58
Parmesan Chicken Cutlets	10	Smoked Trout Frittata with Dill	27
Parmesan Crab Toasts	45	Smoky Chicken Sandwich	30
Parmesan Fish Fillets with Tarragon	20	Smoky Venison Jerky	68
Parmesan Green Bean Casserole	24	Spareribs with Paprika Rub	58
Parmesan Snack Mix	43	Spicy Southwest Seasoning	66
Pea and Potato Samosas with Chutney	32	Spinach and Mushroom Frittata	25
Peach and Apple Crisp with Oatmeal	51	Spinach, Egg and Pancetta Pizza	74
Peach and Blueberry Galette	53	Spring Pea Pizza with Ramps	77
Peach Chicken with Dark Cherry	13	Strawberry Crumble with Rhubarb	50
Peach Fruit Leather	68	Strawberry Roll Ups	68
Pear Pizza with Basil	76	Sugar Roasted Walnuts	41
Pepperoni Pizza Bites with Marinara	41	Swiss Chicken and Ham Casserole	25
Pepperoni Pizza with Mozzarella	72	Tater Tot and Chicken Sausage Casserole	3
Peppery Sausage Casserole with Cheddar	26	Teriyaki Chicken	60
Pizza Margherita	80	Teriyaki Salmon and Bok Choy	19
Porchetta with Lemony Sage Rub	56	Thai Curried Veggies	34
Pork and Turkey Sandwiches	46	Thai-Flavored Brussels Sprouts	36
Pork Jerky	68	Tilapia and Rockfish Casserole	24
Pork Loin Roast with Brown Sugar Brine	61	Tilapia Meunière with Parsley	17
Pork Momos	31	Tuna and Fruit Kebabs with Honey Glaze	17
Pro Dough	71	Tuna and Lettuce Wraps	29
Prosciutto and Bacon Pizza	74	Tuna and Veggie Salad	18
Prosciutto and Fig Pizza	75	Tuna Casserole with Basil	16
Pumpkin Pudding with Vanilla Wafers	55	Tuna Melts with Mayo	41
		Turkey Casserole with Almond Mayo	25
R-T		Turkey Meatloaves with Onion	14
Raspberry Muffins	51	Turkey with Thyme-Sage Brine	61
Ratatouille with Bread Crumb Topping	37		

Turkey-Wrapped Dates and Almonds 46

V-Z

Vanilla Chocolate Cake 53
Vanilla Chocolate Chip Cookies 53
Vanilla Coconut Cookies with Pecans 52
Vanilla Cookies with Chocolate Chips 50
Vanilla French Toast withBourbon 2
Vanilla Pound Cake 54
Vanilla Ricotta Cake with Lemon 55
Vanilla Walnuts Tart with Cloves 51
Vegetable Mélange with Garlic 35
Veggie Salsa Wraps 29
Vinegary Asparagus 35
Vinegary Chicken with Pineapple 13
Whiskey-Basted Prime Rib Roast 56
Zucchini and Onion Pizza 79
Zucchini and Summer Squash Pizza 76
Zucchini Pizza with Pistachios 77

Printed in Great Britain
by Amazon